Scrap Quilt
Celebration

Edited by Karen Bolesta

D1530515

RODALE

RODALE

WE INSPIRE AND ENABLE PEOPLE TO IMPROVE
THEIR LIVES AND THE WORLD AROUND THEM

FOR MORE OF OUR PRODUCTS

WWW.**RODALESTORE**.COM
(800) 848-4735

The writers and editors who compiled this book have tried to make all of the contents as accurate and as correct as possible. Illustrations, photographs, and text have all been carefully checked and cross-checked. However, due to the variability of personal skill, tools, materials, and so on, neither the writers nor Rodale Inc. assumes any responsibility for any injuries suffered or for damages or other losses incurred that result from the material presented here-in. All instructions should be carefully studied and clearly understood before beginning any project.

Printed in the United States of America

Rodale Inc. makes every effort to use acid-free ∞, recycled paper ♻.

The quilt projects in this book were originally published in the Classic American Quilt Collection series, published by Rodale Inc.

Cover design by Christina Gaugler

Illustrations by Mario Ferro and Jackie Walsh (pages 5–11, 22–31, 34–39, 53–63, 66–69, 72–77, 80–85, 100–105, 109–113, 116–123, 126–131, 134–139, 142–145, 147–149, 152–155, 158–163, 176–181, 184–191, 194–201, 204–211, 214–219, 223–226, 227 [squares], 228 [diamonds], 229–233, 236–242, 243 [stitching], 244–246); Sandy Freeman (pages 15–19, 43–49, 89–97, 167–173, 227 [houses], 228 [houses], 243 [piecing])

Photographs by Mitch Mandel/Rodale Images (cover; pages iii, vi, 1, 2, 12, 20, 32, 40, 50, 64, 70, 78, 86, 98, 106, 114, 124, 132, 140, 150, 156, 164, 174, 182, 192, 202, 212, 220, 221); John Hamel/Rodale Images (page i)

Library of Congress Cataloging-in-Publication Data

Scrap quilt celebration / edited by Karen Bolesta.
    p.   cm.
Includes index.
ISBN 1–57954–555–6 paperback
    1. Patchwork—Patterns.   2. Quilting—Patterns.
3. Patchwork quilts.   I. Bolesta, Karen.
TT835 .S35947   2002
746.46'041—dc21   2002069676

Distributed to the book trade by St. Martin's Press

2 4 6 8 10 9 7 5 3 1   paperback

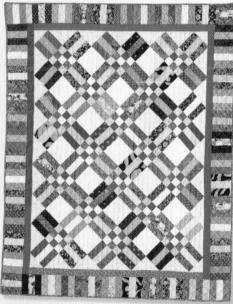

CONTENTS

INTRODUCTION

Everyone who loves quilting loves fabric, from big 4-yard cuts for setting squares and borders to tiny scraps and bits perfect for foundation piecing. And I'm certainly no exception! One of the things that keeps me quilting is the array of gorgeous fabrics available at every turn. I can walk into a quilt shop, spot a bolt of stunning fabric, and instantly know what I want to make. Or I may buy 2 yards of a fabric that's caught my eye and know the yardage will wait patiently in my fabric stash (maybe for years!) because I have to simmer and stew about how I'll use it. There are still other times when creativity strikes and I head upstairs to my sewing room, pull out a couple of long-forgotten and oddly shaped fabric scraps, and whip up a small doll quilt in no time at all.

I figure I'm just like every other quilter out there: We find inspiration in the moment, whether it's in a fabric store or our own fabric stash and whether we have a generous cut of fabric or an overflowing scrap bin to tame. We quilters are inspired by many things—quilts we see in books and magazines that arrive in our mailbox; patterns and designs in everything from carpets and tile to leaves and clouds; and most often, projects we see each other working on at guild meetings, quilting classes, or weekend sewing sessions. When you're surrounded with terrific fabrics, time-honored patterns, and ideas, there's no limit to how many quilts you can create.

I've put together this collection of scrap quilts from some of the most talented quiltmakers in the country to inspire your creativity. Scrap quilts are a perennial favorite of quilters everywhere, and this book showcases the best quilt designs for using up fabric scraps. You're bound to be awed by the ways in which these quilters have combined beloved quilt patterns, such as Log Cabin, Wedding Ring, and Nine Patch, with today's most popular fabrics, such as plaids, batiks, and florals. From hand-dyed fabrics to traditional calicoes, the exciting and contemporary color combinations in these 24 projects will have you racing to your sewing machine.

You may already have a book or two in your library on quilting with scraps, but I guarantee that you'll find great scrap quilts here that will inspire you to explore the topic all over again. Over the years, a vast number of new and different quilt designs—variations on the basic scrap quilt—have evolved, a testament to the unending creativity of quiltmakers. You may think that if you've seen one Star quilt you've seen them all. Think again! You'll be dazzled by the sizzling color combinations quiltmaker Valerie Schadt used in her Feathered World without End quilt on page 50. If you think Wedding Ring quilts are only for the ladies in a quilting bee, turn to page 98 to see Joanne Winn's velvety interpretation of the classic quilt that enjoys such enduring popularity. It's easy to understand why Log Cabin blocks have remained dear to the hearts of quilters through the years: The blocks are quick and easy to cut and piece, and they make great use of scraps of fabric, but don't discount them as showstoppers—just check out June Ryker's incredible Logs Hexagonal design on page 20. It's a scrap lover's dream!

Most of the quilts in this book are easy to make, but some are more time-consuming than others. So for each project in the book, you'll find a skill-level rating to prepare you for what you may encounter. We've worked hard to make sure the step-by-step directions and diagrams are clear and detailed and won't leave you guessing. Many of these quilt designs were long considered to be the true test of expert piecing skills, but we've updated the techniques needed for these patterns to take advantage of the ease and accuracy of rotary cutting and quick piecing.

I hope this collection of quilts will open your eyes as much as it did mine to the unlimited design possibilities of the simple, yet truly American, scrap quilt. And don't be surprised to find that once you make your first scrap quilt, you won't be able to stop. Happy quilting!

—Karen Bolesta

Scrap Quilt Projects

REFLECTIONS

Skill Level: *Intermediate*

I f you love the rich, warm look of nineteenth-century scrap quilts, this elegant beauty will be irresistible. Patricia Mahoney of Santa Maria, California, has employed a treasure-trove of printed fabrics to lift this simple, time-honored pattern to celestial heights. A subtle variation in the choice of setting blocks and a sparkling pieced border helped earn this quilt a well-deserved prize at the 1991 American Quilter's Society Show in Paducah, Kentucky.

BEFORE YOU BEGIN

Although the scrappy look of this quilt does not lend itself to many of the familiar quick-piecing methods, the directions include a variety of quick-cutting techniques that are sure to save you lots of time. Your fabrics can be layered for even more efficient cutting.

Read through "Quiltmaking Basics," beginning on page 221, before you begin this quilt. You'll find lots of helpful hints and tips, in addition to specific instructions concerning the use of the rotary cutter.

CHOOSING FABRICS

Many of the colors and prints sewn into this scrappy quilt are reminiscent of fabrics from past eras, including reproductions of fabrics dating back to the mid- to late-1800s. At first glance, some fabrics in the quilt appear to be solid colors, but closer inspection reveals that they are all prints of varying scale, adding texture and visual interest to the piece. While many of the colors are subdued,

Quilt Sizes

	Double	Queen (shown)
Finished Quilt Size	83¼" × 94½"	94½" × 105¾"
Finished Star Block Size	8"	8"
Number of Star Blocks	35	48

Materials

Fabric	Double	Queen
Assorted light, medium, and dark scraps/prints (*total*)	3¼ yards	4¼ yards
Border stripe print*	2¾ yards	3⅛ yards
Medium-dark print	1¼ yards	2 yards
Medium print	1¼ yards	1¼ yards
Subtle wine print	1⅛ yards	1½ yards
Bright pink print†	—	fat ¼ yard
Light beige subtle print	⅜ yard	⅜ yard
Medium beige print	⅜ yard	⅝ yard
Backing	7¾ yards	8⅔ yards
Batting	91" × 102"	102" × 113"
Binding	⅝ yard	⅝ yard

NOTE: *Yardages are based on 44/45-inch-wide fabrics that are at least 42 inches wide after preshrinking.*

* *For single, continuous border strips. Assumes that both the inner narrow stripe border and the wide outer stripe border will be cut from the same striped fabric. Also assumes that the borders will be cut on the lengthwise grain and that there are four border repeats across the width of the fabric.*

† *Bright pink fabric is not required for the double-size quilt.*

3

Cutting Chart

Fabric	Used For	Strip Width or Pieces	Number to Cut Double	Number to Cut Queen	Second Cut Dimensions	Number to Cut Double	Number to Cut Queen
Assorted prints/scraps	H	2½" squares	108	124			
Wine print	Inner border*	1¼"	8	9			
	F	12½" squares	5	6			
	G	12⅜" squares	2	2			
Medium/ dark print	E (setting square 1)	8½"	5	8	8½" squares	18	29
Medium print	E (setting square 2)	8½"	5	5	8½" squares	18	18
Pink print	E (setting square 3)	8½"	—	1	8½" squares	—	2
Light beige print	I	4⅛"	3	3	4⅛" squares	26	30
Medium beige print	I	4⅛"	3	4	4⅛" squares	27	31
Border stripe	Inner border†	1"	4	4			
	Outer border†	4"	4	4			

You may need to wait before cutting these strips because the width may vary. Refer to the instructions for "Adding the Double Inner Borders," Step 1, page 7.

†*Strips cut on the lengthwise grain. Exact length of these strips will be determined after the quilt top has been assembled.*

Cutting Chart for Individual Star Blocks

Fabric	Used For	Size to Cut	Number to Cut per Star Block
Assorted light, medium, and dark prints/scraps	A	2⅞" squares	4
	B	5¼" squares	1
	C	4½" squares	1
	D	2½" squares	4

NOTE: *Cut all B and D pieces for each Star block from a single fabric, if possible. Cut A and C pieces from two different, contrasting fabrics.*

the quiltmaker avoided a drab appearance by including a sprinkling of pinks, reds, golds, and other light, bright colors, much as her nineteenth-century predecessors might have done.

The placement of value within the Star blocks is varied. In some, dark stars stand out against a lighter background, while in others, the placement of lights and darks is reversed. A few Star blocks contain fabrics with very little difference in value. This mixture adds to the scrappy flavor of the quilt, as well as to its authentic, old-time appearance. To capture a similar look, plan to use *at least* 10 light, 20 dark, and 20 medium-value fabrics.

The quiltmaker used two different medium-scale prints for the setting squares, then tossed in two brighter pink setting squares for an extra spark of color in the center of the quilt. (These pink squares are eliminated in the double-size quilt because of the adjusted layout.)

The setting triangles and inner border are cut from a rich, subtle wine print fabric, which gives the blocks the appearance of floating against the background. A striped border print is used in the outer border and in the narrow strip sewn next to the pieced border.

The pieced border provides a great opportunity to use your scraps! You'll want to include as many different fabrics as you can to make this border twinkle against the darker surrounding borders. The pieced border is finished with triangles sewn from two prints, one slightly darker than the other, but both lighter than most of the colored squares in the border.

To develop your own color scheme, photocopy the **Color Plan** on page 11, and use crayons or colored pencils to experiment with different color arrangements.

Cutting

All measurements include ¼-inch seam allowances. Refer to the Cutting Chart and cut the required number of pieces and strips in the sizes needed. Except for the border stripes, cut all strips across the fabric width (crosswise grain).

No templates are required for this project, since every piece is rotary cut. For easy reference, however, a letter identification for each pattern piece is given in the **Block Diagram** and in the **Queen-Size Assembly Diagram** on page 6.

You will need to cut some of the squares into triangles, as follows:

• For the star points (A triangles), cut the 2⅞-inch squares in half diagonally. Follow the same procedure to cut the two 12⅜-inch squares for the wine print corner triangles (piece G).

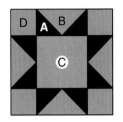

Block Diagram

• For the star background triangles (piece B), cut each of the 5¼-inch squares diagonally in *each* direction.

• For the wine print setting triangles (piece F), cut each of the 12½-inch squares diagonally in each direction.

• For the pieced border triangles (piece I), cut each of the 4⅛-inch squares diagonally in each direction.

Note: Cut and piece a sample block before cutting all the fabric for your quilt.

Piecing the Star Blocks

Each Star block consists of eight matching star points (A), a contrasting star center (C), and four each matching background triangles (B) and squares (D). The placement of lights and darks, as well as the actual fabrics, will vary from block to block. Refer to the **Block Diagram** and lay out each block before you begin to sew, experimenting until you find a color/value arrangement that pleases you and suits your fabrics. The quilt photograph on page 2 and "Choosing Fabrics" on page 3 offer ideas and suggestions.

Step 1. Sew a star point A triangle to each short side of a background B triangle, as shown in **Diagram 1**. Press all the seam allowances toward the A triangles. Make four identical triangle units for each of your blocks.

Diagram 1

Step 2. Sew a triangle unit to the top and bottom edges of a contrasting C square, as shown in **Diagram 2**. Press the seams toward the center square.

Diagram 2

Step 3. Sew a background D square to each end of the remaining triangle units, as shown in **Diagram 3A**. Press the seams toward the squares. Sew one of these strips to each side of the block, as shown in **3B**. Press the seams as desired.

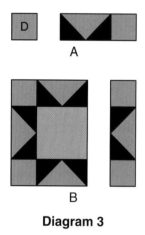

Diagram 3

········Sew Quick·········

Maintain good pressing habits: Be sure to press all seam allowances as you go, pressing toward the darker fabric whenever possible. Use a dry iron, as steam may cause distortion. Be certain that the heat setting is appropriate for the fiber content. Remember that the key word is *press*; do not drag the iron back and forth across the pieces since this, too, can pull them out of shape.

Step 4. Repeat Steps 1 through 3 to make the total number of blocks required for your quilt.

ASSEMBLING THE QUILT TOP

Step 1. Use a design wall or other flat surface to arrange the Star blocks, setting squares (E), setting triangles (F), and corner triangles (G) into diagonal rows, as shown in the **Queen-Size Assembly Diagram**. (You will have a few F triangles left over.) Refer to the **Double-Size Quilt Diagram** on page 9 for assistance in laying out the double-size quilt. In each case, rearrange the Star blocks until you have achieved a balance of color and value that pleases you. The **Queen-Size Assembly Diagram** is color-coded to indicate the placement of each of the three different setting squares.

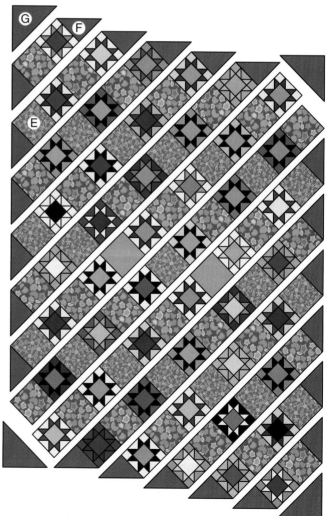

Queen-Size Assembly Diagram

Step 2. Sew the Star blocks, setting squares, and setting triangles together to form diagonal rows, as shown in the **Queen-Size Assembly Diagram**. Press seams toward the setting squares and triangles. Then sew the diagonal rows together, matching seam intersections carefully. Add the four corner triangles, and press the quilt.

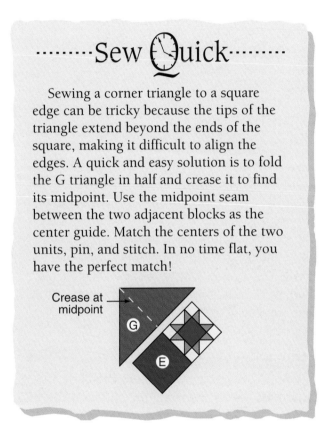

·········Sew Quick·········

Sewing a corner triangle to a square edge can be tricky because the tips of the triangle extend beyond the ends of the square, making it difficult to align the edges. A quick and easy solution is to fold the G triangle in half and crease it to find its midpoint. Use the midpoint seam between the two adjacent blocks as the center guide. Match the centers of the two units, pin, and stitch. In no time flat, you have the perfect match!

Crease at midpoint

ADDING THE BORDERS

The quilt shown has four mitered borders. The wine print and narrow stripe borders are sewn together and added as a single unit. The pieced border is constructed and added next. The wide stripe border is added last.

Adding the Double Inner Borders

Step 1. Check to be sure that your quilt top has been pressed thoroughly. Then measure through the quilt's horizontal and vertical centers to be certain that your quilt measures properly. Before the first border is added, the double-size quilt should measure about $68\frac{1}{2} \times 79\frac{3}{4}$ inches, including the seam allowances. The queen-size quilt should measure $79\frac{3}{4} \times 91$ inches, including the seam allowances. Slight variations are not unusual and can usually be accommodated by easing as the borders are added. If the dimensions of your quilt differ more substantially, adjust the *width* of the innermost (wine print) border to compensate for the difference, so that your pieced border will fit accurately. Refer to the Cutting Chart on page 4 and cut the required number of wine print border strips for the quilt you are making, adjusting the width if necessary.

Step 2. To determine the correct *length* for the first two borders, begin with the vertical measurement of the quilt top determined in Step 1. To this measurement, add two times the finished width of the borders, plus 5 inches ($1\frac{1}{4}$ inches $\times$ 2 = $2\frac{1}{2}$ inches + 5 inches = $7\frac{1}{2}$ inches). This is the length you will need to make both the wine print and the narrow stripe strips for the two innermost side borders. Use the same method to calculate the length of the top and bottom borders, using the horizontal measurement determined in Step 1 as your base.

Step 3. Sew together wine print strips until you have achieved the length required for each border. (For the double-size quilt, each border will require two strips. For the queen-size quilt, the top and bottom borders will each require two strips, and each side border will require $2\frac{1}{2}$ strips.) Trim the strips to the exact length required and press.

Step 4. Cut each 1-inch-wide narrow stripe border in a single, continuous length as required for the side, the top, and the bottom border measurements. The 1-inch width includes the seam allowance.

Step 5. Beginning with the side border strips, pin and sew a wine print and a narrow stripe border strip together lengthwise to form a single side border unit. Press the seam toward the wine strip. Make two of these side border units. In the same manner, pin and sew the top and bottom border strips into units.

Step 6. Pin and sew the four border units to the appropriate sides of the quilt top, positioning the wine print border closest to the center of the quilt, as shown in the **Double-Size Quilt Diagram**. Match and pin the midpoints and attach the borders, stopping ¼ inch from the edge of the quilt, so that all four borders can be mitered later.

Assembling and Adding the Pieced Border

Step 1. Turn a 2½-inch H square on point, and sew a light I triangle to the top right edge and a medium I triangle to the lower left edge to make Unit 1, as shown in **Diagram 4**. Press the seam allowances toward the square, and label these Unit 1. Make the total number of Unit 1 segments required for your quilt size, as indicated in the Border Table. Note that the number of units needed is for *each* of the top, bottom, and side borders.

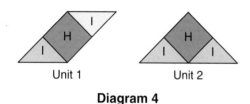

Diagram 4

Step 2. To make Unit 2, sew a medium I triangle to both the bottom left and the bottom right edges of the remaining four H squares, as shown in **Diagram 4**. Press the seam allowances toward the square, and label these Unit 2.

Border Table

	Double	Queen
Total Unit 1	104	120
Total Unit 2	4	4
Top/Bottom Borders (*each*)	24 Unit 1	28 Unit 1
	1 Unit 2	1 Unit 2
Side Borders (*each*)	28 Unit 1	32 Unit 1
	1 Unit 2	1 Unit 2

Step 3. Refer to the Border Table. To assemble each pieced border, sew the required number of Unit 1 segments together along their diagonal edges, as shown in **Diagram 5A**. Finish the right edge of each border with a Unit 2 segment, as shown in **5B**, and press.

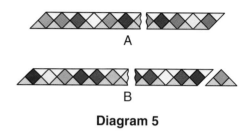

Diagram 5

Step 4. Sew the top, bottom, and side pieced borders to the appropriate sides of the quilt top, positioning the light I triangles closest to the center of the quilt, as shown in the **Quilt Diagrams**. For the best results, match the midpoint of each border to the midpoint of the corresponding edge of the quilt. Pin at the midpoints, and attach the borders, stopping ¼ inch from the edges of the quilt, so that the borders can be mitered after all four are attached.

Adding the Outer Border

Step 1. To determine the correct lengths for the outermost border, measure the quilt vertically and horizontally through its center, including the borders already added. Calculate the lengths of the strips, using the same method and formula as described in Step 2 of "Adding the Double Inner Borders."

Step 2. Cut each 4-inch-wide outer border from the border stripe in a single, continuous length as required for the side, the top, and the bottom border measurements.

Step 3. Sew each of the four borders to the appropriate edge of the quilt top. Match and pin the midpoints and follow the directions for adding mitered borders on page 242.

Step 4. Sew the mitered corners and press the seams open.

QUILTING AND FINISHING

Step 1. Mark the top for quilting. The Star blocks in the quilt shown were quilted in the ditch. Crosshatching of varying widths covers the rest of the quilt.

Step 2. The quilt backing will have to be pieced. **Diagram 6** illustrates the layout for both quilt backs. In each case, seams will run parallel to the top edge of the quilt.

Diagram 6

For the double-size quilt, cut the backing fabric into three equal lengths and trim the selvages. Cut a 30-inch-wide panel from the entire length of two segments, and sew a narrow panel to each side of

Double-Size Quilt Diagram

Queen-Size Quilt Diagram

the full-width piece. Press the seams open.

For the queen-size quilt, cut the backing fabric into three equal lengths and trim the selvages. Cut a 35-inch-wide panel from the entire length of two segments, and sew a narrow panel to each side of the full-width piece. Press the seams open.

Step 3. Layer the backing, batting, and quilt top. Baste the layers together. Quilt by hand or machine, adding any additional quilting designs of your choice as desired.

Step 4. Referring to the directions on page 244, make and attach double-fold binding to finish at a width of ¼ inch. To calculate the amount of binding you will need for the quilt size you are making, add the length of the four sides of the quilt plus 9 inches.

REFLECTIONS

Color Plan

Photocopy this page and use it to experiment with color schemes for your quilt.

MEMORIES OF SS #3

Skill Level: *Intermediate*

The humble Schoolhouse simply glows in Doreen Hugill's colorful mix of madras plaids, charming homespuns, jewel-tone brights, and delicious hand-dyed fabrics. Carefully shaded sashing strips and diagonally cut borders add excitement and motion to this color-splashed wallhanging.

BEFORE YOU BEGIN

Since each Schoolhouse block in this quilt is pieced from a different combination of fabrics, strip piecing is not especially efficient. However, quick cutting is employed to speed construction. With the exception of a few simple shapes that require templates, most of the pieces are strips, squares, and triangles that can be rotary cut. Fabrics can be layered for more efficient cutting.

CHOOSING FABRICS

In terms of color, just about anything goes in this exuberant design! The quiltmaker has fearlessly mixed fire engine red and magenta, teal and chartreuse, fuchsia and orange all in the same quilt. The colorful plaids and single star–studded background fabric pull it all together with great success.

The wonderful diagonal movement in the sashing and borders is created with a combination of subtly shaded and carefully graduated hand-dyed and printed fabrics. The sashing strips and squares grow progressively darker as they move from the upper right

Quilt Size	
Finished Quilt Size	33¼" × 40"
Finished Block Size	6"
Number of Blocks	20

NOTE: In order to maintain the balanced proportions and specific value progressions in this quilt design, no variations in size or layout are provided.

Materials	
Fabric	**Amount**
Assorted madras and homespun plaids	⅔ yard
Assorted bright and neutral prints	⅝ yard
Medium pink mottled solid	¼ yard
Medium rose mottled solid	⅓ yard
Dark red mottled solid	⅓ yard
Tan with navy star print	⅓ yard
Assorted neutral prints	¼ yard
Seven yellow and gold solids, graded from light to dark	⅛ yard each
Backing	1⅓ yards
Batting	40" × 46"

NOTE: Yardages are based on 44/45-inch-wide fabrics that are at least 42 inches wide after preshrinking.

to the lower left corner of the quilt. The diagonally pieced borders and binding intensify this effect. A design wall will come in handy to create a similar effect as you arrange the pieces for this quilt.

To help develop a unique color scheme, photocopy the **Color Plan** on page 19, and use crayons or colored pencils to experiment with different color arrangements.

Cutting Chart

Fabric	Used For	Strip Width	Number of Strips	Second Cut Dimensions	Number to Cut
Medium pink	Borders	3"	1		
	Binding	2½"	1		
Medium rose	Borders	3"	2		
	Binding	2½"	2		
Dark red	Borders	3"	2		
	Binding	2½"	2		
Gold 1 (lightest)	Sashing	1¼"		1¼" × 6½"	6
	Squares	1⅝"	1	1⅝" squares	5
Gold 2	Sashing	1¼"	1	1¼" × 6½"	6
	Squares	1⅝"	1	1⅝" squares	4
Gold 3	Sashing	1¼"	2	1¼" × 6½"	8
	Squares	1⅝"	1	1⅝" squares	5
Gold 4	Sashing	1¼"	2	1¼" × 6½"	9
	Squares	1⅝"	1	1⅝" squares	5
Gold 5	Sashing	1¼"	2	1¼" × 6½"	8
	Squares	1⅝"	1	1⅝" squares	5
Gold 6	Sashing	1¼"	1	1¼" × 6½"	6
	Squares	1⅝"	1	1⅝" squares	4
Gold 7	Sashing	1¼"	1	1¼" × 6½"	6
	Squares	1⅝"	1	1⅝" squares	5
Tan-and-navy print	K and K reverse	Template K		20 each	
	L	2"	1	1¼" × 2"	20
	N	1¾"	2	1¼" × 1¾"	4 each

Cut the following pieces for each Schoolhouse block. In each block, pieces B (door), F (windows), I (roof), and N (chimneys) may be cut from the same brights and neutrals, all different brights and neutrals, or any combination. Refer to the *Block Diagram* and the photograph on page 12 as needed.

Fabric	Used For	Dimensions	Number to Cut per House
Plaids	A	1¼" × 3"	3
	D	1" × 2¼"	3
	F	1" × 3½"	1
	G	1½" × 3½"	1
	J	Template J	1
Bright and neutral prints	B	1½" × 3"	1
	E	1¼" × 2¼"	2
	H	Template H	1
	M	1¼" × 1½"	2
Assorted neutral prints	C	1" × 3¾"	1
	I	Template I	1

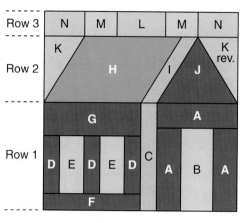

Block Diagram

Cut sizes

A = 1¼" × 3"
B = 1½" × 3"
C = 1" × 3¾"
D = 1" × 2¼"
E = 1¼" × 2¼"
F = 1" × 3½"
G = 1½" × 3½"
L = 1¼" × 2"
M = 1¼" × 1½"
N = 1¼" × 1¾"

CUTTING

All measurements include ¼-inch seam allowances. Refer to the Cutting Chart for the number of strips to cut in the sizes needed. Cut all strips across the fabric width (crosswise grain).

Make templates for pieces H, I, J, and K using the full-size pattern pieces on page 18. Refer to page 224 for complete details on making and using templates. The Cutting Chart indicates how many of each piece to cut with each template. Place the H, I, and K templates *wrong* side up on the wrong side of the fabric to cut those pieces. Turn the K template over to cut K reverse.

Cut each of the 1⅝-inch gold squares in half diagonally to make two triangles, as shown in **Diagram 1.** You will need nine triangles each from Gold 1, 3, 5, and 7; seven triangles from Gold 2 and 6; and ten triangles from Gold 4.

— **Sew Easy** —

It is not always easy to find just the right shades of fabric to show a slow progression of light-to-dark value such as in the sashing strips for this quilt. Sometimes the subtle difference in value from the front to the back of a fabric provides exactly the gradation you seek, so consider using the wrong side of some fabrics.

Note: Cut and piece one sample block before cutting all the fabric for the quilt.

Diagram 1

PIECING THE SCHOOLHOUSE BLOCKS

Refer to the **Block Diagram** as you assemble each block. Each pattern piece is identified by a letter. For ease of construction, the pieces are lettered in the alphabetical order in which they will be sewn. Rotary-cutting dimensions are also given for pieces that do not require a template.

Step 1. Sew a house fabric A to either side of a window fabric B along the longest sides, and press the seams to one side. Then add another A piece to the top of the A/B/A unit, as shown in **Diagram 2.** Stitch a neutral C to the left of the entire unit, as shown. Press the seams toward the newly added strips, and set the unit aside.

Diagram 2

Step 2. Sew three house fabric D pieces to two window fabric E pieces along their longest sides, alternating fabrics in the sequence shown in **Diagram 3.** Press all seams to one side. Add a house fabric F along the bottom edge and a house fabric G along the top edge, as shown, pressing seams toward F and G.

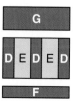

Diagram 3

Step 3. To complete Row 1, join the two units, as shown in **Diagram 4**. Press the seams toward C.

Row 1

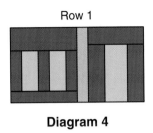

Diagram 4

Step 4. To make the roof section, sew an H, I, and J together, as shown in **Diagram 5**. Add a K and K reverse to either end of the roof, as shown. Press the seams as desired. This completes Row 2.

Row 2

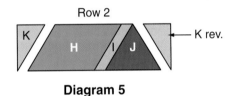

← K rev.

Diagram 5

Step 5. To make Row 3, sew an M chimney to either side of a tan L piece along the shortest sides. Add a tan N to each end of this unit, as shown in **Diagram 6**. Press the seams to one side.

Row 3

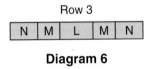

Diagram 6

Step 6. Referring to the **Block Diagram** on page 15, join Rows 1, 2, and 3 of the Schoolhouse block, carefully matching any appropriate seams. Press seams as desired.

Assembling the Quilt Top

Step 1. Refer to the **Assembly Diagram** and use a design wall or other flat surface to lay out the Schoolhouse blocks and sashing strips. The Schoolhouse blocks are arranged in five horizontal rows of four blocks each. The **Assembly Diagram** is coded to indicate where to place the various yellow and gold sashing strips to achieve the desired progression from light to dark.

Step 2. Place the appropriately colored corner triangles to match the adjacent sashing strips to complete the color/value transitions, as shown in the **Assembly Diagram**. You may also find it helpful to refer to the photograph on page 12 as you lay out your quilt top.

Step 3. Sew each pair of corner triangles together along the diagonal seam to make the sashing squares. Press the seams toward the darker triangles. Note that in some cases the two triangles will be cut from the same shade of yellow or gold.

Step 4. Sew the pieced sashing squares and sashing strips together in horizontal rows. Stitch the Schoolhouse blocks and sashing strips in horizontal rows, as shown in the **Assembly Diagram**. Press the seams in opposite directions from row to row.

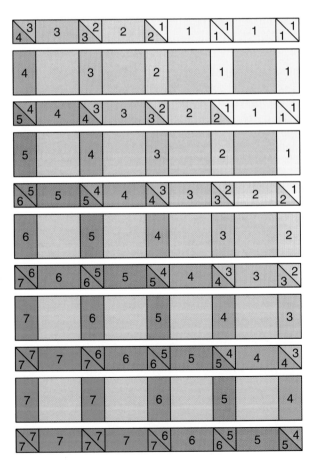

Assembly Diagram

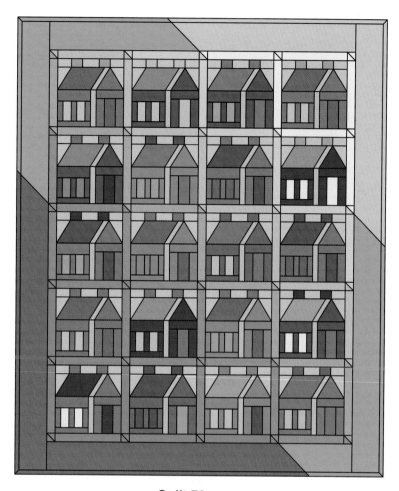

Quilt Diagram

Step 5. Sew the rows together, carefully matching seams. Press as desired.

PIECING AND ADDING THE BORDERS

Step 1. Cut the pink border strip and one rose border strip in half to make two 21-inch-long strips of each. Cut the remaining rose border strip into a 12-inch and a 30-inch piece. Pair the border strips and label them as follows: 21-inch-rose and 21-inch pink—top; 30-inch rose and 21-inch pink—right; 42-inch red and 12-inch rose—bottom; and 42-inch red and 21-inch rose—left.

Step 2. Sew the pairs of strips together, angling the seams, as shown in **Diagram 7**. Press the seams toward the lighter strips.

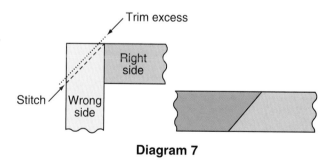

Diagram 7

Step 3. Sew the top and bottom borders to the quilt so the diagonal seams align with the diagonal seams in the sashing squares, as shown in the **Quilt Diagram**. Trim the borders even with the edges of the quilt top. Press the seams toward the borders.

Step 4. Sew the side borders to the quilt, positioning them so the diagonal seams align with the diagonal sashing square seams in the third row from the top. Trim the borders even with the quilt top, and press the seams toward the borders.

QUILTING AND FINISHING

Step 1. Mark the quilt top for quilting. The quilt shown is quilted in the ditch around the houses and along the sashing strips. The roof pieces are quilted to echo the pattern of the fabrics. The interior of the quilt top is quilted in randomly placed diagonal lines that run through the sashing strips, the block backgrounds, and the houses. Double parallel lines through the center of the border strips surround the entire quilt.

Step 2. Trim the selvages from the backing fabric. Layer the backing, batting, and quilt top; baste.

Step 3. Quilt all marked designs, adding any additional quilting as desired.

Step 4. The binding is pieced from the three border fabrics, and the seams are angled to correspond to and match the angles in the borders. Measure the perimeter of the quilt to determine where the binding will change color. Cut the binding strips to the appropriate lengths, leaving enough allowance on each strip so you can angle the seams in the same manner shown in **Diagram 7** on page 17 for the border strips. Attach the binding, aligning the angled seams, as shown in the photo on page 12. Refer to page 244 for additional instructions on making and attaching binding.

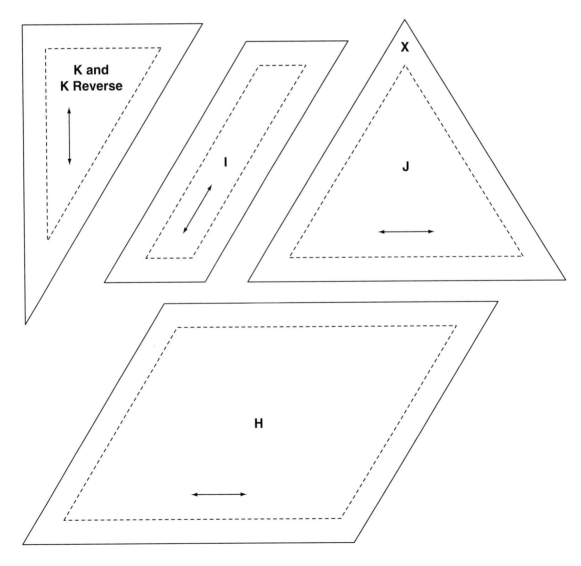

Memories of SS #3

Color Plan

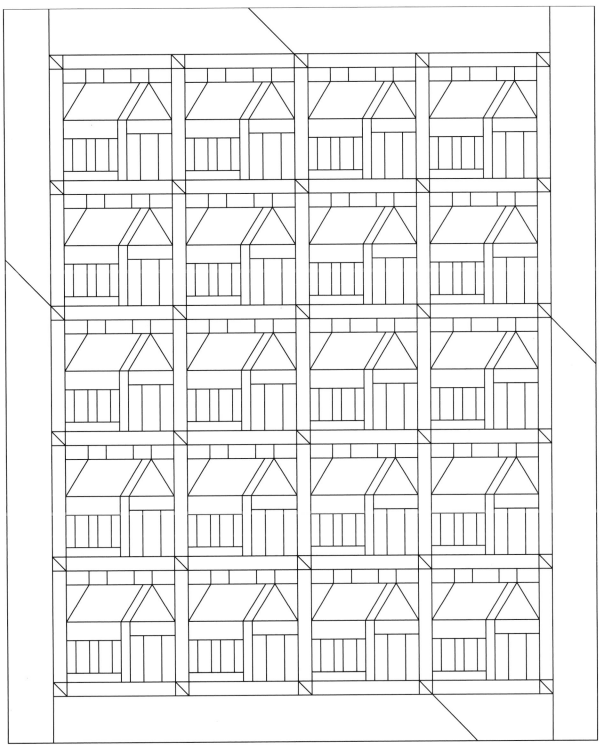

Photocopy this page and use it to experiment with color schemes for your quilt.

LOGS HEXAGONAL

Skill Level: *Challenging*

In a unique twist on tradition, the *Log Cabin* blocks in this quilt by June Ryker of Littleton, Colorado, are transformed into elongated hexagons. Though they look difficult to construct, they are actually pieced in the same manner as a traditional block. The vibrant radiating design in this king-size quilt is achieved by combining full blocks with partial blocks.

BEFORE YOU BEGIN

Although their shape is very unusual, the blocks in this quilt, designed and made by June Ryker, are constructed in the same manner as all other Log Cabin blocks. The directions for this quilt are written based on using the foundation technique, which is an alternative to the technique June used in her original published pattern. Read through "Foundation Piecing," beginning on page 232, to become familiar with the foundation technique.

There are five different foundation templates required for this quilt, as illustrated in the **Block Diagram** on page 22. Blocks A and B are full blocks; they are made from the same template but in two different color combinations. Blocks C1 and C2 are both half blocks, and blocks D and E are partial blocks. Study **Diagram 4** on page 25 to understand how the blocks work together. Prepare a foundation for each block and partial block using the full-size patterns on pages 27–31. Both permanent and removable foundations are suitable for assembling this block.

CHOOSING FABRICS

This quilt is another example of the important role color value plays in the final layout of blocks since the positioning of darks and lights is critical for definition of the flowing design.

To help develop your own unique color scheme

for the quilt, photocopy the **Color Plan** on page 26, and use crayons or colored pencils to experiment with different color arrangements.

Light and dark yardages shown are generous estimates of the total yardage actually used in the

<table>
<tr><td colspan="2">**Quilt Size**</td></tr>
<tr><td>Finished Size</td><td>99" × 99"</td></tr>
<tr><td>**Number of Blocks**</td><td></td></tr>
<tr><td>Full Blocks (A&B)</td><td>48</td></tr>
<tr><td>Half Blocks (C1&C2)</td><td>8</td></tr>
<tr><td>Partial Blocks (D)</td><td>16</td></tr>
<tr><td>(E)</td><td>4</td></tr>
</table>

NOTE: *Because the complex combination of blocks and partial blocks is critical to the overall design of this quilt, no variations in size or layout are provided.*

<table>
<tr><td colspan="2">**Materials**</td></tr>
<tr><td>**Fabric**</td><td>**Amount**</td></tr>
<tr><td>**Light prints**</td><td>7½ yards</td></tr>
<tr><td>**Dark prints**</td><td>8¼ yards</td></tr>
<tr><td>**Solid for centers**</td><td>⅝ yard</td></tr>
<tr><td>**Backing**</td><td>9 yards</td></tr>
<tr><td>**Batting (optional)**</td><td>105" × 105"</td></tr>
<tr><td>**Binding**</td><td>¾ yard</td></tr>
<tr><td>**Foundation material**</td><td>9½ yards</td></tr>
</table>

NOTE: *Yardages are based on 44/45-inch-wide fabrics that are at least 42 inches wide after preshrinking.*

quilt. For a successful scrap quilt, use small amounts of many fabrics.

CUTTING

Referring to the Cutting Chart, cut the number of strips needed. Cut all strips across the fabric width (crosswise grain). The cut sizes for the logs are slightly wider than the finished log size plus ¼-inch seam allowances. With the foundation method, it's easier to work with slightly wider strips. You may wish to decrease the width in ⅛-inch increments as you become more familiar with the technique.

To make the block centers, first make a template of piece 1 using the pattern on page 27, and add ¼-inch seam allowances to all sides. Use the template to cut a piece 1 for each block from the 4½-inch-wide strips. **Note:** Cut and sew one sample block before cutting all the pieces for the quilt.

Cutting Chart

Fabric	Strip Width	Number of Strips
Light prints	1¾"	154
Dark prints	1¾"	168
Solid	4½"	4

The number of dark and light strips needed for logs is estimated based on using full-width yardage. If you are using scraps, the number of strips needed will vary.

MAKING THE FOUNDATIONS

Step 1. The pattern is given full size in seven pieces on pages 27–31. Make a template for each different type of block, as shown in the **Block Diagram.** For best results, first trace all of the

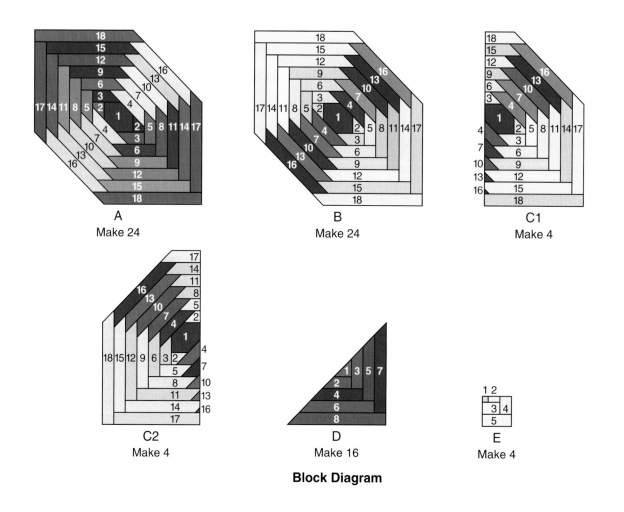

A
Make 24

B
Make 24

C1
Make 4

C2
Make 4

D
Make 16

E
Make 4

Block Diagram

pieces and carefully join them to make the template for the full block, referring to the **Pattern Key** on page 29 for correct placement. The full-block template should measure 12 inches across and 20½ inches from tip to tip. Trace the templates for the half and partial blocks from the completed full-block template. The colored lines on the pattern pieces indicate the various partial templates. Add ¼-inch seam allowances to all sides of each template.

Step 2. Following the instructions on page 234, transfer the patterns to your chosen foundation material. Make sure the marked lines are visible from the back side when you hold the foundation up to the light. Use the **Block Diagram** as a color sample and a reference for piecing order. Cut out the foundations, leaving a bit of extra material on all sides.

PIECING THE BLOCKS

Make a sample A or B block before cutting fabric for the entire quilt. If you experience problems while assembling the block, it may help to increase the width of the fabric strips slightly. Reevaluate your work often. You may find that strip width can be decreased once you are more familiar with the method.

Step 1. Cut a few 1¾-inch-wide strips of each fabric you plan to use in your sample block. Arrange the strips in piles, placing like values together. For a scrappy look, don't be concerned

Premarking your foundation for log color or value can be helpful. For this quilt, an L or a D, written with a permanent marker on specific logs to designate light or dark, would be a quick reference for piecing. Use the **Block Diagram** as a guide to value placement.

with color; just pick up the next strip of the correct value and sew.

Step 2. Place a 2½ × 4½-inch center rectangle right side up on the back of the foundation, covering the entire area of piece 1, as shown in **Diagram 1.** Secure it in place with tape, a bit of glue stick, or a pin.

Hold the foundation up to the light with the back side away from you. A shadow of the rectangle should be visible. It should overlap all lines surrounding piece 1. If it doesn't, reposition the fabric and check again.

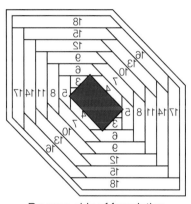

Reverse side of foundation

Diagram 1

Step 3. Add Row 2, beginning with either piece in the row. Place a strip of fabric right side down on top of piece 1, as shown in **Diagram 2A** on page 24. Holding the strip in place, flip the foundation over. Sew along the line separating piece 1 from the piece you are sewing in Row 2, beginning and ending approximately ⅛ inch on either side of the line.

Step 4. Remove the foundation from the machine and flip it to the reverse side. Trim away the excess tail of fabric just past the end of the seam line. Trim the bulk from the seam allowance, then flip the newly sewn piece into a right-side-up position. Finger press firmly in place. If you used tape on piece 1, remove it now. The reverse side of your foundation should now resemble **2B** on page 24. Notice that the unsewn edges of the new log overlap the three unsewn seam lines surrounding the piece's drawn border. Repeat to add the remaining log in Row 2.

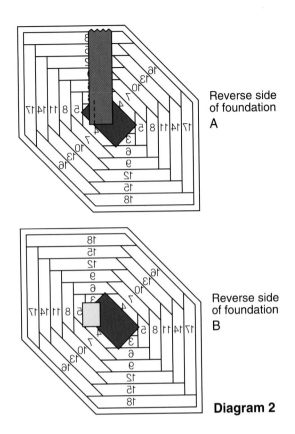

Reverse side
of foundation
A

Reverse side
of foundation
B

Diagram 2

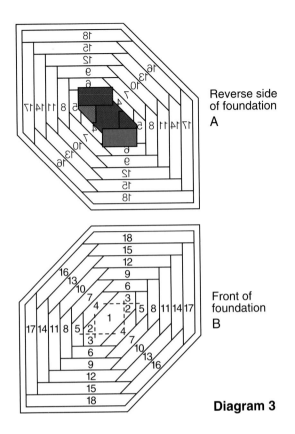

Reverse side
of foundation
A

Front of
foundation
B

Diagram 3

Step 5. Add the two logs in Row 3 in exactly the same manner. Stitch, trim, finger press, and check the width of each new log to make sure it extends past the unsewn seam lines. The reverse side of your foundation will now resemble **Diagram 3A**, and the front of your foundation should now resemble **3B**, with sewn seam lines crisscrossing each other. These crisscrossing seam lines help to reinforce the seams and add stability.

Step 6. All remaining logs are added in the same way. Although the block may look different from other foundation-based blocks, there is actually no difference in the way logs are added. Keep working your way outward until the last logs in Row 18 are sewn. Press the completed block lightly, then cut on the outer line of seam allowance, removing excess fabric.

Step 7. Repeat Steps 2 through 6, making the required number of full, half, and partial blocks. The piecing process for the half and partial blocks is the same as for the full blocks. Always begin with the lowest-numbered piece and work your way to the outside.

ASSEMBLING THE QUILT TOP

Step 1. Use a design wall or flat surface to arrange your blocks, referring to **Diagram 4** and the **Quilt Diagram** as guides to block placement.

Step 2. You will begin assembling the quilt at its center, radiating outward as you work. Join the blocks in the order listed below. Sew only to the outside seam line of the foundation; leave the seam allowances free. Backstitch at the beginning and the end of the seam. Pivot blocks to set in seams where necessary. (For details on setting in seams, see page 227 in "Quiltmaking Basics.")

◆ Sew four A blocks together at the quilt's center.
◆ Sew a B block into each corner.
◆ Sew two A blocks to each side.
◆ Sew two B blocks to each corner.
◆ Sew three A blocks to each side.

Quilt Diagram

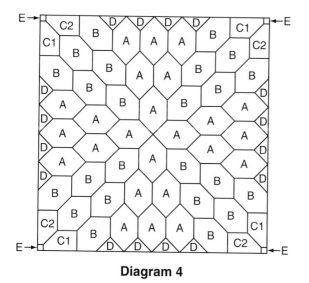

Diagram 4

✧ Sew three B blocks to each corner.

✧ Sew partial blocks C1, C2, D, and E around the outside edge to complete the quilt top.

Step 3. Tear away all removable foundations. Press seams.

QUILTING AND FINISHING

Step 1. Mark the quilt top for quilting, if desired. The quilt shown was quilted down the center of each log.

Step 2. The backing for this quilt should measure approximately 108 inches square. Cut the 9-yard piece of backing fabric into three equal lengths, and trim the selvages. Sew the segments together lengthwise. Press the seams open.

Step 3. Layer the backing, batting if used, and quilt top, centering the batting and quilt top on the backing. Trim approximately 9 inches of excess backing fabric from each side of the quilt. Baste the layers together. Quilt as desired.

Step 4. Referring to the directions on page 244 in "Quiltmaking Basics," make and attach double-fold binding. You will need approximately 405 inches of binding.

LOGS HEXAGONAL

Color Plan

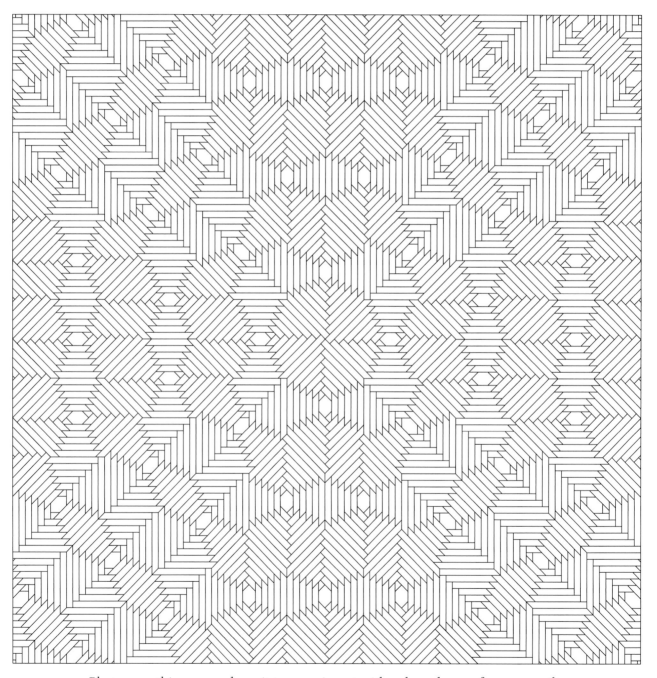

Photocopy this page and use it to experiment with color schemes for your quilt.

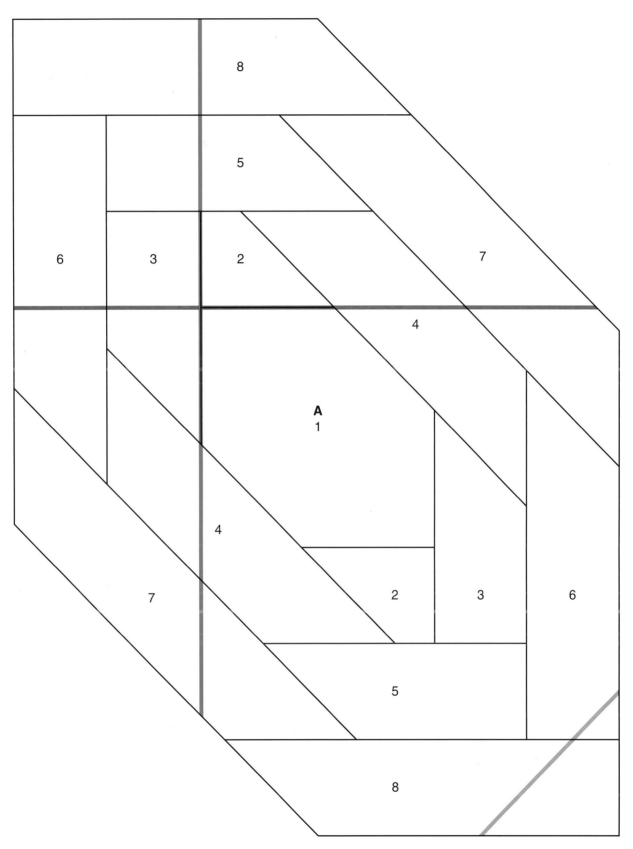

Pattern shown is the mirror image of the finished block.

16   **B** 13   10   10   **C** 13   16

Patterns shown are the mirror images of the finished block.

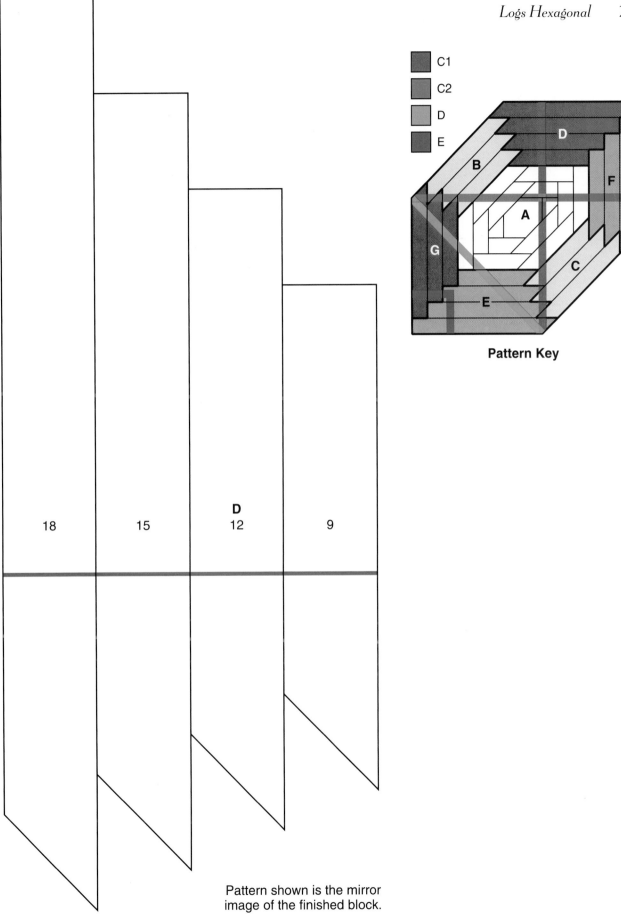

C1
C2
D
E

Pattern Key

18　　15　　**D**
12　　9

Pattern shown is the mirror
image of the finished block.

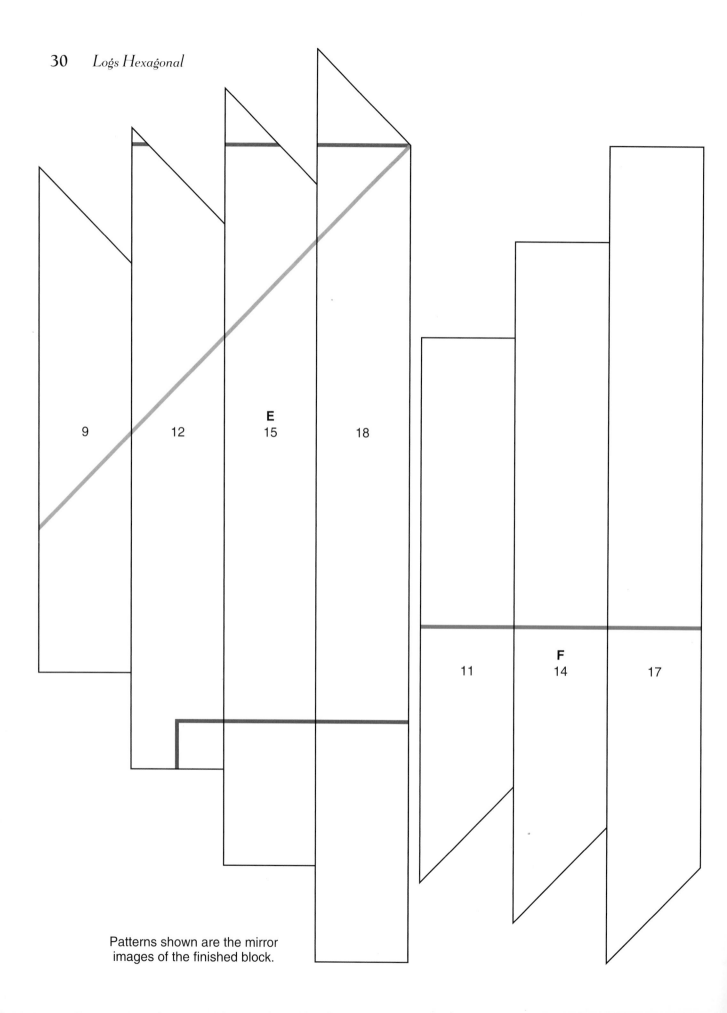

9

12

E
15

18

F
14

11

17

Patterns shown are the mirror
images of the finished block.

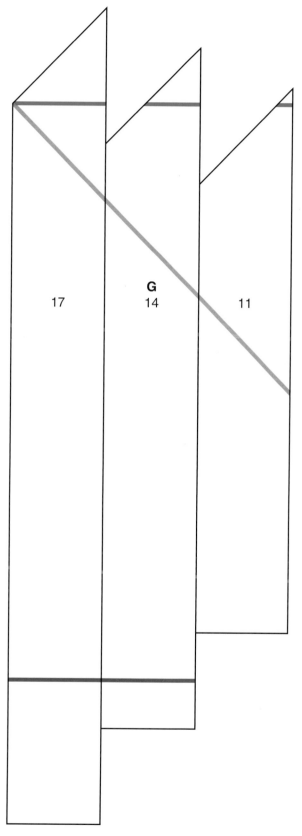

17

G
14

11

Pattern shown is the mirror image of the finished block.

SPARKLE PLENTY

Skill Level: *Challenging*

Sparkling Amish solids color this contemporary Amish-look quilt. Quiltmaker Joan Dyer of Redondo Beach, California, was inspired by a 1930s-era pinwheel quilt and chose orchid and navy to flavor her version of large and small pinwheels. Joan made this queen-size quilt as a wedding gift for her eldest daughter, but the directions also include a wallhanging that is equally suitable for gift giving.

BEFORE YOU BEGIN

Triangle squares are used to assemble the large, on-point orchid and navy pinwheel blocks and the multicolored pinwheel block sashing that surrounds them.

Two quick-piecing methods are described on pages 225–227. The large pinwheels are assembled using the single square method. The single square method and the grid method are both suitable for the small pinwheels. We recommend you read the instructions for both methods before choosing fabrics or starting this project.

CHOOSING FABRICS

To make a quilt similar to the one shown, choose light orchid and navy fabrics for the large pinwheel blocks. The light orchid fabric is repeated in the middle border, the navy in the wide, outer border. A medium orchid fabric is used in the inner border.

In the quilt shown, the quiltmaker used many subdued Amish colors in the small pinwheels, but added sparkle by scattering an occasional vivid dark or light solid

Quilt Sizes

	Wallhanging	Queen (shown)
Finished Quilt Size	70¼" × 70¼"	93" × 115½"
Finished Block Size		
Large Pinwheel	12"	12"
Small Pinwheel	4"	4"
Number of Blocks		
Large Pinwheel	5	18
Large Half-Pinwheel	4	10
Small Pinwheel	60	175
Number of Triangle Squares		
Large Pinwheel	20	72
Large Half-Pinwheel	4	10
Small Pinwheel	240	700

Materials

Fabric	Wallhanging	Queen
Navy	2¾ yards	5¼ yards
Light orchid	1⅛ yards	3 yards
Medium orchid	1⅛ yards	1½ yards
Assorted darks	1⅛ yards	2¼ yards
Assorted lights and medium lights	1⅛ yards	2¼ yards
Backing	4½ yards	8½ yards
Batting	77" × 77"	99" × 122"
Binding	⅝ yard	⅞ yard

NOTE: *Yardages are based on 44/45-inch-wide fabrics that are at least 42 inches wide after preshrinking.*

Cutting Chart

Fabric	Used For	Strip Width	Number to Cut Wallhanging	Queen
Navy	Large pinwheels	6⅞"	2	6
	Corners and half-pinwheels	9¾"	1	4
	Outer border	9"	7	11
Light orchid	Large pinwheels	6⅞"	2	6
	Corners and half-pinwheels	9¾"	1	4
	Middle border	1½"	6	9
Medium orchid	Inner border corners	3⅜"	4	4
	Inner border half-pinwheels	3⅜"	4	10
Assorted colors	Small pinwheels	See "Making the Small Pinwheels"		

throughout the blocks. For the small pinwheels, select a variety of solids, half of them dark shades, the rest light to medium-light in value.

Collect as many colors as possible to re-create the sparkling effect of the pinwheels. For example, the yardage requirement for the assorted dark solids for the wallhanging is 1⅛ yards. Buy ⅛ yard of nine different dark fabrics to get the most impact for your money. For the queen size, quarter-yard cuts of fabric will be more economical. Buy ¼ yard of nine different dark solids to reach the 2¼ yards needed.

To help you create your own unique color scheme, photocopy the **Color Plan** on page 39, and use crayons or colored pencils to experiment with different color arrangements.

CUTTING

All measurements include ¼-inch seam allowances. Referring to the Cutting Chart, cut the required number of strips in the widths needed. Cut all strips across the fabric width.

The inner border pieces are cut from strips. When you have cut the number of strips listed in the Cutting Chart, refer to the instructions here to cut the individual pieces. Refer to "Making the Small Pinwheels" to cut the small pinwheel blocks.

• Cut the 6⅞-inch navy and light orchid strips into 6⅞-inch squares.

• Cut the 9¾-inch navy and light orchid strips into 9¾-inch squares.

• Cut the 3⅜-inch medium orchid inner border corner strips into 15⅜-inch lengths.

• Cut the 3⅜-inch medium orchid inner border half-pinwheel strips into 23⅞-inch lengths.

Note: Cut and piece one sample pinwheel in each size before cutting all of the fabric for the quilt.

MAKING THE LARGE PINWHEELS

Each large pinwheel block is made up of four triangle squares, as illustrated below.

Large Pinwheel Block Diagram

Step 1. Refer to the Quilt Sizes chart on page 33 to determine the number of large triangle squares and pinwheel blocks you need for your quilt size. Refer to "Method 2: Single Squares from Squares" on page 226 to make the triangle squares for your quilt, using the 6⅞-inch navy and light orchid squares. Press the seams and trim the tips as shown in the basic instructions.

Step 2. Position four of the large triangle squares as shown in **Diagram 1A**, then sew pairs together as indicated. Press the center seam in each pair in opposite directions, then match the seams carefully and sew the two units together. Leave the final seam unpressed for now. The finished block should look like **1B**. Repeat to make the number of whole blocks required. (You will have triangle-squares left over; set them aside. They will be used to assemble the half-pinwheel blocks.)

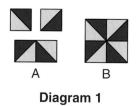

Diagram 1

MAKING THE HALF-PINWHEELS

Step 1. Cut the 9¾-inch light orchid and navy squares in half diagonally twice, as shown in **Diagram 2**.

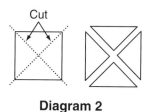

Diagram 2

Step 2. Use one of the leftover orchid/navy triangle squares for each half-pinwheel block. Position the triangle square, an orchid triangle, and a navy triangle, as shown in **Diagram 3**. Be sure to match the edges of the triangles with the triangle squares as shown, then sew them together. Press the seams toward the navy fabric. Set aside the leftover navy and orchid triangles to be used in the quilt's corners.

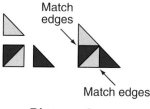

Diagram 3

PREPARING THE INNER BORDERS

Step 1. Fold each 3⅜ × 23⅞-inch medium orchid strip in half crosswise, wrong sides together, matching the edges exactly. Press the strip to mark the center and help the edges adhere to each other. Use your rotary cutter and ruler to make a 45-degree cut across the ends opposite the folds, beginning precisely at the lower corner of the strip, as shown in **Diagram 4**. Open the strip. Repeat for all of the strips.

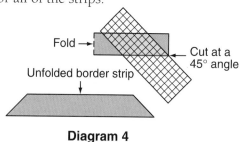

Diagram 4

Step 2. Sew a medium-orchid strip to each large half-pinwheel block, matching the center crease to the center of the pinwheel block (see **Diagram 5**). Press the seam toward the border strip. Repeat for the remaining half-pinwheels.

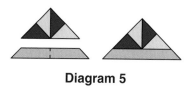

Diagram 5

MAKING THE SMALL PINWHEELS

Each small pinwheel block is made up of four triangle squares, as shown below.

Small Pinwheel Block Diagram

Step 1. Refer to the Quilt Sizes chart on page 33 to determine the number of triangle squares you need to make the small pinwheel blocks. For good contrast, be sure each triangle square pairs a dark fabric with a light or medium-light fabric. To make triangle squares, refer to the assembly methods on pages 225–227. If you are using the grid method, use a 2⅞-inch grid, and cut each piece of yardage in half lengthwise twice so you are working with pieces about 10 inches wide to keep the grid at a manageable size. If using the single square method, cut 2⅞-inch squares.

Step 2. Select four triangle squares and position them with the dark triangles oriented as shown in **Diagram 1** on page 35. Sew the blocks together and press in the same manner as for the large pinwheel blocks, leaving the final seam unpressed.

ASSEMBLING THE CORNER UNITS

Step 1. Fold each 3⅜ × 15⅜-inch medium orchid strip in half and make a 45-degree cut through the ends as described in Step 1 of "Preparing the Inner Borders."

Step 2. Match the centers and sew a trimmed border strip to the longest side of a light orchid triangle to create one-half of a corner unit, as shown in **Diagram 6**. Press the seam toward the border strip. Repeat for the three remaining light orchid triangles. Sew a trimmed border strip to each navy triangle to create the other half of a corner unit, pressing the seam toward the navy triangle.

Step 3. Sew the light orchid and navy units together in pairs, as shown in **Diagram 7**. Make four corner units, matching the seams carefully where border strips meet. Press seams toward the navy unit.

Diagram 6   **Diagram 7**

ASSEMBLING THE QUILT

Step 1. Use a design wall or a flat surface to lay out the quilt in diagonal rows, as shown in the **Wallhanging Assembly Diagram** or the **Queen-**

Size Assembly Diagram. Reposition and rotate the small pinwheels until you're satisfied with the appearance of the quilt; be sure to keep all the dark colors in the same position when rearranging, and avoid positioning light orchid and navy fabrics against their counterpart panels in the large blocks.

Wallhanging Assembly Diagram

Step 2. Assemble the components of the diagonal rows by first sewing together each group of three small pinwheels that separates the large pinwheels. As you align each group for stitching, press the seams that were previously left unpressed so that adjoining blocks have seams facing in opposite directions. Sew the three-pinwheel strips to the sides of the large pinwheels, matching the center and end points carefully, as shown in **Diagram 8**. Press the seams toward the sashing strips.

Diagram 8

Step 3. Sew together the long rows of small pinwheels to create sashing strips that separate the diagonal rows of blocks. For the wallhanging, you'll have two rows of five small pinwheels, and two rows of 13 small pinwheels. For the queen size, you will have two rows of five small pinwheels, two rows of 13 small pinwheels, two rows of 21 small pinwheels, and one row of 25 small pinwheels.

Step 4. For the wallhanging, work from the upper left corner and sew the first sashing strip, made of five small pinwheels, to the pinwheel block with sashing. Sew the half-pinwheels to the ends of the pinwheel block row. Sew the corner pinwheel on last. Press. Repeat for the lower right corner. For the center row, sew the long sashing strip to the sides of the pinwheel block row. Sew the upper left and lower right units to the center row, then sew on the corner setting triangles. Press.

Step 5. For the queen size, work from the upper left corner and sew the first sashing strip to the pinwheel block with sashing. Sew the half-pinwheels to the ends of the pinwheel block row. Sew on the corner pinwheel, matching the center point to the center of the adjoining sashing strip.

Queen-Size Assembly Diagram

Press. Sew the next two rows of sashing strips and pinwheel blocks together, matching the seams carefully and pressing them toward the sashing strips. Sew the half-pinwheels to the ends of each row to create the upper left unit. Repeat to assemble the lower right unit of the quilt.

Sew the largest sashing row to the bottom of the upper left corner. Sew the two assembled units together. Sew on the remaining corner pinwheels, matching the center points to the centers of the adjoining sashing strip. Press.

ATTACHING THE BORDERS

Step 1. Measure the quilt top vertically through the center. To this measurement add two times the finished width of the middle border, plus 5 inches (add a total of 7 inches), to allow for the miter. Use the 1½-inch-wide light orchid strips to assemble two side borders this length. Then measure the quilt top horizontally through the center and use the remaining 1½-inch-wide light orchid strips to assemble top and bottom borders this exact length.

Step 2. Pin and sew the four border strips to the quilt top, beginning and ending the seams ¼ inch from the edge of the quilt. Press the seams toward the border. For instructions on mitering, refer to page 242.

Step 3. Add the side outer borders first (see the **Queen-Size Quilt Diagram** on page 38). Measure the quilt top vertically through the center. Use the 9-inch-wide navy strips to make two border strips this length.

Step 4. Fold a strip in half crosswise and crease. Unfold it and position it right side down along one side of the quilt, with the crease at the vertical midpoint. Pin at the midpoint and ends first, then along the length of the entire side, easing in fullness. Sew the border to the quilt top. Repeat on the opposite side of the quilt.

Step 5. Measure the width of the quilt top through the horizontal center of the quilt, including side borders. Use the remaining 9-inch navy strips to assemble two strips this exact length. Sew to the top and bottom of the quilt as described in Step 4.

Queen-Size Quilt Diagram

QUILTING AND FINISHING

Step 1. Mark the quilt top for quilting. The quilt shown features a feather wreath in each large pinwheel block, a cable design in the inner borders, and a floral design in the outer borders. Individual patches were quilted in the ditch.

Step 2. To make the backing for the wallhanging, cut the fabric crosswise into two equal pieces, and trim the selvages. Cut one of the pieces in half lengthwise and sew one half to each side of the full-width piece, as shown in **Diagram 9**. Press the seams open. For the queen-size quilt, cut the backing fabric crosswise into three equal pieces, and trim the selvages. Sew the pieces together lengthwise. Press the seams open.

Step 3. Layer the quilt top, batting, and backing. Baste the layers together and quilt as desired.

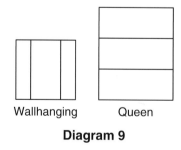

Wallhanging   Queen
Diagram 9

Step 4. Referring to the directions on page 244, make and attach double-fold binding. To calculate the amount of binding needed for the quilt size you are making, add the length of the four sides of the quilt, plus 9 inches.

SPARKLE PLENTY

Color Plan

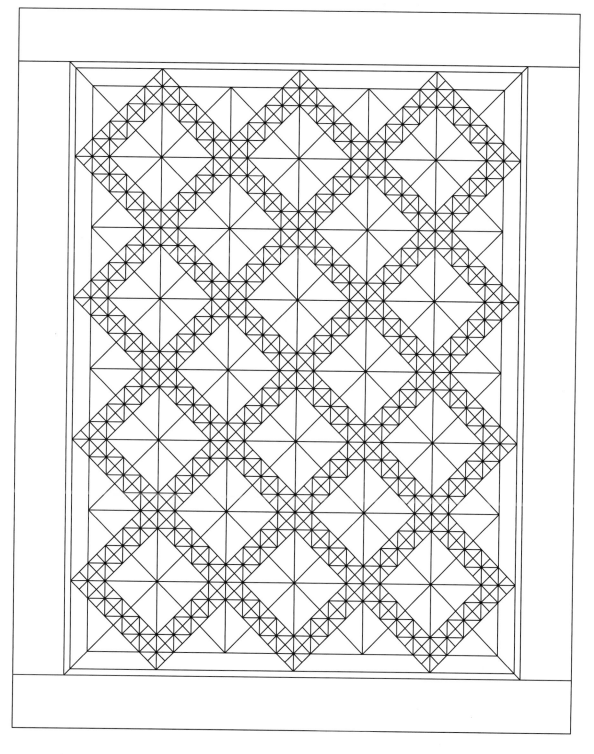

Photocopy this page and use it to experiment with color schemes for your quilt.

HOUSE MEDALLION

Skill Level: *Intermediate*

*T*his quilt has a personality all its own, with its grab bag of striking, simple-to-piece borders. A carefree mix of brightly colored, boldly patterned stripes, checks, and polka dots lend Susan Bengtson's original design a decidedly festive air. The generously sized lap quilt doubles as a cozy, bed-size coverlet or as a large wallhanging that will steal the spotlight in any family room or den.

BEFORE YOU BEGIN

With its wide variety of fabrics and techniques, this quilt will give you the chance to try many things. It's rated intermediate simply because each successive border adds something new in terms of pattern or technique. The construction is simple enough, however, that a beginner can feel confident while broadening and sharpening her piecing skills.

Except for a few simple shapes that require templates, all of the pieces are strips, squares, and triangles that can be rotary cut. In addition, an easy strip-piecing technique is provided for making the checkerboard border.

Directions for two size variations are provided. The smaller wallhanging finishes with the first sawtooth border—a perfect size for a gift.

"Set-In Seams," beginning on page 227, provides general information about making the Schoolhouse block, as well as for more details on rotary cutting and strip-piecing techniques.

CHOOSING FABRICS

The variety of modern polka dots, stripes, and checks complements

Quilt Sizes

	Wallhanging	Lap (shown)
Finished Quilt Size	36½" × 36½"	64" × 64"
Finished Block Size		
Schoolhouse	9"	9"
Star		6"
Number of Blocks		
Schoolhouse	4	4
Star		28

Materials

Fabric	Wallhanging	Lap
Red polka dot	¼ yard	⅝ yard
Red check	¼ yard	¼ yard
Assorted pink and red dots, stripes, and checks	⅓ yard	⅝ yard
Assorted tan, brown, and black dots, stripes, and checks	¾ yard	1⅞ yards
Brown-on-tan dots		¾ yard
Tan stripe	⅝ yard	¾ yard
Black solid	⅛ yard	¼ yard
Gold solid	⅛ yard	¼ yard
Tan and brown solids	⅛ yard	⅛ yard
Assorted bright dots, stripes, and checks	½ yard	1¾ yards
Backing	1¼ yards	4 yards
Batting	43" × 43"	70" × 70"

NOTE: *Yardages are based on 44/45-inch-wide fabrics that are at least 42 inches wide after preshrinking.*

Cutting Chart

Fabric	Used For	Strip Width	Number to Cut Wallhanging	Lap	Second Cut Dimensions
Red polka dot	Border 1	2½"	2	2	
	Border 3	2"		6	
Red check	Border 2	1½"	4	4	
Pinks and reds	Sawtooth borders	2⅞"	3	6	2⅞" squares
Assorted tans, browns, and blacks	Checkerboard border	2"	4	4	
	Sawtooth borders	2⅞"	3	6	2⅞" squares
	Stars	2⅜"		1	2⅜" squares
	Stars	3½"		1	3½" squares
	On-point border	5½"		4	5½" squares
	On-point border	3"		1	3" squares
Black solid	Stars	4¼"		1	4¼" squares
	Stars	2"		1	2" squares
Brown-on-tan dots	Stars	4¼"		3	4¼" squares
	Stars	2"		5	2" squares
Brights	Checkerboard border	2"	8	8	
	Stars	2⅜"		6	2⅜" squares
	Stars	3½"		2	3½" squares
	On-point border	3½"		5	3½" squares

From the assorted tan, brown, and black prints and black and gold solids, cut the following pieces for each of the four Schoolhouse blocks. Refer to the *Schoolhouse Block Diagram* and the photograph on page 40 as needed.

Fabric	Used For	Dimensions	Number to Cut per House
House print 1	A	2" × 5"	2
	C	1½" × 5"	1
	H	Template H	1
House print 2	F	1½" × 4"	2
	D	1¼" × 4"	1
	G	1½" × 5"	2
Roof print	I	Template I	1
	K	1½" × 1½"	2
Door and window solid	B	2" × 5"	1
	E	1⅜" × 4"	2
Sky solid	L	1½" × 3"	1
	J and J reverse	Template J	1 each

the eclectic mix of traditional quilt block patterns in this happy-go-lucky quilt. The prints are from a single fabric line, so they coordinate effortlessly, which brings order to what might have been an otherwise dizzying array.

Brights, primaries, and jewel tones work especially well in this design. Neutrals such as tan, brown, and black add a calming influence. You might choose to work strictly in dots and geometrics or to add other prints and patterns. Draw

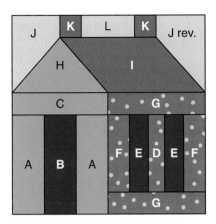

Schoolhouse Block Diagram

Cut sizes

A = 2" × 5"
B = 2" × 5"
C = 1½" × 5"
D = 1¼" × 4"
E = 1⅜" × 4"
F = 1½" × 4"
G = 1½" × 5"
K = 1½" × 1½"
L = 1½" × 3"

your selection from one fabric line or rely on a mixture from your scrap bag.

To develop a unique color scheme for the quilt, photocopy the **Color Plan** on page 49, and use crayons or colored pencils to experiment with different color arrangements.

CUTTING

All measurements include ¼-inch seam allowances. Refer to the Cutting Chart and cut the required number of strips and squares in the sizes needed. Cut all strips across the fabric width.

Make templates for pieces H, I, and J, using the full-size pattern pieces on page 48. Refer to page 224 for complete details on making and using templates. The Cutting Chart indicates how many of each piece to cut with each template. Place the templates wrong side up on the wrong side of the fabric to cut pieces, except for J reverse. Turn the J template over to cut piece J reverse.

You will need to cut some of the squares into triangles, as follows:

• For the Sawtooth borders, cut the 2⅞-inch assorted red, pink, tan, and brown squares in half diagonally, as shown in **Diagram 1A.** You'll need 68 red and pink triangles and 68 tan and brown triangles for the wallhanging. You'll need 168 red and pink and 168 brown and tan triangles for the lap quilt.

• For the bright Stars, cut the 4¼-inch brown-on-tan dot squares diagonally in half in each di-

rection to make 96 triangles, as shown in **1B.** Cut the 2⅜-inch assorted bright squares in half once diagonally to make 192 triangles.

• For the dark Stars, cut the 2⅜-inch black and brown print squares in half diagonally to make 32 triangles. Cut the 4¼-inch black solid squares diagonally each way to make 16 triangles.

• For the on-point borders, cut the 5½-inch tan and brown squares diagonally in both directions to make 104 Y triangles. Cut the 3-inch tan and brown squares in half diagonally to make 16 Z triangles.

Note: Cut and piece a sample Schoolhouse and Star block before cutting fabric for all of the blocks in the quilt.

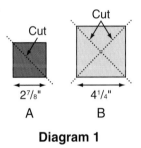

Diagram 1

ASSEMBLING THE SCHOOLHOUSE BLOCKS

Refer to the **Schoolhouse Block Diagram** as you assemble each block. Each pattern piece is lettered in the alphabetical order in which it will be sewn. Cutting dimensions are also provided for pieces that are rotary cut. For either quilt size, you will need four Schoolhouse blocks. While the houses are made from different fabrics, each house uses four fabrics, as specified in the Cutting Chart.

Step 1. Sew an A piece to either side of a B piece along the long edges, then add a C piece to the top of the unit, as shown in **Diagram 2** on page 44. Press all seams to one side.

Step 2. Sew an E piece to either side of a D piece. Add an F piece to either end of the unit, referring to **Diagram 3** on page 44. Sew a G piece to the top and bottom of the unit, as shown. Press all seams to one side.

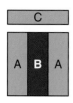
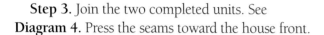
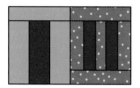

Diagram 2

Diagram 3

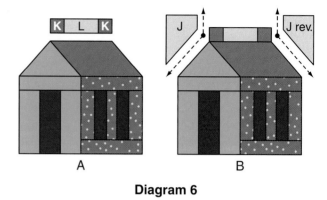

A   B

Diagram 6

Step 3. Join the two completed units. See **Diagram 4.** Press the seams toward the house front.

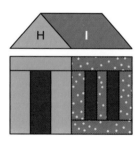

Diagram 4

Step 4. Sew an H piece to the left side of an I piece, as shown in **Diagram 5.** Press the seams toward I. Stitch this roof unit to the top edge of the house, as shown. Press the seams as desired and set aside.

Diagram 5

Step 5. Sew a K piece to either side of an L piece, as shown in **Diagram 6A.** Press the seams away from L. Pin, then stitch this chimney unit to the top edge of the roof, as shown. Press the seams as desired. Set in the J and J reverse pieces, as shown in **6B.** For J, begin stitching ¼ inch from the raw edge at the point where H, I, and K meet. Attach J reverse in the same manner. In each case, stitch outward in the direction indicated by the arrows. Press the seams away from the J pieces. Refer to page 227 for additional information on set-in seams.

Step 6. Repeat Steps 1 through 5 to make a total of four Schoolhouse blocks.

ASSEMBLING THE QUILT CENTER

Step 1. Use a design wall or other flat surface to lay out the four Schoolhouse blocks in two rows of two blocks each, as shown in the **Quilt Diagram.** Sew the blocks in horizontal rows, pressing the seam allowances in opposite directions from row to row. Sew the rows together, carefully matching seams. Press.

Step 2. Cut each of the 2-inch-wide red polka dot Border 1 strips in half to yield four strips that each measure approximately 21 inches long.

Step 3. Measure the four-block Schoolhouse unit from top to bottom, taking the measurement through the center, not along the sides. Trim two of the Border 1 strips to this length.

Step 4. Fold one strip in half crosswise and crease. Unfold it and position it right side down along one side of the four-block unit, with the midpoints and ends matching. Pin, easing in fullness if necessary. Sew the border to the quilt top, using a ¼-inch seam allowance. Press the seams toward the border strip. Repeat on the opposite side.

Step 5. Add the remaining border strips to the top and bottom edges of the quilt top in the same manner, except this time measure the quilt through its horizontal center and include the side borders.

Quilt Diagram

PIECING AND ADDING THE CHECKERBOARD BORDER

Step 1. Cut all of the 2-inch-wide strips for the checkerboard border in half so they are approximately 21 inches long. Sew the strips together in sets of three, referring to **Diagram 7.** The strips should contrast in value or color or both. Press the seams in one direction. Using a rotary cutter and ruler, square up one end of each strip set. Cut 2-inch-wide segments from the strip sets, as shown, until you have cut 68 segments.

Step 2. Sew the segments together, mixing fabrics and turning alternating segments so that adjoining seams are pressed in opposing directions. See **Diagram 8.** For either quilt, make two borders with 14 segments and two borders with 20 segments.

Step 3. Sew the 14-segment borders to the quilt sides, followed by the 20-segment top and bottom borders, matching the corner seams. Press seams toward the inner border. See "Sew Easy" on page 46 for tips on fitting pieced borders.

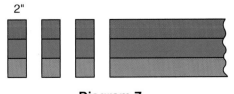

Diagram 7

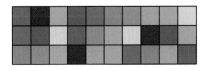

Diagram 8

ADDING THE RED BORDER 2

Following the procedure described in Steps 3 and 4 of "Assembling the Quilt Center" on page 44, add the red side Border 2 strips, followed by the top and bottom Border 2 strips, to the quilt top. Refer to the **Quilt Diagram** on page 45.

MAKING AND ADDING THE SAWTOOTH BORDER

Step 1. Sew the red and pink triangles to the tan and brown triangles, as shown in **Diagram 9**, to make triangle squares. Make 68 for the wallhanging and 168 for the lap quilt. Press the seams toward the red and pink triangles.

Step 2. To make Sawtooth Border 1, sew the triangle-square units into strips, as shown in **Diagram 10**. Make two strips with 16 triangle squares each for the side borders and two strips with 18 triangle squares each for the top and bottom borders. Make sure that the triangle points change direction at the middle of each border, as shown here and in the **Quilt Diagram** on page 45.

Diagram 9   **Diagram 10**

Step 3. Sew a Sawtooth Border 1 strip to each side of the quilt with the red and pink triangle edges aligned with the red check border. Press the seams toward the red check border. Add the top and bottom Sawtooth Border 1 strips in the same manner.

If you are making the wallhanging, proceed to "Quilting and Finishing" on page 48. If you are making the lap quilt, continue on with Step 4.

Step 4. The Sawtooth Border 2 is made exactly the same way as Sawtooth Border 1, except each side contains more triangle squares. You will need to make two strips with 24 triangle squares each for the side borders and two strips with 26 triangle squares each for the top and bottom borders. Again, be sure to change the direction of the

triangles at the midpoint of each border. Press the seams in one direction and set the borders aside.

— Sew Easy —

When joining two smaller triangles to a larger one, such as in the Star blocks, the resulting seams form an X. Stitch carefully through the center of the X when adding this pieced unit to the block for a perfect point where the two units meet.

The same principle holds true when piecing triangle squares into rows, as in the Sawtooth borders. Stitch through the X formed by the seams on the strip of triangle squares when attaching the border for more perfect points.

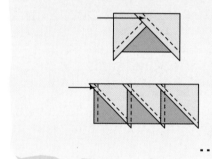

MAKING AND ADDING THE STAR BORDER

The blocks are all pieced in the same manner, as shown in the **Star Block Diagram**, but they are shaded in two different value arrangements. Make 24 blocks with brown-on-tan dot backgrounds, bright triangle points, and a contrasting center square. Make four blocks with black solid backgrounds, using a mix of black and tan prints for the points and centers.

Star Block Diagram

Step 1. Sew a bright triangle to each short side of a tan triangle, as shown in **Diagram 11A.** Press the seams toward the bright fabric. Make four identical units for each block. Sew a triangle unit to the top and bottom edge of a contrasting bright square, as shown. Press the seams toward the center square.

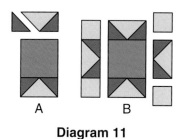

Diagram 11

Step 2. Sew a tan square to each end of the remaining two triangle units, as shown in **11B.** Press the seams toward the squares. Sew one of these strips to each side of the block. Press the seams as desired. Repeat to make 24 bright Star blocks.

Step 3. Make four dark Star blocks following Steps 1 and 2 above, substituting black solid for the tan polka dot pieces and black and tan polka dots and checks for the bright fabrics.

Step 4. Sew six bright Star blocks together in a row to make a border strip. Press the seams as desired. Make four of these border strips.

Step 5. Sew one border to each side of the quilt top, carefully matching the outer seams between the Star blocks with the seams of Sawtooth Border 1.

Step 6. Sew a dark Star block to each end of the remaining two bright Star borders, and sew these borders to the top and bottom edges of the quilt, matching seams. Press as desired.

Adding Sawtooth Border 2

Referring to the **Quilt Diagram** on page 45, sew a Sawtooth Border 2 to each side of the quilt top in the same manner as for Sawtooth Border 1. Press, then repeat for the top and bottom of the quilt. Press.

Assembling and Attaching the Final Borders

Step 1. You will need to piece the red polka dot Border 3 strips to fit the quilt. Cut two of the strips in half crosswise and add a half strip to each of the remaining four strips.

Step 2. Add the borders in the same manner as for red Borders 1 and 2. Add the side borders first, followed by the top and bottom borders. Press the seams toward the red borders.

Step 3. To assemble the on-point outer border, sew a tan or brown print Y triangle to two opposite sides of a 3½-inch bright print square, as shown in **Diagram 12A.** Press the seams toward the triangles. Make 48 of these units.

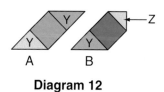

Diagram 12

Step 4. Sew Y and Z triangles to opposite sides of a bright print square, as shown in **12B.** Press the seam allowances toward the triangles. Make eight of these units.

Step 5. Sew 11 Y/square/Y units together to form a long border strip. Add a Y/square/Z unit to each end of the strip, and finish the strip by adding another Z triangle. See **Diagram 13.** Press the seams as desired. Make two of these border strips for the side borders.

Diagram 13

Step 6. Make the top and bottom borders in the same manner, using 13 Y/square/Y units per strip.

Step 7. Sew the side borders to the quilt top, followed by the top and botton borders. Refer to the **Quilt Diagram** on page 45.

QUILTING AND FINISHING

Step 1. Mark the quilt top for quilting. The quilt shown is machine quilted in the ditch around most of the key shapes.

Step 2. For the lap quilt, you will need to piece the backing. Cut the backing fabric in half crosswise, and trim the selvages. Cut one piece in half lengthwise and sew one half to each side of the full-width piece. Press the seams away from the center panel. See page 243 for more information on pieced quilt backs. For the wallhanging, simply trim the selvages of the backing fabric.

Step 3. Layer the backing, batting, and quilt top; baste. Hand or machine quilt as desired.

Step 4. Referring to page 244, make and attach double-fold binding from the tan stripe fabric. Make about 154 inches for the wallhanging and 264 inches for the lap quilt.

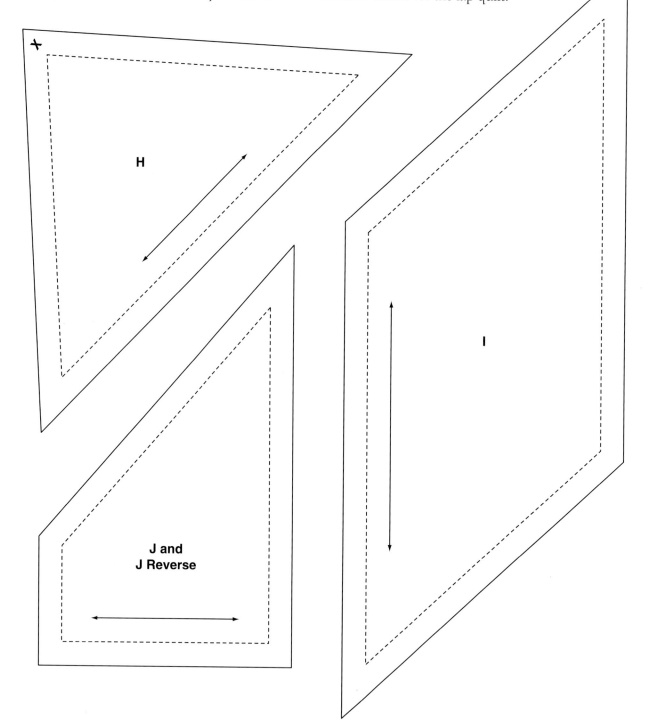

HOUSE MEDALLION

Color Plan

Photocopy this page and use it to experiment with color schemes for your quilt.

FEATHERED WORLD WITHOUT END

Skill Level: *Challenging*

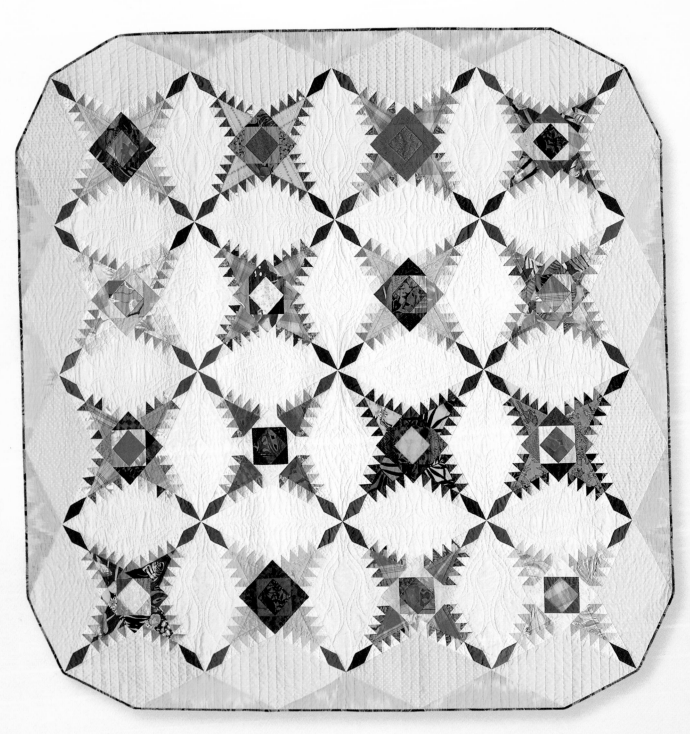

*H*ere's a quilt that positively glows! Valerie Schadt of Fayetteville, New York, teams the traditional World without End and the classic Feathered Star and gives new life to both with a selection of carefully placed and decidedly nontraditional fabrics. Our easy-to-follow foundation method allows you to piece this stunner with minimal fuss and maximum accuracy.

BEFORE YOU BEGIN

Although this quilt *is* challenging, with its many small pieces and set-in seams, foundation piecing makes it easy to achieve accurate results. The block is assembled as a series of three different units, which are pieced over paper foundations. These foundations are then sewn together to construct the blocks. To complete the quilt, large diamonds are set into the angles between the blocks.

Preparing foundations does take time, but there are benefits to offset the extra preparation. Since there is no need to cut pieces to exact sizes, cutting time is greatly decreased. If you position pieces correctly and sew carefully on the marked lines, you'll find that the finished units fit together perfectly.

To make the task even easier, we've included lots of tips and illustrations along with our usual step-by-step instructions. If you haven't tried foundation piecing, be sure to read through the instructions carefully before beginning this project.

If you are new to the process and would like to try foundation piecing on a small scale, we've given directions to make a wallhanging version of this design. Try the larger quilt if you are an experienced foundation piecer or if you're feeling up to the challenge of a more ambitious project.

Although not quite large enough to qualify as a true bedspread, it is the perfect decorative cover for a double or queen bed when paired with a dust ruffle and pillow shams—hence our designation as bed topper.

Quilt Sizes		
	Wallhanging	**Bed Topper (shown)**
Finished Quilt Size	40" × 40"	72" × 72"
Finished Block Size	16"	16"
Number of Blocks	4	16

Materials		
Fabric	**Wallhanging**	**Bed Topper**
Assorted dark, light, and medium prints and solids	1¾ yards	5 yards
Medium yellow solid	1⅛ yards	1⅞ yards
Very light yellow solid	⅝ yard	⅝ yard
Deep gold mottled print or solid	⅜ yard	⅝ yard
Dark yellow solid	*	2½ yards
Light yellow solid	*	1¼ yards
Backing	2¾ yards	4½ yards
Batting	47" × 47"	79" × 79"
Binding	⅜ yard	⅝ yard

NOTE: *Yardages are based on 44/45-inch-wide fabrics that are at least 42 inches wide after preshrinking.*

* *Light yellow and dark yellow solid fabrics are not required for the wallhanging.*

51

Cutting Chart

Fabric	Used For	Strip Width or Pieces	Number to Cut Wallhanging	Bed Topper
Assorted lights, mediums, and darks	F	3½" squares	4	16
	G	3⅛" squares	8	32
	H	4" squares	8	32
	Feathers for Foundations B, C	2"	*	*
Assorted lights and mediums	Large triangle for Foundation C	3¾"	*	*
Medium yellow	D	Template D	8	12
Very light yellow	D	Template D	4	4
Gold	E	Template E	4	12
Dark yellow	D	Template D	—	16
Light yellow	D	Template D	—	8

* You may wish to wait to cut these strips until you begin piecing the Foundation B and C units. This will allow you to determine how many strips you wish to cut from each fabric. As a rule of thumb, the Foundation B and C units for each block will require approximately two 2-inch-wide light and two 2-inch-wide dark strips for the feathers, and one 3¾-inch-wide strip for the large triangle pieces. These strips can be uniform within the block, or completely scrappy.

Refer to "Quiltmaking Basics," beginning on page 221, for techniques to assist you with this project.

CHOOSING FABRICS

The blocks in this quilt are pieced in warm and scrappy combinations of red, orange, and yellow. Blue—whether pale or deep—provides the cool contrast. The placement of lights and darks varies from block to block, with one notable exception. All of the diamond star tips are very dark prints, which creates a secondary star motif and enhances the illusion of curves in the design.

While the tiny triangles, or "feathers," do not need to be so consistently dark, it is important for them to stand out from the block backgrounds. To achieve this contrast, keep the background fabrics fairly light in value and relatively subtle in terms of print.

You can make the blocks in this quilt as uniform or as scrappy as you please. This quiltmaker has pieced all of the Foundation B and C units in a single block from the same group of fabrics, but each block is different from its neighbor. She's included lots of "surprise" fabrics to give the traditional pattern up-to-the-minute appeal.

In the quilt shown, the large diamonds separating the blocks progress from the lightest yellow in the center to dark yellow as you move toward the quilt's perimeter. Deep gold half-diamonds finish the outer edges of the quilt. Whether you choose yellow or another color for the diamonds, it is important that you maintain this light-to-dark progression in order to give the quilt its "lit from within" appearance.

To develop your own color scheme, photocopy the **Color Plan** on page 63, and use crayons or colored pencils to experiment with different color arrangements.

CUTTING

All measurements include ¼-inch seam allowances. For easy reference, the **Block Diagram**, the **Foundations Diagram**, and the **Assembly Diagrams** on pages 58 and 59 are all keyed to identify the various pieces and units by letter or name. Refer to the Cutting Chart and cut the required number of strips and pieces in the sizes needed. Cut all strips across the width of the fabric (crosswise grain).

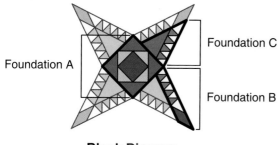

Block Diagram

Make templates for pieces D and E from the patterns and instructions on page 60. For more information about making templates, see page 224.

You will need to cut some of the squares into triangles for the Foundation A units, as follows:

• For the G triangles, cut each print and solid 3⅛-inch square in half once diagonally.

• For the H triangles, cut each of the assorted print and solid 4-inch squares in half once diagonally.

Note: We recommend that you cut and piece a sample block before cutting all of the fabric for the quilt.

Block Component Chart

	Wallhanging	Bed Topper
Number of Foundation A Units	4	16
Number of Foundation B Units	16	64
Number of Foundation C Units	16	64

········Sew **Q**uick········

When a pattern requires larger-than-usual templates, such as the D and E setting diamonds in this design, freezer paper makes a good, inexpensive choice for template material. The freezer paper template can be pressed directly onto the fabric, then removed and reused a number of times before it requires replacement. Fabric can be stacked to cut more than one layer at a time, saving additional time and money. Cut carefully so that you do not slice away slivers of the paper pattern.

PIECING THE FEATHERED STARS

Each block in this quilt requires one Foundation A unit, four Foundation B units, and four Foundation C units. The **Foundations Diagram** is labeled to identify the three different foundation units and their various component parts.

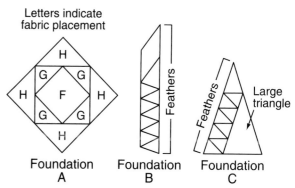

Foundations Diagram

Preparing the Foundations

Before you begin piecing, you need to prepare all of the base foundations required for the quilt. Refer to the Block Component Chart and trace the required number of Foundation A, B, and C units from the pattern on pages 61 and 62.

Although foundations can be made from either fabric or paper, we recommend that you use paper foundations for this quilt. The weight and stability of the paper helps to prevent the stretching and distortion that sometimes occurs with fabric foundations. In addition, paper is comparatively inexpensive and readily available.

Many types of paper are suitable for foundations. Newsprint is an excellent choice because it is sturdy enough to hold up to handling and stitching, but it tears away easily after the quilt is finished. Blank newsprint is available from office supply stores in pads of many sizes, so it is easy to draft large patterns (larger than a copier can reproduce). Other possible choices include onion skin paper, tracing paper, and copier paper.

One method to avoid tracing each pattern individually is to use a hot iron transfer pen. Draw the full-size image onto tracing paper, then iron it onto the foundation paper. The image can usually be ironed onto a foundation material five or six times. Retrace the original transfer for additional ironings, taking care to mark over the existing lines exactly. It's a good idea to piece one block before making all your copies.

A photocopier can also be used to duplicate your foundations, but you need to take the following precautions to be sure that you don't distort your patterns:

• Make sure the copier is set to reproduce the image at exactly 100 percent.

• Use only the original drawing from the book to make photocopies. Copies of copies are more likely to become distorted.

• Compare each copy with the original pattern. If you find you are having problems with distortion, position the original pattern as close to the center of the copied page as possible. This will often eliminate the distortion.

Piecing on a Foundation

If you look at Foundations A through C on pages 61–62, you'll see that the only seam allowance included is the one around the outer perimeter of the pattern. The outer line will eventually be the cutting line and will allow you to ac-

curately trim away excess fabric once the unit is pieced. All other lines on the foundation are sewing lines. Seam allowances are created when you overlap pieces for sewing. The foundations are not removed until the entire quilt is assembled.

Try to follow the same guidelines for grain placement that you would normally use when piecing. When possible, the fabric straight of grain should be parallel with the outer edge of the block.

Cut out each paper foundation prior to piecing, adding at least ¼ inch of additional paper around all the sides.

Although it's not a critical point for symmetrical patterns like Foundation A, keep in mind that the printed sides of the asymmetrical B and C foundations are a mirror image of how the finished unit will look.

Piecing the Foundation A Units

Step 1. The Foundation A unit forms the square-within-a-square at the center of each block. Position a 3½-inch F square right side up on the reverse (unprinted) side of the foundation, centering it over the lines for piece 1, as shown in **Diagram 1.** To check placement, hold the foundation up to the light, with the printed side away from you. The edges of the fabric should overlap the seam lines for the center patch. Hold the square in place with a pin or a dab of glue stick.

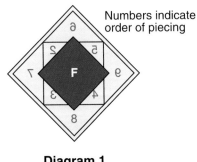

Diagram 1

Step 2. Select four G triangles to surround the center square. These triangles can be cut from the same fabric, or they can be totally scrappy. To sew piece 2, place a G triangle right side down on the

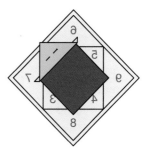

Diagram 3

— Sew Easy —

When working with foundations, you'll find it easier to align the fabric pieces if you can see the printed lines from both sides of the foundation paper. If the paper is transparent or very lightweight, the lines will probably be visible. If not, place each foundation printed side down on a light box (or against a window), and sketch lightly over the seam lines to give yourself the basic guidelines.

reverse side of the foundation, aligning its longest edge with one side of the center F square, as shown in **Diagram 2A**. Secure the triangle in place, and turn to the printed side of the foundation. Using a stitch length of 14 to 18 stitches per inch, sew directly on the line that separates piece 1 from piece 2, beginning and ending the seam approximately ⅛ inch on either side of the line, as shown in **2B**.

Step 4. To add piece 3, place another G triangle right side down, aligning its longest edge with the center square, as shown in **Diagram 4A**. Turn to the printed side of the foundation, and sew directly on the line that separates piece 1 from piece 3, beginning and ending the seam approximately ⅛ inch on either side of the line, as shown in **4B**. Turn the foundation over and trim, flip, finger press, and pin as you did previously.

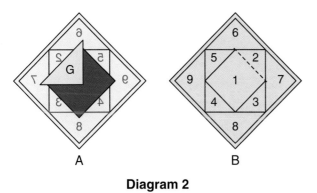

A

B

Diagram 2

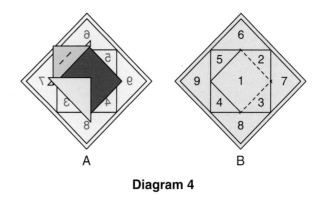

A

B

Diagram 4

Step 3. Turn to the reverse side of the foundation. Trim the excess seam allowance between the newly sewn patches if necessary, then flip the triangle into a right side up position. Finger press and pin in place. The reverse side of the foundation should resemble **Diagram 3**. Make sure the short sides of the triangle overlap the seam lines around its outer edges by enough to create a stable seam allowance when those seams are sewn.

Step 5. Add pieces 4 and 5 in the same manner, trimming seam allowances and finger pressing each in place. The unprinted side of the foundation should now resemble **Diagram 5**.

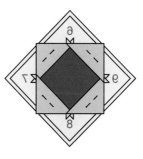

Diagram 5

Step 6. Select four H triangles to complete the outer ring of the Foundation A unit. These triangles may all be cut from the same fabric or may be totally scrappy. Place a triangle right side down on the pieced unit, aligning its longest edge as shown in **Diagram 6A.** Use the intersection of pieces 2 and 5 as a guide to placement. Make sure the long edge of the new piece (piece 6) overlaps the seam by approximately ¼ inch. Turn to the printed side of the foundation, and sew on the line separating pieces 2 and 5 from piece 6. Flip piece 6 right side up, finger pressing it in place. The reverse side of the foundation should resemble **6B.**

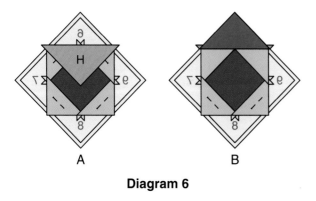

Diagram 6

Step 7. Add the remaining H triangles as described in Step 6, working around all sides of the pieced unit. When all four are sewn to the foundation, press it lightly on the pieced side. Turn it over and use scissors or a rotary cutter to cut on the outermost lines, trimming away excess fabric. The unit is a perfect square-in-a-square with a ¼-inch seam allowance surrounding it.

Step 8. Repeat to assemble one Foundation A unit for each block in your quilt.

Piecing the Foundation B Units

Step 1. To piece a Foundation B unit, select dark and light 2½-inch-wide strips from the fabrics cut for feathers. Place a dark strip right side up on the reverse side of the foundation, covering all of piece 1, as shown in **Diagram 7A.** Be sure all edges of the strip extend past the seam lines. Place a light strip right side down on top of it and pin it in place, as shown in **7B.**

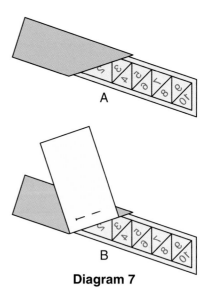

Diagram 7

Step 2. Turn to the printed side of the foundation and sew on the line separating piece 1 from piece 2, stopping and starting approximately ⅛ inch on either side of the line, as shown in **Diagram 8A.** Turn to the reverse side and trim away the excess seam allowance and any extra tails of fabric. Finger press piece 2 into a right side up position and pin. The pieced side of the foundation should resemble **8B.**

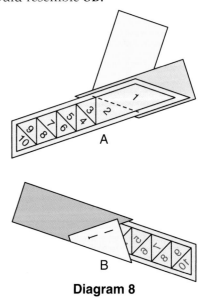

Diagram 8

Step 3. To add piece 3, position a dark strip face down on top of piece 2 as shown in **Diagram 9A.** Secure the fabric and turn to the printed side

······Sew Quick·······

As you begin piecing the Foundation B and C units, label the foundations with the words "light," "medium," or "dark," as shown on the patterns on page 62. Once you've completed a few units, the labels probably won't be necessary. Keep in mind that the printed side of the foundation is a mirror image of the finished side.

of the foundation. Sew on the line separating piece 2 from piece 3. Flip, trim, finger press, and pin, as shown in **9B**. Add all remaining pieces in the same manner. When you reach the end of the strip, press the pieced side of the foundation lightly, then use scissors or a rotary cutter to trim on the outermost line of the foundation.

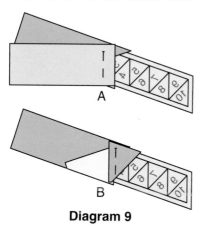

Diagram 9

Step 4. Repeat Steps 1 through 3 to assemble four Foundation B units for each block.

Piecing the Foundation C Units

Step 1. Foundation C is assembled in basically the same manner as Foundation B. Begin at piece 1 with a light strip, then alternate darks and lights until you reach piece 9. The triangles are sewn in the opposite direction as those in Foundation B, so that seams will be pressed in opposite directions when the pieces are joined.

Step 2. To add piece 10, position a 3¾-inch-wide strip of medium value fabric right side down on the reverse side of the foundation, as shown in **Diagram 10**. Flip the foundation over to the printed side, and sew on the line separating piece 10 from the light and dark triangles. Trim the excess fabric and seam allowances, and flip and finger press piece 10 in place. Press the unit on the pieced side, and trim on the outermost line of the foundation.

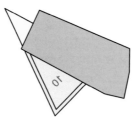

Diagram 10

——— Sew Easy ———

Individual preferences vary! As you begin constructing the Foundation B and C units, you may prefer to cut individual pieces from fabric strips as you go, rather than working with the entire strip. Experiment to find the most comfortably sized "scrap" to use for each shape in the foundation unit. Once you've determined what size suits you best, you can begin segmenting entire strips in advance.

Step 3. Repeat Steps 1 and 2 to assemble four Foundation C units for each block in your quilt.

ASSEMBLING THE BLOCK

Step 1. Set your sewing machine to its normal stitch length. Matching seams carefully, sew a Foundation B unit to a Foundation C unit, as shown in **Diagram 11** on page 58. The foundation papers provide a good guide when matching pieces, but be sure to check individual seam placement. Repeat, connecting all B and C foundations in the same manner.

Diagram 11

Step 2. Sew a Foundation B/C unit to one side of a Foundation A unit, as shown in **Diagram 12A.** Begin ¼ inch from the raw edge at the foundation's marked seam, take three stitches, and backstitch, taking care not to stitch back into the seam allowance. Complete the seam, ending with a backstitch ¼ inch from the raw edge, at the end of the marked seam line. Sew the remaining three Foundation B/C units to the other three sides of Foundation A in the same manner to complete the block, as shown in **12B.**

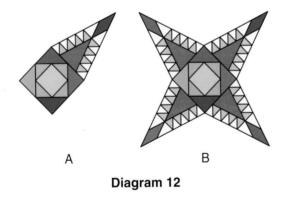

A   B

Diagram 12

Step 3. Repeat Steps 1 and 2 to assemble the required number of blocks for your quilt.

ASSEMBLING THE QUILT

Step 1. Use a design wall or other flat surface to arrange the blocks, as shown in the **Wallhanging** and **Bed Topper Assembly Diagrams.** Place the large yellow D diamonds between the blocks, as shown. The lightest yellow diamonds will be at the center of the quilt, with the diamonds be-

coming progressively darker as you move toward the outer edges. Place the gold E half-diamonds around the outer edges of the quilt. Refer to the photograph on page 50 as needed.

Step 2. Sew the vertical D diamonds to the sides of the blocks, as indicated in the **Wallhanging** and **Bed Topper Assembly Diagrams**, pivoting to set in the pieces. For additional instructions on set-in seams, see page 227 in "Quiltmaking Basics."

Step 3. Set in the horizontal diamonds in the same manner. You will be connecting the rows as you work.

Step 4. Use the same method to set in the E half-diamonds to finish the edges of the quilt.

Step 5. Remove all foundation papers and press the quilt.

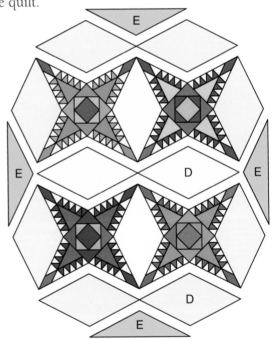

Wallhanging Assembly Diagram

QUILTING AND FINISHING

Step 1. Mark the top for quilting. The quilt shown was quilted with a stylized pineapple motif surrounded by leaves in the center of each block. The rest of the quilt is channel quilted.

Bed Topper Assembly Diagram

Step 2. Regardless of which quilt you are making, you will need to piece the backing. **Diagram 13** illustrates the layout for both size quilt backs.

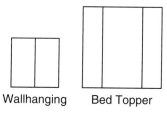

Wallhanging   Bed Topper

Diagram 13

For the wallhanging, cut the backing fabric in half crosswise and trim the selvages. Cut a 25-inch-wide panel from the entire length of each piece. Sew the two panels together lengthwise, as shown. Press the seam open.

For the topper, cut the backing fabric in half crosswise and trim the selvages. Cut two 20-inch-wide pieces from the entire length of one piece of backing fabric, and sew a narrow panel to each side of the full-width piece, as shown. Press the seams open.

Step 3. Layer the backing, batting, and quilt top, and baste the layers together. Quilt by hand or machine, adding additional quilting as desired.

Step 4. Referring to the directions on page 244 in "Quiltmaking Basics," make and attach double-fold binding to finish at a width of ¼ inch. To calculate the amount of binding you will need for the quilt size you are making, add the length of the four sides of the quilt plus 9 inches.

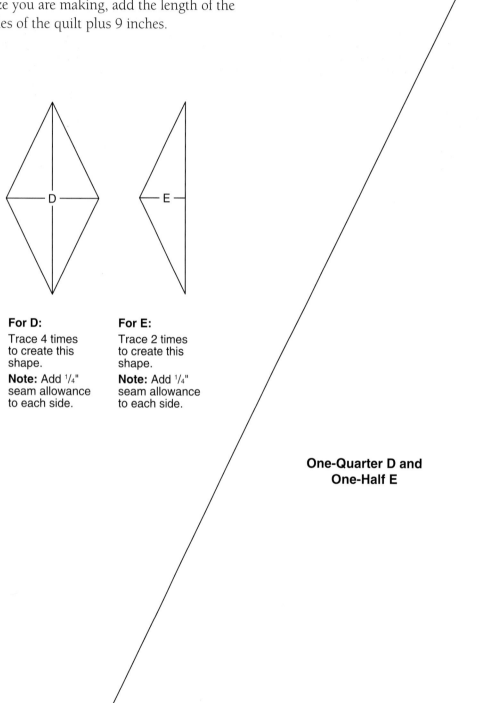

For D:
Trace 4 times to create this shape.
Note: Add ¼" seam allowance to each side.

For E:
Trace 2 times to create this shape.
Note: Add ¼" seam allowance to each side.

One-Quarter D and One-Half E

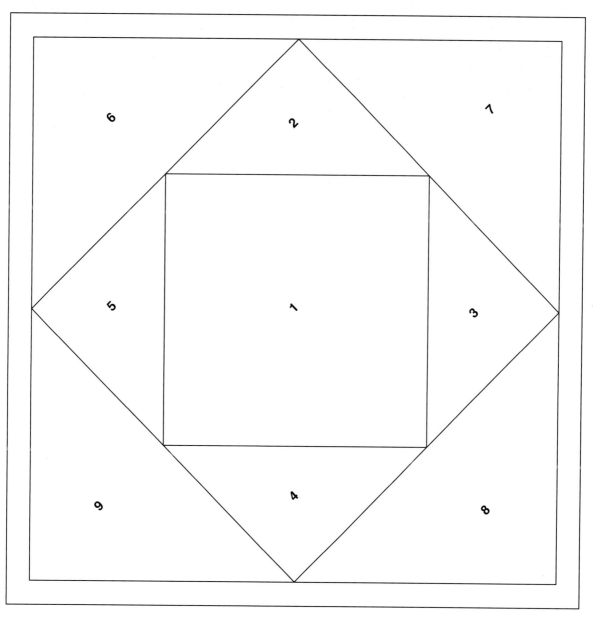

Foundation A

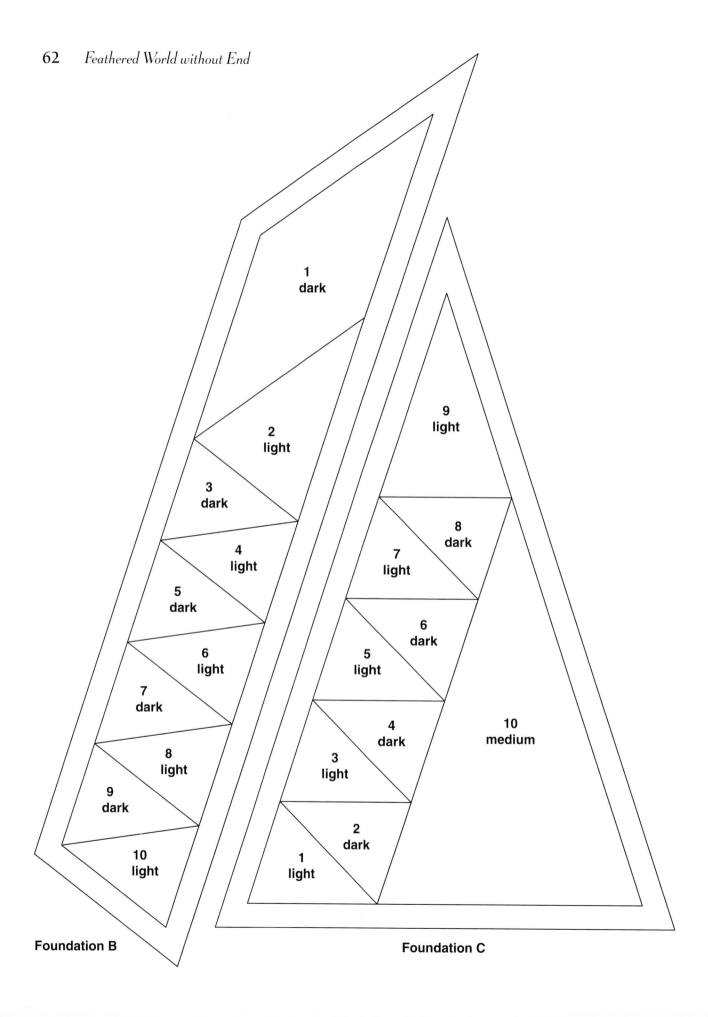

Foundation B

Foundation C

Feathered World without End

Color Plan

Photocopy this page and use it to experiment with color schemes for your quilt.

IS THIS WEDDED BLISS?

Skill Level: *Intermediate*

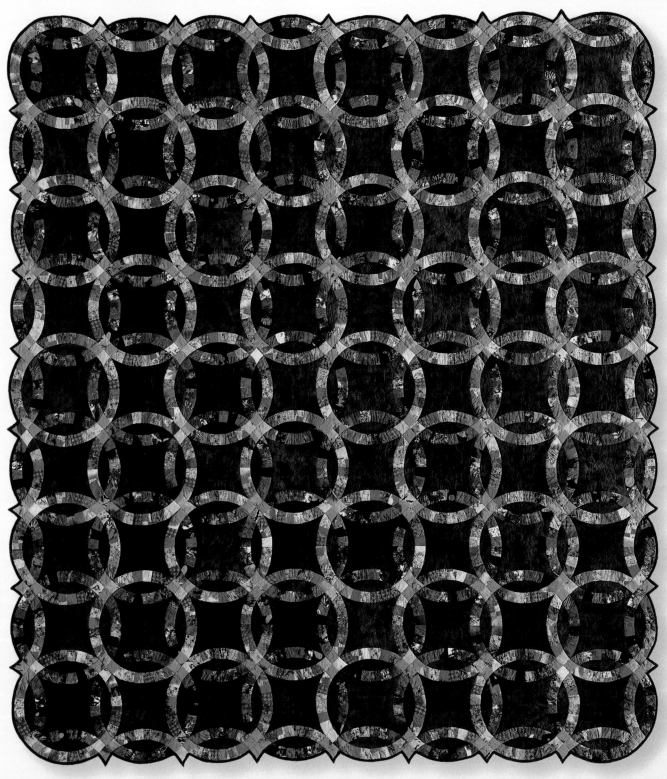

*M*aureen Carlson of Illinois created this regal double-size *Wedding Ring* quilt. The quilt's full name, "Is This Wedded Bliss, or Have I Dyed and Gone to Heaven?" says it all. It is heavenly, and the lush purple fabric Maureen hand dyed is a big part of the quilt's appeal. What better fabrics to contrast with the velvety texture of hand-dyed cotton than splashy batiks!

BEFORE YOU BEGIN

If this is your first Double Wedding Ring quilt, be sure to read "Sewing Curved Seams," beginning on page 229, before starting the project. Although every Double Wedding Ring quilt has the same look, each quilt may be constructed differently, so read the instructions carefully.

You will need to make templates for pattern pieces A, B, C, D, and E on page 21. For information on making and using templates, see page 224 in "Quiltmaking Basics."

CHOOSING FABRICS

The quiltmaker hand dyed her own fabric for the background and melons in this quilt. If you like the hand-dyed look but don't want to do it yourself, check your local quilt shop, which may carry hand-dyed fabrics. You could also choose a solid fabric for the background. The rings were pieced from an assortment of purchased batik fabrics in shades varying from pink to rose to wine, with occasional vibrant blues, oranges, greens, and blue-greens added for visual appeal. Batiked fabrics are readily available, so you can choose from a variety of colors and designs.

Quilt Sizes		
	Wallhanging	**Double (shown)**
Finished Quilt Size	33½" × 33½"	81" × 90½"
Finished Ring Diameter	15"	15"
Number of Rings	12	72
Number of Pieced Arcs	62	322

Materials		
Fabric	**Wallhanging**	**Double (shown)**
Purple hand-dyed solid	1⅜ yards	7½ yards
Assorted batiks	1⅝ yards	7⅔ yards
Pink batik	¼ yard	¾ yard
Green batik	¼ yard	¾ yard
Backing	1¼ yards	7⅞ yards
Batting	42" × 42"	89" × 99"
Binding	¾ yard	1 yard

NOTE: *Yardages are based on 44/45-inch-wide fabrics that are at least 42 inches wide after preshrinking. Be sure to check the width of hand-dyed fabrics before purchasing them because sometimes they are sold in narrower widths. Adjust your yardages if necessary.*

CUTTING

All measurements include ¼-inch seam allowances. Referring to the Cutting Chart, cut the required number of pieces for your quilt size.

Cutting Chart

Fabric	Used For	Piece	Number of Pieces	
			Wallhanging	Double
Purple	Background	A	12	72
	Melons	B	31	161
Pink batik	Connecting wedges	C	36	176
Green batik	Connecting wedges	C	36	176
Assorted batiks	Outer wedges of arcs	D	62	322
	Outer wedges of arcs	D reverse	62	322
	Inner wedges of arcs	E	248	1,288

Note: Cut and piece one sample ring before cutting all of the fabric for the quilt.

PIECING THE ARCS

Step 1. Stack the D, D reverse, and E pieces in separate piles. Begin each pieced arc with a D piece. To the right of it, sew a succession of four E pieces. End the arc with a D reverse piece. As you sew, be sure the pieces are oriented so that curves arc in the same direction, as shown in **Diagram 1.** Gently press all seams in the same direction, taking care not to stretch the unit. Repeat until you've assembled all arcs required for your quilt.

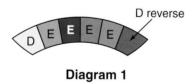

Diagram 1

Step 2. Center and sew a pieced arc to one side of each purple B melon, as shown in **Diagram 2.** Refer to page 229 for specific information and tips on assembling the curved pieces common to most Double Wedding Ring quilts. Press seams toward the melons. You will use half of the pieced arcs for this step.

Diagram 2

Step 3. Sew a green batik C piece to each D end of the remaining arcs, as shown in **Diagram 3.** Sew a pink batik C piece to each D reverse end of the arcs, as shown. Gently press the seams in the same direction as other seams in the arc.

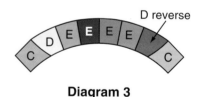

Diagram 3

——— Sew Easy ———

Make sure you mix up your assortment of fabrics for a pleasing overall use of color. For example, if you have selected a few hot colors, as in the quilt shown, use them randomly and sparingly for a hit of electric blue here and a spot of tangerine there.

Step 4. Center and sew these longer pieced arcs to the arc/melon units you already assembled, as shown in **Diagram 4**. Press all seams toward the melons. Again, refer to page 229 for further help with sewing curved seams.

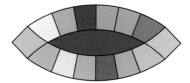

Diagram 4

ASSEMBLING THE QUILT TOP

Step 1. Use a design wall or other flat surface to lay out the completed arc/melon units and the A background pieces in rows, as shown in the **Partial Assembly Diagram**. Note that the orientation of arc/melon units changes from row to row, so refer to the diagram or the photograph on page 64 for directional placement of the pink and green tips of the arc/melon units. For the double-size quilt, you will have nine horizontal rows of eight rings each. For the wallhanging, you will have four horizontal rows of three rings each. The C pieces shown will be added after the rows are assembled.

Step 2. Sew the units into horizontal rows. You will need to start and stop stitching ¼ inch from

each end of the arcs as you attach them to the purple background pieces. Refer to page 231 for more information on sewing curved pieces into rows.

Step 3. Sew the rows together, starting and stopping your seams ¼ inch from the end of each arc, to complete the quilt top.

Step 4. After the quilt top is assembled, set in the remaining C pieces where the arcs intersect around the perimeter of the quilt, referring to the **Partial Assembly Diagram**. Be sure that the square corner of all of the C pieces points in toward the quilt. Notice that the colors alternate from row to row.

QUILTING AND FINISHING

Step 1. Mark the quilt top for quilting. The quilt shown was hand quilted with a floral motif in the center of each ring. It was also quilted in the ditch around each ring.

Step 2. The backing for the wallhanging is made from a single panel of 42-inch-wide fabric. Trim the selvages and press the 1¼-yard length of backing fabric.

Step 3. For the double-size quilt, cut the backing fabric into three equal lengths, and trim the selvages. Cut a 29-inch-wide panel from two of the lengths, then sew one panel to each side of

Partial Assembly Diagram

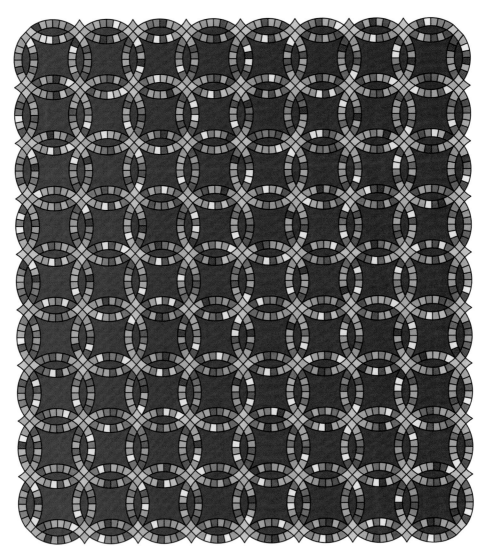

Double-Size Quilt Diagram

the full-width panel, as shown in **Diagram 5**. Press the seams open.

Step 4. Layer the backing, batting, and quilt top, and baste. Quilt as desired.

Step 5. Use narrow bias binding to bind the quilt. See page 246 for details on making bias binding and applying it around curves.

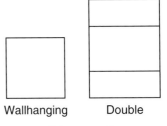

Wallhanging   Double

Diagram 5

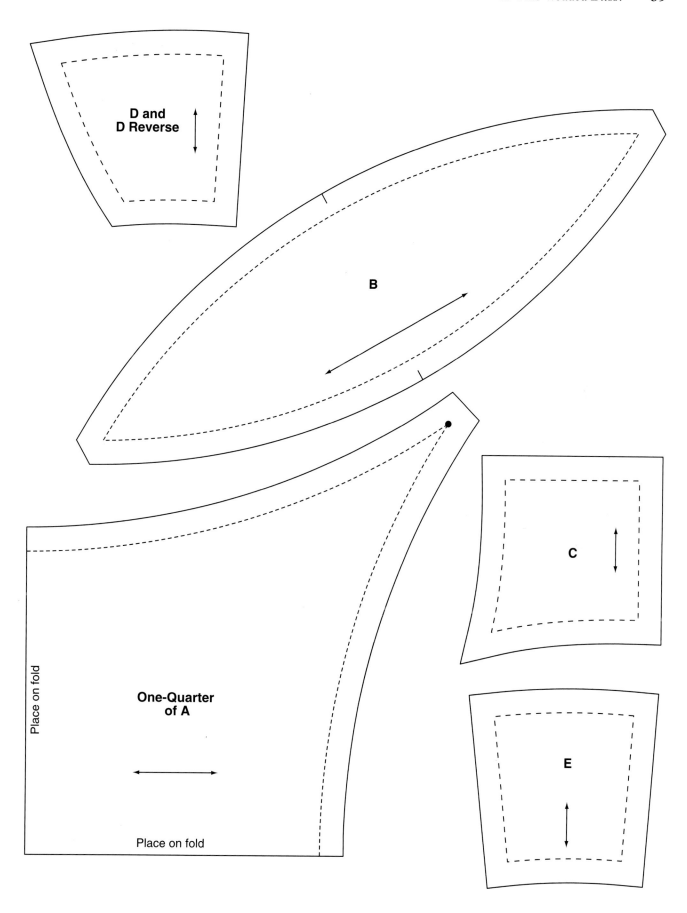

D and
D Reverse

B

C

Place on fold

One-Quarter
of A

Place on fold

E

OKLAHOMA NINE PATCH

Skill Level: *Easy*

This dynamic scrap quilt was inspired by a photo in a book on Oklahoma heritage quilts. Since the pattern could not be identified, the quiltmaker, Carolyn Miller, of Santa Cruz, California, named it in honor of its source. In this double-size version, the interaction of black and white creates a striking three-dimensional effect and forms a perfect backdrop for the explosion of color resulting from the dozens of scrap fabrics used.

BEFORE YOU BEGIN

Each Double Nine-Patch block in this quilt is composed of five Nine-Patch blocks and four triangle squares. The directions are written based on using an easy strip-piecing technique for making the Nine-Patch blocks. Strips of fabric are sewn together into strip sets. The strip sets are then cut apart and resewn into blocks. Read through the general construction directions beginning on page 143, for further details on strip piecing.

The directions for making the triangle squares are based on using the grid method. You will cut 10½-inch strips into squares, layer two squares together, and then mark and cut the grid as directed.

CHOOSING FABRICS

If you want to re-create the look of the quilt shown, use as many different fabrics as possible for the Nine-Patch blocks. The directions are written so that each pair of dark and light strips will result in three Nine-Patch blocks.

Quilt Sizes

	Lap	Double (shown)
Finished Quilt Size	57" × 79½"	79½" × 102"
Finished Block Size		
Double Nine Patch	11¼"	11¼"
Small Nine Patch	3¾"	3¾"
Triangle Squares	3¾"	3¾"
Number of Blocks		
Double Nine Patch	24	48
Small Nine Patch	120	240
Triangle Squares	96	192

Materials

Fabric	Lap	Double
Assorted darks	2⅛ yards	4 yards
Assorted lights	2⅛ yards	4 yards
Black	1⅝ yards	2⅝ yards
White	1⅛ yards	2 yards
Dark print	1⅛ yards	1½ yards
Backing	5 yards	7½ yards
Batting	63" × 86"	86" × 108"
Binding	⅝ yard	¾ yard

NOTE: *Yardages are based on 44/45-inch-wide fabrics that are at least 42 inches wide after preshrinking.*

For best results, use two new fabrics for each pair. If you do use a fabric more than once, be sure to pair it up with a different fabric each time.

To help develop your own

Cutting Chart				
Fabric	Used For	Strip Width	Number of Strips	
			Lap	Double
Assorted darks	Strip sets	1¾"	40	80
Assorted lights	Strip sets	1¾"	40	80
Black	Triangle squares	10½"	3	6
	Inner border	2½"	7	9
White	Triangle squares	10½"	3	6
Dark print	Outer border	4½"	7	9

unique color scheme for the quilt, photocopy the **Color Plan** on page 77, and use crayons or colored pencils to experiment with different color arrangements.

Light and dark yardages shown are generous estimates of the total yardage used in the quilt. Since small amounts of many fabrics are a key ingredient for a successful scrap quilt, you will likely begin with more yardage than indicated, but not all of it will be used.

CUTTING

All measurements include ¼-inch seam allowances. Referring to the Cutting Chart, cut the required number of strips in the width needed. Cut all strips across the fabric width (crosswise grain).

Cut the black and white fabrics for the triangle squares into 10½-inch-wide strips, then cut the strips into 10½-inch squares. Pair up one white and one black square for each grid of triangle squares.

Note: Cut and piece one sample block before cutting all the fabric for the quilt.

PIECING THE BLOCKS

Each Double Nine-Patch block is made up of five Nine-Patch blocks and four triangle squares, as illustrated in the **Block Diagram**. The scrappy Nine-Patch blocks are assembled using easy strip-piecing techniques. The triangle squares are made using the grid method.

Block Diagram

Making the Triangle Squares

Step 1. Working on the wrong side of a 10½-inch white square, use a pencil or permanent marker to draw a grid of four 4⅝-inch squares, as shown in **Diagram 1A**. Draw the grid so that it is at least ½ inch from the raw edges of the fabric. Referring to **1B**, carefully draw a diagonal line through each square in the grid.

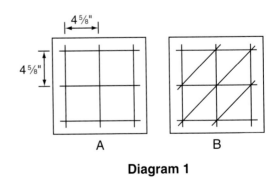

Diagram 1

Step 2. Place the white square right sides together with a 10½-inch black square. Using a ¼-inch seam allowance, stitch along both sides of the diagonal lines, as shown in **Diagram 2**. Use the edge of your presser foot as a ¼-inch guide, or draw a line ¼ inch from each side of the diagonal line.

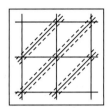

Diagram 2

Step 3. Use a rotary cutter and ruler to cut the grid apart. See page 223 in "Quiltmaking Basics" for complete details on rotary cutting. Cut on all the marked lines, as indicated in **Diagram 3A**. Carefully press the triangle squares open, pressing the seam toward the dark fabric. Trim off the triangle points at the seam ends, as shown in **3B**. You will get eight triangle squares from each grid, which is enough for two blocks. Continue marking and cutting triangle squares until you have made the number required for the quilt size you are making.

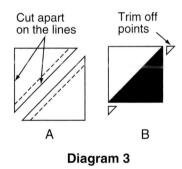

Diagram 3

Piecing the Nine-Patch Blocks

Each Nine-Patch block requires two different segment variations, as shown in **Diagram 4**. There are two A segments and one B segment in each block. The directions given here will allow you to piece three blocks at one time from the same two fabrics.

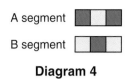

Diagram 4

Step 1. The blocks are assembled using a strip-piecing technique. Refer to the Cutting Chart to determine the total number of light and dark strips required to make the Nine-Patch blocks for your quilt. Cut the strips from an assortment of fabrics, then separate them into light and dark piles.

Step 2. Select a dark strip and a light strip from the piles. From the dark strip, cut two 10¾-inch-long pieces and one 5½-inch-long piece. From the light strip, cut one 10¾-inch piece and two 5½-inch pieces. Set the remaining pieces of strips aside.

Step 3. To make the A segments, use a ¼-inch seam to sew a dark 10¾-inch-long strip to each side of the light 10¾-inch-long strip, as shown in **Diagram 5A**. Press the seams toward the dark strips.

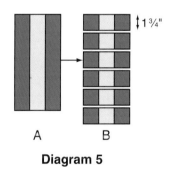

Diagram 5

Step 4. Using a rotary cutter and ruler, square up one end of the strip set. Cut 1¾-inch segments from the unit, as shown in **5B**; you should be able to cut six segments.

Step 5. To make the B segments, sew the light 5½-inch-long strips to each side of the dark 5½-inch-long strip, as shown in **Diagram 6A** on page 74. Press the seams toward the dark strip.

Step 6. Using a rotary cutter and ruler, square up one end of the strip set. Cut 1¾-inch segments from the strip set, as shown in **6B;** you should be able to cut three segments.

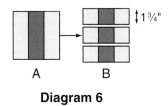

Diagram 6

Step 7. Sew two A segments and one B segment together, as shown in **Diagram 7,** matching seams carefully. Since the seam allowances are pressed in opposite directions, the intersections should fit together tightly. Stitch, using ¼-inch seam allowances. Repeat with the remaining segments.

Diagram 7

Step 8. Repeat Steps 2 through 7, piecing three Nine-Patch blocks from each pair of strips until you have completed the number of Nine-Patch blocks required for your quilt.

ASSEMBLING THE DOUBLE NINE-PATCH BLOCKS

Step 1. Lay out five small Nine-Patch blocks and four triangle squares in three rows, as shown in **Diagram 8,** making sure the triangle squares are positioned correctly. Sew the blocks into rows, pressing the seams toward the triangle squares.

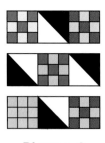

Diagram 8

Step 2. Sew the rows together, matching seams carefully. Press.

Step 3. Repeat, assembling the required number of Double Nine-Patch blocks for your quilt.

ASSEMBLING THE QUILT TOP

Step 1. Use a design wall or other flat surface to lay out the Double Nine-Patch blocks, as shown in the **Quilt Diagram.** The quilt shown in the diagram is the double size, which has eight rows of six blocks each. The layout for the lap-size quilt is the same, except there are six rows of four blocks each. Pay attention to the orientation of the quilt blocks; every other block is turned 90 degrees.

Step 2. Referring to the **Assembly Diagram,** sew the blocks together in rows, pressing the seams in opposite directions from row to row. Sew the rows together, matching seams carefully. Press.

Assembly Diagram

Quilt Diagram

ADDING THE BORDERS

Step 1. For either quilt, the 2½-inch-wide black inner border strips must first be joined end to end to achieve the necessary length. For the lap-size quilt, sew two strips together for each side border. For the top and bottom borders, cut one strip in half crosswise, and sew one half to each of the two remaining full-length strips. For the double-size quilt, sew eight strips together in pairs, making four long border strips. Cut the remaining strip in half crosswise, and sew one half each to two of the long border strips.

Step 2. Add the top and bottom borders first. Measure the width of the quilt top, taking the measurement through the horizontal center of the quilt rather than along the top or bottom. Trim the two shorter black border strips to this exact length.

Step 3. Fold one trimmed strip in half crosswise and crease. Unfold it and position it right side down along the top edge of the quilt, with the crease at the vertical midpoint. Pin at the midpoint and ends first, then along the length of the entire end, easing in fullness if necessary. Sew the border to the quilt top using a ¼-inch seam allowance. Press the seam toward the border. Repeat on the bottom edge of the quilt.

Step 4. Measure the length of the quilt, taking the measurement through the vertical center of the quilt and including the top and bottom borders. Trim the remaining black border strips to this exact length.

Step 5. Fold one strip in half crosswise and crease. Unfold it and position it right side down along one side of the quilt top, matching the crease to the horizontal midpoint. Pin at the midpoint and ends first, then across the entire length of the quilt top, easing in fullness if necessary. Stitch, using a ¼-inch seam allowance. Press the seam allowance toward the border. Repeat on the opposite side of the quilt.

Step 6. In the same manner, piece together the 4½-inch-wide outer border strips to get four long borders. Measure and add the borders to the quilt top, adding the top and bottom borders first, then the side borders.

QUILTING AND FINISHING

Step 1. Mark the quilt top for quilting. The quilt shown has outline quilting in the triangle squares and a large X quilted through the center of each Nine-Patch block. A diagonal grid in the borders completes the design.

Step 2. Regardless of which quilt size you've chosen to make, the backing will have to be pieced. **Diagram 9** illustrates the two quilt backs.

To make the backing for the lap-size quilt, divide the backing fabric crosswise into two equal pieces, and trim the selvages.

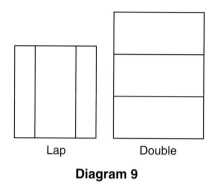

Lap   Double

Diagram 9

Step 3. Cut one of the pieces in half lengthwise, and sew one half to each side of the full-width piece. Press the seams open.

Step 4. To make the backing for the double-size quilt, divide the fabric crosswise into three equal pieces, and trim the selvages. Sew the three pieces together along the long sides, then press the seams open.

Step 5. Layer the quilt top, batting, and backing, and baste. Quilt as desired.

Step 6. Referring to the directions on page 244 in "Quiltmaking Basics," make and attach double-fold binding. To calculate the amount of binding needed for the quilt size you are making, add up the length of the four sides of the quilt and add 9 inches. The total is the approximate number of inches of binding you will need.

OKLAHOMA NINE PATCH

Color Plan

Photocopy this page and use it to experiment with color schemes for your quilt.

SUMMER NIGHT

Skill Level: *Intermediate*

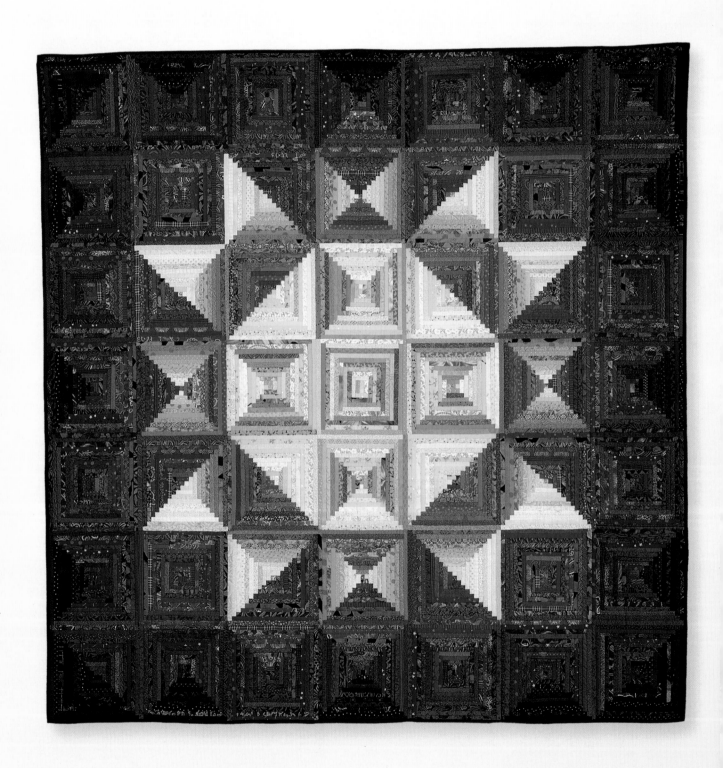

The memory of a childhood friend and long summer evenings spent playing outside inspired quiltmaker Karen K. Stone to create *Summer Night*, a wonderful example of how the traditional Log Cabin block can be used to create a striking, contemporary quilt. Careful use of color and value create a starburst center and subtle shading around this wallhanging's perimeter.

BEFORE YOU BEGIN

The directions for this quilt are written based on using the foundation technique, which will make piecing the narrow (½-inch finished width) logs easier. Read through "Foundation Piecing," beginning on page 232, to become familiar with the technique. Prepare a foundation for each block using the pattern on page 84. The pattern given is reduced; enlarge it 150 percent before tracing.

Either permanent or removable foundations will work equally well for this block, but permanent foundations may add enough depth to eliminate the need for batting.

CHOOSING FABRICS

The key to this quilt lies in very careful color placement. While it could technically be called a two-color quilt (blue and yellow), it is actually comprised of many different fabrics in shades of gold, light and medium yellows, and medium and dark blues. The subtle variations in color and value add to the overall impact of the quilt.

There are nine different color variations of the basic block, as illustrated by **Diagram 1** on page 80. Study the photo on the opposite page and the **Quilt Diagram** on page 83 to understand how the blocks work together.

To help develop your own unique color scheme

Quilt Size	
Finished Quilt Size	74" × 74"
Finished Block Size	10½"
Number of Blocks	49

NOTE: *Because specific color and value placement is critical to the overall design of this quilt, no variations in size or layout are provided.*

Materials	
Fabric	**Amount**
Light yellows	2 yards
Medium yellows and golds	2 yards
Medium blues	7 yards
Dark blues	1¾ yards
Backing	4¾ yards
Batting	80" × 80"
Binding	⅝ yard
Foundation material	5¼ yards

for the quilt, make several photocopies of the **Color Plan** on page 85, and use crayons or markers to experiment with different color arrangements. Even if you choose to make a quilt exactly like the one shown, actually filling in the colors will help you gain a better understanding of the design and will make assembly easier.

79

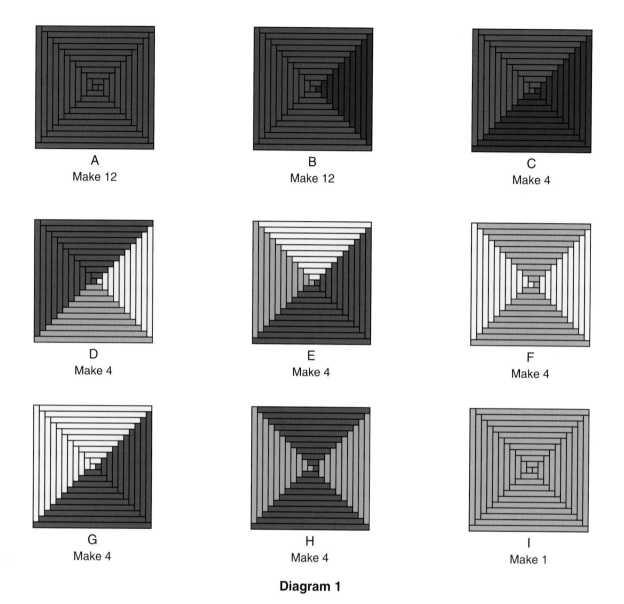

A
Make 12

B
Make 12

C
Make 4

D
Make 4

E
Make 4

F
Make 4

G
Make 4

H
Make 4

I
Make 1

Diagram 1

CUTTING

Referring to the Cutting Chart, cut the number of strips needed. Cut all strips across the fabric width (crosswise grain). **Note:** Cut and sew one sample block before cutting all the pieces for the quilt.

The pieces in the block have a finished width of ½ inch. If you were piecing traditionally, you would cut 1-inch-wide strips. For the foundation method, begin by cutting 1¼-inch strips from the fabrics. You may wish to decrease that width in ⅛-inch increments as you become more familiar with the technique, but don't cut pieces less than 1 inch wide.

The number of dark and light strips needed for logs is estimated based on using full-width yardage. If you are using scraps, the number of strips needed will vary.

Cutting Chart

Fabric	Strip Width	Number of Strips
Light yellows	1¼"	40
Medium yellows and golds	1¼"	46
Medium blues	1¼"	180
Dark blues	1¼"	36

MAKING THE FOUNDATIONS

Step 1. The block pattern is given on page 84. Enlarge the pattern 150 percent before tracing it. **Note:** The pattern is given without seam allowances; be sure to add a ¼-inch seam allowance to all sides of the completed template.

Step 2. Following the instructions on page 234, transfer the pattern to your chosen foundation material. Make sure the marked lines are visible from the back side when you hold the foundation up to the light. Notice that the front of each foundation is a mirror image of the finished block, and always keep that in mind as you sew the logs to the foundation.

Use the **Block Diagram** as a reference for piecing order. Cut out the foundations, leaving a bit of extra material on all sides.

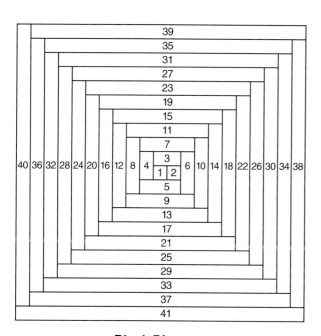

Block Diagram

PIECING THE BLOCKS

Make a sample block before cutting fabric for the entire quilt. If you experience problems while assembling the block, increase the strip width. Using strips slightly wider than necessary can be a real time-saver since not as much precision is needed when positioning them for sewing. Reevaluate your work often. You may find that strip width can be decreased again once you are more familiar with the method.

Select one of the blocks shown in **Diagram 1** and cut several strips of the fabrics used in that block. Refer to the diagram for correct color placement as you piece your sample block.

Step 1. Cut a 1¼-inch square from the strip of fabric reserved for piece 1. Place the square right side up on the reverse side of the foundation, aligning it so that the square covers the entire area of piece 1, as shown in **Diagram 2**. Secure in place with tape, a bit of glue stick, or a pin. **Note:** Only the center portion of the block is shown in **Diagrams 2** through **6**. The complete block contains 41 logs, as shown in the **Block Diagram**.

Hold the foundation up to the light with the back side away from you. You should be able to see a shadow of the center square. Check to make sure it extends past all lines surrounding piece 1. If it doesn't, reposition the square and check it again.

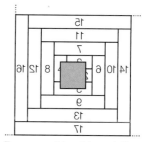

Reverse side of foundation
(center of block shown only)

Diagram 2

Step 2. Place the fabric strip for piece 2 right side down on the reverse side of the foundation, as shown in **Diagram 3A** on page 82. Align the piece with the lower and left edges of piece 1. (Remember that the back of your foundation is a mirror image of the front.) Holding the fabric in position, flip the foundation to the front side and sew on the line separating pieces 1 and 2, as shown in **3B.** Begin and end the line of stitches approximately ⅛ inch on either side of the line.

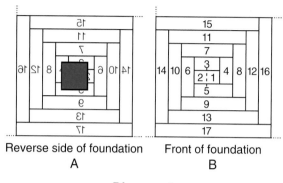

Reverse side of foundation   Front of foundation
              A   B

Diagram 3

Step 3. Remove the foundation from the machine and flip it to the back side. Trim the seam allowance if necessary to reduce bulk. If you used tape to secure the center piece, remove it now. Flip piece 2 into a right-side-up position, finger pressing it into place. The reverse of your foundation should now look like **Diagram 4.** Notice that the unsewn edges of piece 2 overlap the three unsewn seam lines surrounding the piece's drawn border.

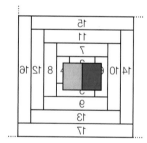

Reverse side of foundation

Diagram 4

Step 4. For piece 3, place a strip of fabric right side down, as shown in **Diagram 5A.** Holding the strip in place, flip the foundation over and sew on the line separating pieces 1 and 2 from piece 3, again beginning and ending approximately ⅛ inch on either side of the line. Remove the foundation from the machine and flip it to the back side. Cut away the excess tail of fabric, trimming just past the end of the line of stitches.

Flip piece 3 into a right-side-up position, finger pressing it into place, as shown in **5B.**

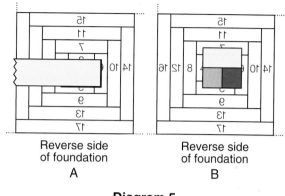

Reverse side   Reverse side
of foundation   of foundation
       A   B

Diagram 5

Step 5. Piece 4 is added next. Position a strip right side down on the reverse side of your foundation. Hold the fabric in place, flip to the front of the foundation, and sew on the line separating pieces 1 and 3 from piece 4. Remove from the machine, trim the excess fabric, and flip piece 4 into a right-side-up position. Finger press firmly into place. Check to make sure all unsewn edges of piece 4 overlap seam lines around the piece's border.

The front of your foundation should now look like the one illustrated in **Diagram 6.** So far, you have sewn three seams. Notice that they cross each other. This crisscrossing will continue, helping to reinforce the seams in your foundation block.

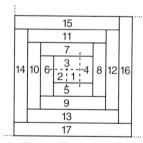

Front of foundation

Diagram 6

Step 6. Add all remaining logs in exactly the same manner. Remember to trim excess bulk from seam allowances, finger press each piece into place, and check to make sure the new piece overlaps all unsewn seam lines before adding the next log.

After you have added piece 41, press the block with a warm iron, then cut on the outer line of the seam allowance.

Step 7. Repeat Steps 1 through 6 to make the correct number of blocks in each color variation shown in **Diagram 1** on page 80. Pin a letter label to each group of blocks as you complete it.

ASSEMBLING THE QUILT TOP

Step 1. The blocks are arranged in seven rows, each containing seven blocks. Referring to **Diagram 1** on page 80, **Diagram 7,** and the **Quilt Diagram,** lay out the blocks. **Diagram 1** shows the nine block variations used; **Diagram 7** and the **Quilt Diagram** show the position of the blocks in the layout. Check to make sure the blocks are turned the right way to accurately create the design.

Step 2. Sew the blocks into rows. Tear away removable foundations from seam allowances where blocks were joined. To help you match seams perfectly, be sure to press seam allowances of adjoining rows in opposite directions.

C	B	A	B	A	B	C
B	A	E	H	D	A	B
A	D	G	F	G	E	A
B	H	F	I	F	H	B
A	E	G	F	G	D	A
B	A	D	H	E	A	B
C	B	A	B	A	B	C

Diagram 7

Note: If permanent foundations create too much bulk when pressed in one direction, press the seams open. Be sure to pin and match seams carefully when rows are sewn together.

Step 3. Sew the rows together, carefully matching seams where blocks are joined.

QUILTING AND FINISHING

Step 1. Mark the quilt top for quilting, if desired. The quilt shown is quilted in the ditch along all seam lines.

Quilt Diagram

Step 2. To piece the backing, cut the 4¾-yard length of backing fabric in half crosswise, and trim the selvages. Divide one piece in half lengthwise, and sew one half to each side of the full-width piece. Press the seams open.

Step 3. Layer the backing, batting if used, and quilt top, and baste the layers together. Quilt as desired.

Step 4. Referring to the directions on page 244 in "Quiltmaking Basics," make and attach double-fold binding. You will need approximately 305 inches of binding.

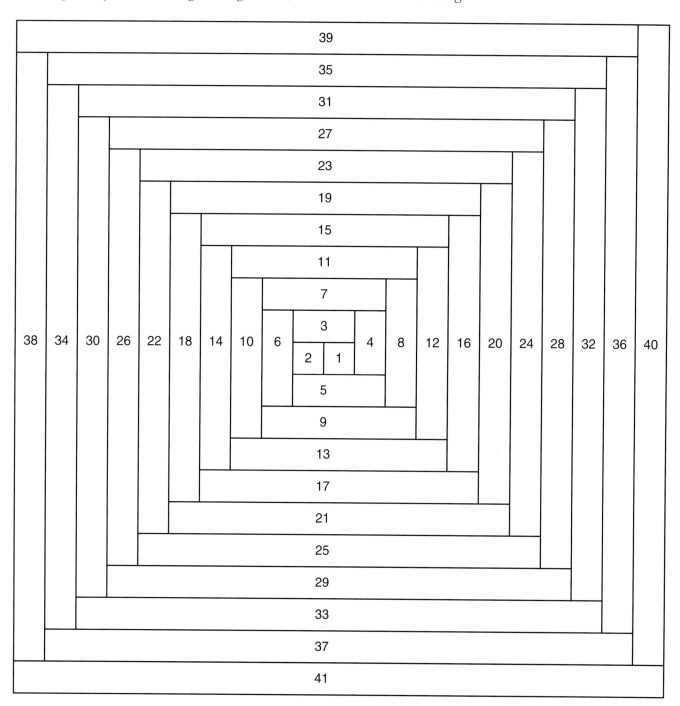

Block Pattern

Pattern shown is the mirror image of the finished block.
Note: Pattern is reduced. Enlarge it 150 percent before tracing.

SUMMER NIGHT

Color Plan

Photocopy this page and use it to experiment with color schemes for your quilt.

ANTIQUE INDIGO SCHOOLHOUSES

Skill Level: *Intermediate*

A cherished collection of vintage blue fabric takes center stage in this spiffy version of the Schoolhouse pattern, made by Sally Tanner. The country-fresh color scheme creates a clean, crisp image and is an ideal choice for this classic mix of piecework and appliqué. A simple but stunning ribbon border on this twin-size quilt provides the perfect complement.

BEFORE YOU BEGIN

The instructions for this quilt are written based on quick-cutting techniques. With the exception of a few simple shapes that require templates, most of the pieces can be rotary cut. Fabrics can be layered for even more efficient cutting.

Like the other Schoolhouse blocks in this book, the pieced blocks in this quilt are perfect for machine work. There is one basic difference: In this variation, the window sashes are appliquéd in place. The "Sew Easy" box on page 90 offers tips for making the neat, narrow fabric strips ideally suited for this purpose.

Read through "Set-In Seams," beginning on page 227, before you begin this quilt. In addition to specific instructions concerning use of the rotary cutter, you'll find information and hints designed to help in the construction of the basic Schoolhouse block.

CHOOSING FABRICS

Here is the perfect opportunity to use up bits and scraps of those

Quilt Sizes

	Twin (shown)	Double
Finished Quilt Size	64½" × 76½"	76½" × 88½"
Finished Block Size	10"	10"
Number of Blocks	20	30

Materials

Fabric	Twin	Double
Muslin	2⅞ yards	4 yards
Assorted blue print scraps	2 yards	3 yards
Navy print	1⅞ yards	2 yards
Ecru with navy dots	⅓ yard	⅜ yard
Backing	4 yards	5⅓ yards
Batting	73" × 85"	85" × 97"

NOTE: Yardages are based on 44/45-inch-wide fabrics that are at least 42 inches wide after preshrinking.

sentimental fabrics you've been saving for an extra-special project. In fact, the quiltmaker chose this particular variation of the School-house block and designed the wonderfully scrappy pieced border to make use of the small-est, precious bits of her prized an-tique fabrics. Blues can range from royal to Williamsburg, navy to

powder—or anything in between.

You might choose to make all of the houses from the same blue fabric or mix and match as this quiltmaker has done. She pieced each Schoolhouse block from its own blue print, but you can combine different blue fabrics in a single block to make the best use of the material on hand.

			Number of Strips			Number to Cut	
Fabric	Used For	Strip Width	Twin	Double	Second Cut Dimensions	Twin	Double
Navy	Border 4	4½"	8	9			
Muslin	Border 1	2½"	7	9			
	Border 3	2½"	8	9			
	Sashing	2½"	10	15			
	E	5"	1	2	2" × 5"	20	30
	H	1½"	3	4	1½" × 4½"	20	30
	K	1"	3	5	1" × 6¼"	20	30
	L	1¾"	4	5	1¾" × 3½"	40	60
	P	1¼"	4	5	1¼" × 6½"	20	30

Fabric	Used For	Piece or Dimensions	Number to Cut per House
Each blue print	A	Template A	1
	C	Template C	1
	F	1½" × 2"	2
	G	1¾" × 4½"	2
	I	1" × 4"	1
	J	1¾" × 4"	1
	M	1½" × 3½"	1
	N	1½" × 4"	2
	O	1¾" × 5½"	2
	Window sashing	⅞" × 10½"	1
Muslin	B	Template B	1
	D	Template D	1
	D reverse	Template D	1

Fabric	Used For	Piece	Number to Cut Twin	Double
Ecru with navy dots	X	Template X	72	88
Blue prints	Y	Template Y	36	44
	Y reverse	Template Y	36	44
	Z	Template Z	4	4

Should blue not be your cup of tea, any other two-color scheme would be equally attractive. For the true free spirit, a total scrap bag approach would be handsome as well.

To develop your own color scheme for the quilt, photocopy the **Color Plan** on page 95, and use crayons or colored pencils to experiment with different color arrangements.

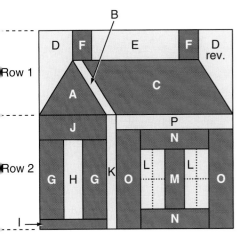

Block Diagram

Cut sizes

E = 2" × 5"
F = 1½" × 2"
G = 1¾" × 4½"
H = 1½" × 4½"
I = 1" × 4"
J = 1¾" × 4"
K = 1" × 6¼"
L = 1¾" × 3½"
M = 1½" × 3½"
N = 1½" × 4"
O = 1¾" × 5½"
P = 1¼" × 6½"

CUTTING

All measurements include ¼-inch seam allowances. Refer to the Cutting Chart and cut the required number of pieces or strips in the sizes needed. Cut all strips across the fabric width (crosswise grain).

For ease of construction, rotary-cutting dimensions as well as a letter identification are given for each pattern piece in the **Block Diagram** that is rotary cut. For example, the piece labeled G, which is 1¾ × 4½ inches, does not require a template to cut. The letter label is simply given for easy reference. Because some of the pieces are very similar but not identical, it will be helpful for you to label your stacks of pieces by their letters.

Make templates for pieces A, B, C, D, X, Y, and Z using the full-size pattern pieces on pages 96–97. Refer to page 224 for complete details on making and using templates. The Cutting Chart indicates how many of each piece to cut with each template. Place the B, C, Y, and Z templates wrong side up on the fabric to cut pieces B, C, Y, and Z. Turn the Y template over to cut Y reverse pieces. Reserve a 27-inch square of navy fabric for bias binding.

Note: Cut and piece one sample block before cutting all the fabric for the quilt. You may also want to piece together a few of the ribbon border pieces to test your templates for accuracy before cutting all of the X, Y, and Z pieces.

PIECING THE SCHOOLHOUSE BLOCKS

Refer to the **Block Diagram** as you assemble each block. Note that all of the house pieces for a single block are cut from the same blue fabric. You may find it helpful to lay out all the pieces for one block before stitching any of the units together.

Step 1. Sew an A, B, and C piece together in sequence, as shown in **Diagram 1**. Press the seams toward B.

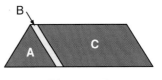

Diagram 1

Step 2. Sew a blue F chimney to either side of a muslin E strip, as shown in **Diagram 2**. Press the seams toward the chimneys. Stitch this pieced strip to the top edge of the roof, as shown. Press the seams as desired.

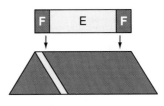

Diagram 2

Step 3. Set in the muslin D and D reverse pieces, as shown in **Diagram 3**. For D, begin stitching ¼ inch from the raw edge at the point where the A, B, and F pieces meet. For D reverse, begin stitching ¼ inch from the raw edge at the point where C and F meet. In each case, stitch outward in the direction indicated by the arrows.

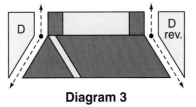

Diagram 3

Press the seams away from the D pieces. Refer to page 227 for additional information on pivoted, or set-in, seams. This completes Row 1. Set aside.

Step 4. For the front of the house, sew a blue G piece to either side of a muslin H piece along their longest sides, as shown in **Diagram 4.** Press the seams toward the blue pieces.

Diagram 4

Step 5. Add a blue I piece along the bottom edge and a blue J piece along the top edge of the house front, as shown in **Diagram 5.** In each case, press the seam toward the newly added piece.

Complete the house front by adding a muslin K piece along the right edge, as shown. Press the seam away from the K piece. Set the completed unit aside.

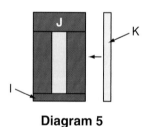

Diagram 5

Step 6. The window sashing is appliquéd to the muslin L pieces before the windows are pieced into the Schoolhouse block. Refer to "Sew Easy" for tips on making the appliqué window sashing strips. Use the $7/8 \times 10^{1}/_2$-inch strips cut and set aside for this purpose to make window sashings that finish about $3/8$ inch wide. Cut each finished sashing strip into two $3^{1}/_2$-inch-long segments and two $1^{3}/_4$-inch-long segments.

Step 7. Finger press the L pieces lengthwise and crosswise to mark both the horizontal and vertical midpoints, as shown in **Diagram 6A.** Center a $1^{3}/_4$-inch-long window sashing strip over

the crosswise crease on an L piece and use your preferred method of appliqué to stitch the strip in place. Repeat to stitch a $3^{1}/_2$-inch-long strip in position over the lengthwise crease, as shown in **6B.** Repeat to make the second window block.

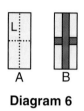

Diagram 6

— **Sew Easy** —

Bias bars, ideal for making narrow bias strips, are useful when making straight-grain strips, too, which means they're perfect for making the window sashing in this quilt.

To use the bars, fold and press the cut strip with *wrong* sides together, aligning the lengthwise raw edges. Use your sewing machine to make a $1/8$-inch seam along the raw edge.

Run the appropriate size rod into the tunnel created by the seam. Adjust the strip so that the seam is centered over one flat side of the rod and press the seam allowance to one side. Use a touch of spray starch for a nice, crisp finish. Remove the rod carefully; if it's metal, it may be hot!

Place the finished strip, seam allowance down, on the quilt block. Pin or baste in place, and you're ready to appliqué.

Step 8. Sew an appliquéd L piece to either side of a blue M piece, as shown in **Diagram 7.** Press the seams toward the blue fabric. Add an N piece along the top and bottom edges of this new unit, as shown. In each case, press the seams toward the newly added piece.

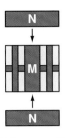

Diagram 7

Step 9. Stitch a blue O piece to the left and right sides of the window unit, as shown in **Diagram 8.** Press the seams toward the newly added pieces. Complete the side of the house by adding a muslin P strip along the top edge of the unit. Press the seam away from P.

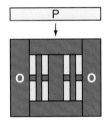

Diagram 8

Step 10. Join the two completed units, as shown in **Diagram 9,** to complete Row 2. Press the seam toward the side of the house. Then, re-ferring to the **Block Diagram** on page 89, sew Rows 1 and 2 together to complete the Schoolhouse block, carefully matching the seams where the roof and house meet. Press the seam in either direction.

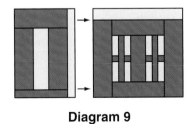

Diagram 9

Step 11. Repeat Steps 1 through 10 to make 20 blocks for the twin-size quilt or 30 blocks for the double-size quilt.

ASSEMBLING THE QUILT TOP

Step 1. From the 2½-inch-wide muslin sashing strips, cut 10½-inch-long pieces for horizontal sashes. You will need 16 pieces for the twin-size quilt and 25 pieces for the double-size quilt.

Step 2. Regardless of the size quilt you are making, you will need to piece the vertical sashing strips to achieve the necessary length. Join the remaining 2½-inch-wide muslin strips in pairs. For the twin size, you will need three long vertical sashing strips; for the double size, you will need four. Trim these long pieced strips to fit your vertical rows, which should be 58½ inches for the twin-size quilt and 70½ inches for the double-size quilt.

Step 3. Refer to the **Twin-Size Assembly Diagram** and use a design wall or other flat surface to lay out the Schoolhouse blocks and the sashing strips in vertical rows. The twin-size quilt will have four vertical rows of five blocks each, separated by short horizontal sashing strips, as shown. The double-size quilt will have five vertical rows of six blocks each, separated by sashing strips. Sew the Schoolhouse blocks and horizontal sashing strips

Twin-Size Assembly Diagram

together in rows. Press the seams toward the Schoolhouse blocks.

Step 4. Join the rows and the vertical sashing strips, taking care to align blocks horizontally before pinning and stitching. Ease as necessary for a proper fit. Press seams away from the sashing.

Adding the Mitered Borders

The quilt shown has a series of four borders. Two are muslin, one is pieced, and the outer border is a blue print. All borders are mitered.

Step 1. For the first muslin border, the strips need to be pieced. For the twin size, sew two $2\frac{1}{2}$-inch-wide muslin strips together with a diagonal seam for a side border, and press the seams as desired. Make another long border strip in the same manner and trim both strips to the length of your quilt top plus two times the border width plus 5 inches for mitering. For the top and bottom borders, cut one of the remaining $2\frac{1}{2}$-inch-wide muslin strips in half, and sew one half to each of the remaining two strips. Press the seams. Trim the borders to the width of your quilt top plus two times the border width plus 5 inches, as for the side borders.

For the double size, sew the $2\frac{1}{2}$-inch-wide muslin border strips together in pairs to make four long strips. Measure the width of quilt top through the center, and add two times the border width plus 5 inches to the total. Trim two strips to this length for the top and bottom borders. Cut the remaining $2\frac{1}{2}$-inch muslin strip in half, and sew one half to each of the remaining long strips. Measure the length of the quilt through the center, and add two times the border width plus 5 inches. Trim the strips to this length for the top and bottom borders.

Step 2. Fold a side border in half crosswise and crease. Unfold it and position it right side down along one side of the quilt top, with the crease at the quilt's midpoint. Pin and sew the border in place, using a $\frac{1}{4}$-inch seam allowance. Begin and end sewing $\frac{1}{4}$ inch from the raw edge of the quilt

top. Repeat on the opposite side. Do not trim the border even with the edges of the top and bottom of the quilt top.

Step 3. Repeat the process described in Step 2 to attach the top and bottom borders to the quilt top. Finish the border by mitering the corners, referring to page 242 for complete instructions.

Assembling the Pieced Border

Step 1. Sew an ecru print X triangle to either side of a blue print Z piece, as shown in **Diagram 10**. Press the seams toward Z. Make four of these units and set them aside.

Diagram 10

Step 2. Sew blue print Y and Y reverse pieces to either side of an ecru print X, as shown in **Diagram 11**. Press the seams away from X. For the twin quilt, make a total of 36 such units; for the double quilt, make a total of 44.

Diagram 11

Step 3. Join the Y/X/Y reverse units into strips, using an ecru X piece to link the units, as shown in **Diagram 12**. For the twin-size quilt, make four strips of four units each for the top and bottom borders, and four strips of five units each for the side borders. For the double quilt, make a total of four strips of five units each and four strips of six units each.

Diagram 12

Step 4. Referring to **Diagram 13**, sew a long, Y/X/Y reverse strip to each side of a previously

Diagram 13

pieced X/Z/X unit. Be sure each of the long strips is the same length. Press the seams away from the X pieces. Make four of these long border units. Note that each finished border strip has a Y piece at one end and a Y reverse piece at the other end, so each border is already angled for mitering.

Step 5. Referring to the **Quilt Diagram** on page 94, sew one of the longer pieced border strips to each side of the quilt top. The strip should be positioned so that the narrowest exposed side of piece Z is closest to the center of the quilt. Since the corners will be mitered, begin and end sewing

········Sew Quick········

When attaching long sashing strips between rows of blocks, it can be tricky aligning the blocks from row to row. Here's a quick and easy way to mark the points for matching on the sashing strips.

Layer a couple of strips (as many as you can snip through with your scissors), then use your rotary ruler to measure the distance from one block to the next. For instance, in this quilt, the finished blocks are 10 inches square. First measure ¼ inch from one end of the strips (for the seam allowance) and make a small snip at the edge of the sashing strip. Measure 10 inches from the first snip and make another small cut in the sashing strips. Measure the finished width of the horizontal sashing strips (2 inches in this case) and snip again. Continue measuring the 10 inches then 2 inches and making snips. Repeat for the other side of the strips, then pin the strips to the rows of quilt blocks, matching the snips with the seam intersections.

¼ inch from the raw edge as these border strips are added.

Step 6. In a similar manner, sew the shorter pieced border strips to the top and bottom edges of the quilt top.

Step 7. Complete the border by sewing the angled seams to join the Y and Y reverse pieces in each corner.

Adding the Outer Borders

Step 1. Both the outer muslin and navy print borders must be pieced in the manner described in Step 1 of "Adding the Mitered Borders" to achieve the proper lengths. For the twin-size quilt, you can simply join pairs of like-color border strips for each side of the quilt. For the double size, the top and bottom borders are made by joining two strips, but the side borders each require two and a half strips. To determine the length needed for the borders, measure the quilt through the vertical and horizontal center. Add 5 inches to each length for mitering. Trim all borders to the lengths you calculated.

Step 2. Sew a side muslin border to the corresponding navy border to make a border unit. Press the seam toward the navy strip. Make two of these border units. Sew the top and bottom muslin borders to the top and bottom navy borders in the same manner.

Step 3. Referring to the **Quilt Diagram** on page 94, position each border unit so that the muslin strip is closest to the center of the quilt and the blue strip is on the outside. Sew the border strips to the edges of the quilt top. Be sure to start and stop sewing ¼ inch from each end of the quilt top.

Step 4. Miter the corner seams, mitering both borders in one step. Refer to page 242 for more details on mitering borders.

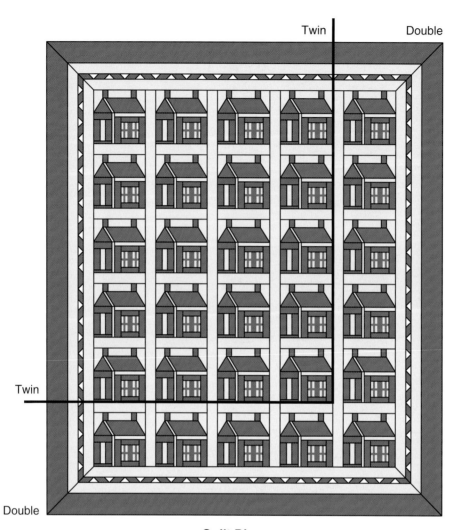

Quilt Diagram

QUILTING AND FINISHING

Step 1. Mark the quilt top for quilting. In the quilt shown, each Schoolhouse block is outline quilted, with additional diagonal line quilting in the roof of each house. The pieced border is quilted in the ditch. The sashing and the unpieced borders are quilted in a diamond pattern.

Step 2. Regardless of which size quilt you've chosen to make, you'll need to piece the backing. For either quilt, cut the backing fabric in half crosswise, and trim the selvages. Cut one piece in half lengthwise, and sew one half to each side of the full-width piece. Press the seams away from the center panel. For the twin size, the seams will

run parallel to the top and bottom of the quilt. For the double size, the seams will run parallel to the sides of the quilt. Refer to page 243 for more information on pieced backings.

Step 3. Layer the backing, batting, and quilt top, and baste the layers together.

Step 4. Quilt all marked designs, adding any additional quilting as desired.

Step 5. Referring to the directions on page 244, make and attach double-fold bias binding. Use the square of navy print fabric that has been set aside for this purpose. For the twin size, you will need about 292 inches of double-fold bias; for the double size, you will need about 340 inches.

ANTIQUE INDIGO SCHOOLHOUSES

Color Plan

Photocopy this page and use it to experiment with color schemes for your quilt.

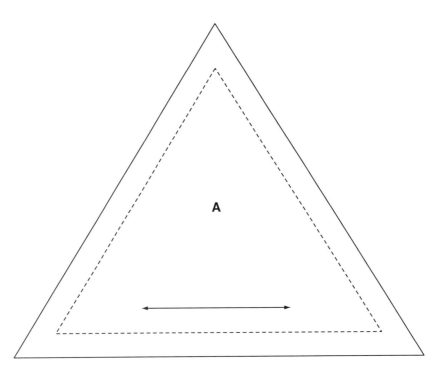

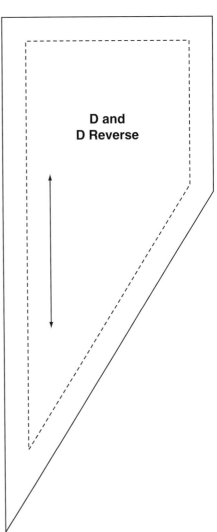

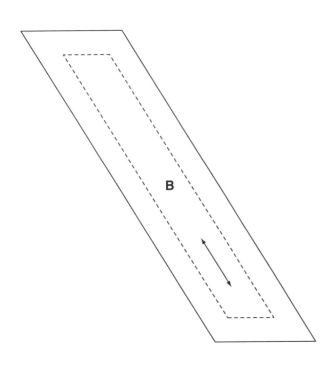

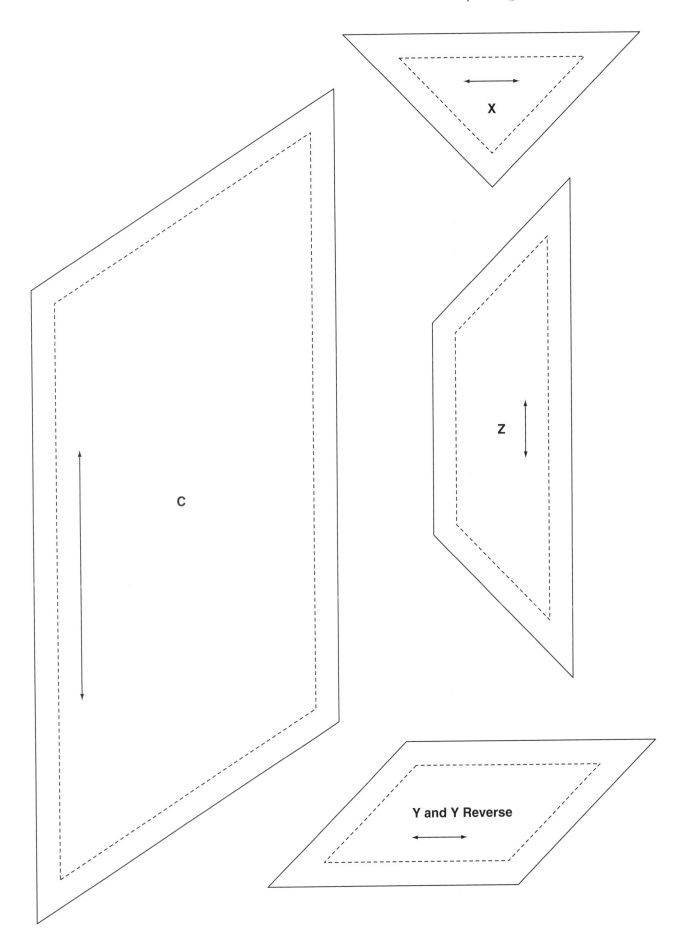

X

Z

C

Y and Y Reverse

CRAZY WEDDING RING

Skill Level: *Intermediate*

Joanne Winn's *Crazy Wedding Ring* wallhanging creatively combines the best of the old with the best of the new. Scraps of fabrics sewn to foundation pieces in the crazy-quilting style popular in the Victorian age are enhanced with decorative stitching. Joanne's updated technique lets you take advantage of the wonderful decorative machine stitches and threads available today to create a vintage look. The real surprise is that the curved piecing associated with a Wedding Ring quilt has been completely eliminated! The crazy-pieced melons are appliquéd by hand or machine to a continuous background.

BEFORE YOU BEGIN

Unlike traditional Wedding Ring quilts, the Crazy Wedding Ring requires only one template, the melon. However, we recommend that you make two plastic templates, one that includes the seam allowance and one that doesn't. The melon pattern is on page 105. The template with the 1/4-inch seam allowance will be used for tracing paper foundation pieces. The finished-size template will be used to mark the turn-under line for appliqué. Refer to page 224 in "Quiltmaking Basics" for more information on making and using templates.

Freezer paper, blank newsprint, onionskin, and heavy tracing paper all work well for foundation piecing, and they can be torn away easily after your pieces are sewn. Trace and cut out 49 melons for the wallhanging or 220 melons for the queen-size quilt.

CHOOSING FABRICS

Both the borders and melons in this quilt are crazy pieced.

Quilt Sizes

	Wallhanging (shown)	Queen
Finished Quilt Size	47½" × 55½"	99½" × 99½"
Finished Ring Size	11"	11"
Number of Melons	49	220

Materials

Fabric	Wallhanging	Queen
Ivory for background	1⅜ yards	7½ yards
Assorted fabric scraps for patchwork and binding	2¾ yards	6½ yards
Muslin foundation for borders	⅔ yard	1⅝ yards
Backing	3⅛ yards	9⅓ yards
Batting	55" × 63"	108" × 108"
Machine embroidery thread		
Freezer paper or tracing paper for foundations		

NOTE: *Yardages are based on 44/45-inch-wide fabrics that are at least 42 inches wide after preshrinking.*

For this technique, an assortment of many fabrics will give you the best results. Fat eighths, fat quarters, scraps, and precut squares will all work well. Choose solids, small-scale prints, prints with contrast, and large, splashy prints that resemble tapestry. Don't worry as much about color as about the variety of fabrics. This quilt was made with many dark, muted fabrics of similar color value, but the random addition of both light and vibrant pieces will give the quilt pizzazz.

You will also need to choose several threads for machine embroidery. You may use traditional cotton or cotton-covered polyester threads, or try rayon threads that highlight the colors in your fabrics to make a more dramatic statement.

CUTTING

The yardage requirements given are estimates and will likely vary depending on the size of your crazy pieces and waste from trimming excess seam allowances when piecing. The method of crazy piecing requires cutting as you go rather than precutting pieces. Only the background fabric and border foundation pieces will need to be cut to a predetermined size. These pieces will be cut later, when you are ready to assemble the quilt top.

PIECING THE MELONS

Step 1. Choose a fabric to begin your first melon, and cut an approximately 3 × 3½-inch rectangle from it. Position the piece right side up on your paper foundation, as shown in **Diagram 1.** A portion of the fabric may extend beyond the edge of your foundation. This excess fabric will be trimmed away later.

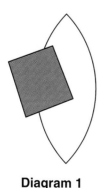

Diagram 1

— Sew Easy —

If you are using freezer paper as your foundation, be sure to sew the fabric to the matte (nonshiny) side of the paper. Otherwise, when you flip and press your pieces, your iron will stick to the plastic coating on the paper. To keep the coated side from sticking to your ironing board when you press, simply lay a scrap of muslin on your ironing board.

Step 2. Choose another fabric and cut a rectangle from it, making sure that one side is about as long as the right edge of your first rectangle. Position the rectangle right side down along the right edge of the first piece, matching the raw edges, as shown in **Diagram 2A.** Using a ¼-inch seam allowance, sew the two pieces to the foundation paper. Flip the second fabric over so both pieces are right side up, as shown in **2B.** Press the seam lightly after the addition of this and each new piece.

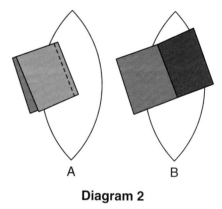

A   B

Diagram 2

Step 3. Choose a third fabric and cut a piece from it that is large enough to cover the top portion of the melon. Position it right side down, aligned flush with the top raw edge of the first two pieces, as shown in **Diagram 3A.** Stitch the layers together with a ¼-inch seam allowance, then flip the new piece so it is right side up. See **3B.**

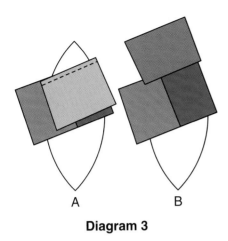

A   B

Diagram 3

━━ Sew Easy ━━

To add decorative machine stitching between pieces, it is best to do it after each seam. Otherwise, the edges of the seam will be covered by more pieces, making it harder to stitch a neat, stable line. By stitching before your next piece is added, the starting and stopping points of the stitching will be covered by consecutive pieces.

Step 4. The fourth fabric will cover the remaining section of the melon, so cut a piece that will cover the foundation after the piece is flipped into place. Position the piece right side down, with the bottom edge flush with the edge of pieces 1 and 2. Stitch, then flip the piece right side up. Your melon should now resemble **Diagram 4.**

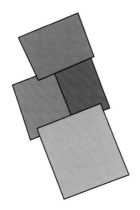

Diagram 4

Step 5. For appliquéing, you will need to mark the finished-size melon shape on your crazy-pieced melon. If you plan to use the freezer paper method described on page 231, turn the melon over and trace the finished-size template onto the freezer paper foundation. Trim away the excess fabric to the outside line, then trim the freezer paper to the inside line, as shown in **Diagram 5.** Press the fabric seam allowance toward the freezer paper.

If you plan to do needle-turn appliqué, first trim away the excess fabric from your foundation piece. Then trace the finished-size melon onto the right side of the fabric. You may trim the seam allowance to a scant ¼ inch from the drawn line if you prefer.

If you are using decorative stitching, don't forget to add this along the seams of the last pieces you added. When all stitching is complete, remove the foundation paper.

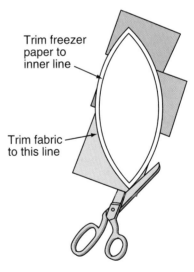

Trim freezer paper to inner line

Trim fabric to this line

Diagram 5

Step 6. Repeat Steps 1 through 5 to assemble 49 melons for the wallhanging or 220 melons for the queen-size quilt.

Remember that no two melons are exactly alike, as shown in the photograph on page 98. The instructions give an example of one way to position your fabrics for sewing. You may choose to use triangles or other shapes for some of your pieces.

Some of your melons may have more pieces than the one illustrated here. Just remember that each new piece should overlap all outside edges of the fabrics it is being sewn to.

PREPARING THE MELONS FOR APPLIQUÉ

The melons will all be appliquéd to a solid background, so the outer seam allowance of each must be turned under. See page 231 for a suggested technique to help you prepare accurately shaped melons.

ASSEMBLING THE QUILT TOP

Step 1. For the wallhanging, trim the 1⅜-yard piece of solid ivory background fabric to 40½ × 48½ inches. The background for the queen-size quilt must be 88½ inches square, so it will have to be pieced. Cut the 7½-yard piece of solid ivory fabric crosswise into three equal panels, and trim all of the selvages. Choose one panel for the center section of the background and measure its width. Subtract that width from 88½ to determine the remaining width necessary. Divide the result by two and add ½ inch for seam allowances.

Using a 42-inch center panel as an example: 88½ − 42 = 46½ ÷ 2 = 23¼ + ½ = 23¾ inches.

Trim the remaining two panels to the width you just calculated. Sew a narrow panel to each lengthwise side of the full-width panel and press the seams open. Trim the full-size background piece to 88½ inches long.

Step 2. To position the melons correctly, you must accurately mark the back-ground. Draw a grid with a pencil or other removable marker that reflects the distance between melon centers. To do so, draw a horizontal and vertical line beginning at the upper left corner of your background, each beginning 4 inches from the outer edge of the fabric. Continue drawing horizontal and vertical lines, parallel to and 8 inches away from the first lines, as shown in **Diagram 6.**

For the wallhanging, draw five vertical lines and six horizontal lines. For the queen-size quilt, your grid should have 11 vertical and 11 horizontal lines. By starting your grid 4 inches from the edge, you will end up with a 2½-inch border of background fabric remaining around the outside edge of the quilt top once the melons are centered over the grid lines.

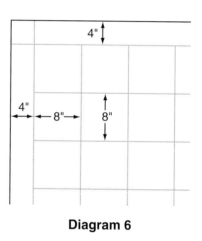

Diagram 6

— Sew Easy

Instead of marking a grid on the background fabric, you may want to press your fabric into rows the width of the grid. Measure and mark the folds, then press the fabric accordion style to define the grid.

Step 3. Use a design wall or other flat surface to position the melons on the grid, referring to the **Wallhanging Diagram** on page 104. Hold the melons in place temporarily with a pin in case you want to move them around. The points of each melon should align with your drawn lines, as shown in **Diagram 7**. Continue adding melons until you are pleased with the layout, then appliqué them to the background.

For the queen-size quilt, it might be more manageable to appliqué a few rows at a time. If you

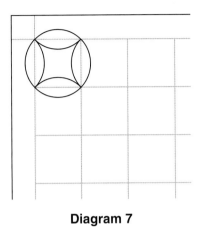

Diagram 7

decided to use the freezer paper appliqué method, remember to remove the paper after appliquéing each melon.

········Sew Quick········

You may find it easier to fuse the melons to your background using lightweight fusible web as an alternative to the appliqué method described on page 231. This method is quick and easy, and it is particularly suitable for a wallhanging that won't be handled as much as a bed quilt. Use the finished-size template to trace melons onto the fusible web. Cut them out and follow the manufacturer's directions for fusing. After fusing the melons to the background, you can use decorative stitches along the edges to secure them.

MAKING AND ATTACHING THE BORDERS

The quilt borders are also pieced on a foundation in the same random-piecing manner as the melons. We recommend that you use a fabric foundation instead of paper for the borders. The fabric foundation will remain permanently in the quilt, giving it extra stability.

Step 1. For the wallhanging, cut muslin border strips 4 inches wide. For the queen-size quilt, cut border strips 6 inches wide. To determine the length of the side borders, measure the length of your quilt top, taking the measurement through the vertical center of the quilt rather than along the sides. Add approximately 1½ inches to that measurement, and cut (or piece together) two long muslin strips to this length. Measure the width of the quilt in a similar manner, adding two times the width of the side borders plus 1½ inches. Cut or piece together two muslin foundation strips to this length.

Use the crazy-piecing technique to cover the muslin foundations, adding decorative stitching as you go, if desired. Trim the completed side borders to the exact length of your quilt measurement.

Step 2. Fold one side border in half crosswise and crease. Unfold it and position it right side down along one side of your quilt top, with the crease at the horizontal midpoint. Pin at the midpoint and ends first, then along the length of the entire side, easing in fullness if necessary. Sew the border to the quilt top using a ¼-inch seam allowance. Repeat on the opposite side of the quilt.

Step 3. Trim the top and bottom borders to the width of your quilt. Fold the top border in half crosswise and crease. Unfold it and position it right side down along one end of your quilt top, with the crease at the vertical midpoint. Pin at the midpoint and ends first, then along the length of the entire side, easing in fullness if necessary. Sew the border to the quilt top using a ¼-inch seam allowance. Repeat on the bottom of the quilt.

QUILTING AND FINISHING

Step 1. Mark the quilt top for quilting. The quilt shown was machine quilted with clear nylon thread in the ditch of each crazy piece. In addition, an undulating feather border was quilted in the background fabric between the outer rows of

Wallhanging Diagram

rings and the crazy quilt border. The center of each ring was quilted with a flower surrounded by four leaves.

Step 2. To piece the backing for the wallhanging, cut the backing fabric in half, and trim the selvages. Cut two 12-inch-wide panels from one segment, and sew a narrow panel to each side of the full-width panel, as shown in **Diagram 8.** Press the seams open.

Step 3. To piece the backing for the queen-size quilt, cut the backing fabric into three equal lengths, and trim the selvages. Cut a 32-inch-wide

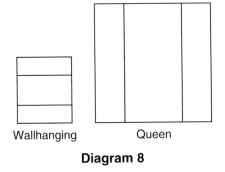

Wallhanging   Queen
Diagram 8

panel from two of the pieces, and sew one of these to each side of the remaining full-width piece, as shown. Press the seams open.

Step 4. Layer the quilt top, batting, and backing, and baste the layers together. Quilt as desired.

Step 5. The quilt shown has a pieced binding, made from scraps of the fabrics used in the quilt. Referring to the directions on page 244 in "Quiltmaking Basics," make straight-grain double-fold binding, piecing together short strips of a variety of fabrics. The length of your strips can vary, but they should all be the same width (about 2½ inches). Keep adding strips until you have the length needed to bind your entire quilt.

To calculate the approximate number of inches of binding needed for the quilt size you are making, add the length of the four sides of the quilt plus 9 inches.

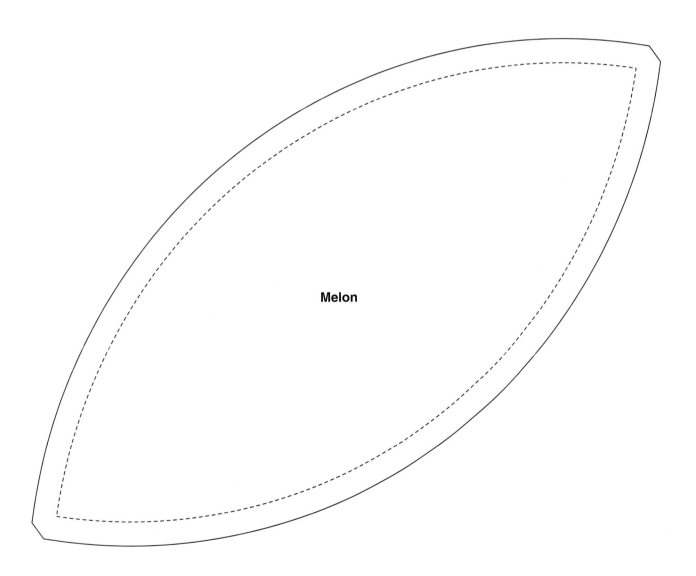

Melon

SUMMER'S END

Skill Level: *Intermediate*

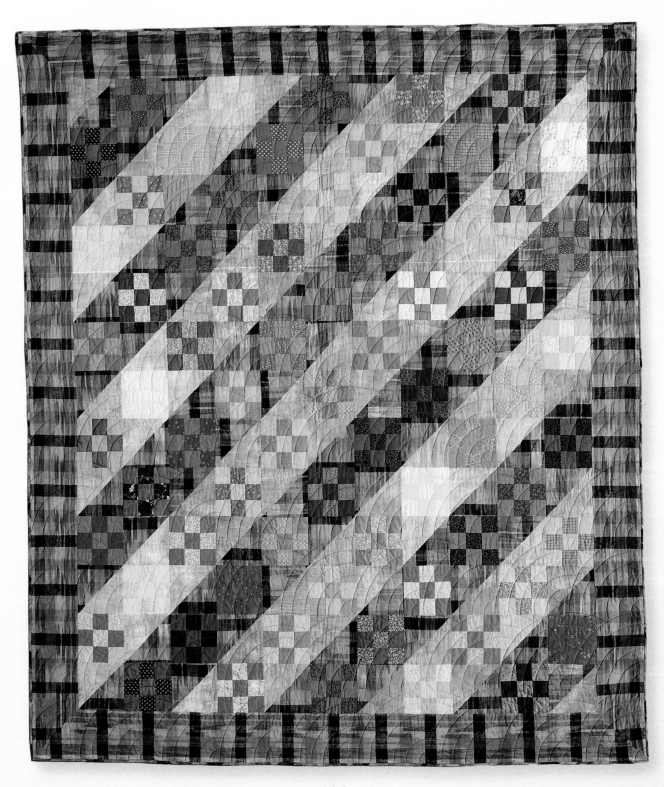

Although it's composed of basic Nine-Patch blocks in a classic Straight Furrows setting, this vibrant quilt by Judy Miller comes alive through the masterful use of color. Made as a fun end-of-summer project using fabric purchased at summer sales, the twin-size quilt's focal point is a bold madras plaid used in the border and as one half of the triangle squares. The fabrics used in the Nine-Patch blocks and the other half of the triangle squares echo the many colors in the plaid, resulting in a complex yet harmonious burst of color.

Before You Begin

The directions for this quilt are written based on using an easy strip-piecing technique for making the Nine-Patch blocks. Strips of fabric are sewn together into strip sets. The strip sets are then cut apart and resewn into blocks. Read through the general construction directions beginning on page 143, for further details on strip piecing.

The directions for making the triangle squares call for layering two squares of fabric and stitching them together on the diagonal. The squares are then cut apart on the diagonal, resulting in two triangle squares.

Quilt Sizes

	Twin (shown)	Double	Queen
Quilt Size	78" × 90"	84" × 102"	90" × 102"
Finished Block Size	6"	6"	6"
Number of Blocks			
Nine Patch	71	90	97
Triangle Squares	72	90	98

Materials

Fabric	Twin	Double	Queen
Dark plaid	3 yards	3¾ yards	4 yards
Assorted lights	2¾ yards	3⅜ yards	3⅝ yards
Assorted darks	2¾ yards	3⅜ yards	3⅝ yards
Light hand-dyed fabric	1⅜ yards	1¾ yards	2 yards
Backing	7½ yards	7⅞ yards	8⅝ yards
Batting	84" × 96"	90" × 108"	96" × 108"
Binding	¾ yard	⅞ yard	⅞ yard

Note: Yardages are based on 44/45-inch-wide fabric that is at least 42 inches wide after preshrinking.

Choosing Fabrics

To re-create the look of this quilt, you'll need to select your fabrics very carefully. In fact, we've given this quilt an Intermediate skill rating simply because of the challenge presented by coordinating the fabrics as successfully as this quiltmaker has done.

First, choose a gorgeous plaid—one with a wide range of colors. The plaid is used in the border as well as in the dark half of the triangle squares.

Next, select the prints and solids for the Nine-Patch blocks.

Cutting Chart

Fabric	Used For	Strip Width	Number of Strips		
			Twin	Double	Queen
Dark plaid	Triangle squares	6⅞"	6	8	9
	Border	6½"	9	10	10
Assorted lights	Strip sets	2½"	36	45	49
Assorted darks	Strip sets	2½"	36	45	49
Light hand-dyed fabric	Triangle squares	6⅞"	6	8	9

While there are many different colors used in the quilt, each individual Nine-Patch block is made from two different values of the same color. In some blocks the fabrics are very close in value, while in others they have greater contrast. You'll need a selection of light and dark fabrics to create the distinct light and dark rows. For best results, choose small amounts of a wide variety of fabrics in colors that complement the plaid.

Finally, select a fabric for the light half of the triangle squares. The quiltmaker used a hand-dyed fabric with muted splashes of color that repeat those found in the plaid, but in pastel tones. You can choose a similar hand-dyed fabric or substitute one of the new commercial prints that resemble hand-dyed fabric.

To help develop your own unique color scheme for the quilt, photocopy the **Color Plan** on page 113, and use crayons or colored pencils to experiment with different color combinations.

The light and dark yardages shown are generous estimates of the total yardage actually used in the quilt. Since small amounts of many different fabrics are key here, you will likely begin with more yardage than indicated, but not all of it will be used.

CUTTING

All measurements include ¼-inch seam allowances. Referring to the Cutting Chart, cut the required number of strips in the width needed. Cut

Sew Easy

The piecing instructions for the Nine-Patch blocks make it easy to take advantage of scraps you have on hand. For example, two 8-inch squares in contrasting shades will yield two Nine-Patch blocks.

all strips across the fabric width (crosswise grain).

The number of strips required is based on using full-width fabric (at least 42 inches wide). If you use shorter strips, either to obtain greater variety or to use up scraps, the number of strips required will vary.

Cut the plaid and the hand-dyed fabric for the triangle squares into 6⅞-inch-wide strips, then cut the strips into 6⅞-inch squares. Pair up a square of each fabric for each pair of triangle squares.

Note: Cut and piece one sample block before cutting all the fabric for the quilt.

PIECING THE BLOCKS

In this quilt, Nine-Patch blocks alternate with triangle squares. The blocks are illustrated in the **Block Diagram.** There are two variations of the Nine-Patch blocks; the difference between them lies in the placement of the light and dark fabrics. The Nine-Patch blocks are assembled using easy strip-piecing techniques. The method used to make the triangle squares eliminates the need to cut individual triangles.

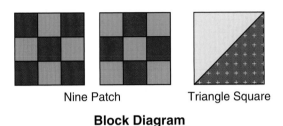

Nine Patch   Triangle Square
Block Diagram

Making the Triangle Squares

Step 1. Working on the wrong side of a $6\frac{7}{8}$-inch square of hand-dyed fabric, use a pencil or permanent marker to draw a diagonal line from corner to corner, as shown in **Diagram 1A.**

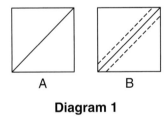

A   B
Diagram 1

Step 2. Position the marked square right sides together with a plaid square. Using a ¼-inch seam allowance, stitch along both sides of the diagonal line, as shown in **1B.** Use the edge of your presser foot as a ¼-inch guide, or draw a line ¼ inch from each side of the diagonal line.

Step 3. Using a rotary cutter and ruler, cut the squares apart on the diagonal line, as shown in **Diagram 2A.** See page 223 in "Quiltmaking Basics" for complete details on rotary cutting. Carefully press the triangle squares open, pressing the seam toward the plaid fabric. Trim off the triangle points at the seam ends, as shown in **2B.** You will get two triangle squares from each pair of squares cut in this manner. Continue marking and

cutting triangle squares until you have made the number required for the quilt size you are making.

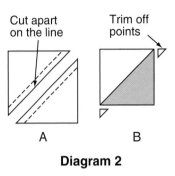

Cut apart on the line   Trim off points
A   B
Diagram 2

Piecing the Nine-Patch Blocks

Each Nine-Patch block requires two different segment variations, as shown in **Diagram 3.** One block variation uses two A segments and one B segment, while the other variation uses two B segments and one A segment. Following these directions, you'll cut three each of the two different segments—enough to assemble two blocks. When the blocks are later combined with others in the quilt top, their similarity won't be noticeable, keeping the scrappy look of your quilt intact.

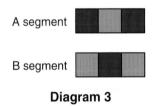

A segment
B segment
Diagram 3

Step 1. The blocks are assembled using a strip-piecing technique. Referring to the Cutting Chart, cut the total number of strips required to make the Nine-Patch blocks for your quilt. Select a pair of cut strips of different value, and cut three $2\frac{1}{2} \times 8$-inch strips from each. Keep in mind that you'll need blocks that are distinctly light and blocks that are distinctly dark in order to create the effect of light and dark rows.

Step 2. Sew a dark 8-inch strip to each side of a light 8-inch strip, as shown in **Diagram 4A** on page 110. Press the seams toward the dark strips.

Step 3. Use your rotary cutter to square up one end of the sewn unit, then cut three 2½-inch-wide segments from it, as shown in **4B**.

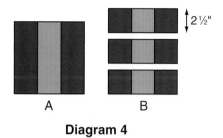

Diagram 4

Step 4. Sew a light 8-inch strip to each side of a dark 8-inch strip, as shown in **Diagram 5A**. Press the seams toward the dark strip.

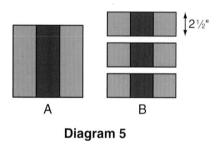

Diagram 5

Step 5. Use your rotary cutter to square up one end of the sewn unit, then cut three 2½-inch-wide segments from it, as shown in **5B**.

Step 6. Referring to the **Block Diagram** on page 109 for correct placement, position your sewn segments into three rows for each block. Sew the blocks together, matching seams carefully. Since the seam allowances on the segments are pressed in opposite directions, the intersections should fit together tightly. Stitch, using a ¼-inch seam allowance. Press.

Step 7. Repeat Steps 1 through 6 with other fabric combinations until you have assembled enough light and dark blocks for your quilt.

ASSEMBLING THE QUILT TOP

Step 1. Use a design wall or other flat surface to lay out the blocks, referring to the **Quilt Diagram**

for the correct layout. The quilt shown in the diagram is the twin-size quilt, which has 13 rows of 11 blocks each. The layout for the double- and queen-size quilts is the same, except that the double size has 15 rows of 12 blocks each, and the queen size has 15 rows of 13 blocks each. When placing blocks, make sure the light half of each triangle square is positioned against a light Nine-Patch block and the dark half is positioned against a dark Nine-Patch block.

Step 2. When you are satisfied with the layout, sew the blocks together in rows, as shown in the **Assembly Diagram**. Press the seams in opposite directions from row to row.

Step 3. Sew the rows together, carefully matching seams where blocks meet. If you've

Assembly Diagram

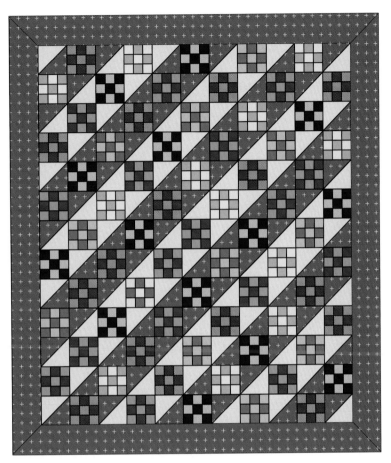

Quilt Diagram

pressed the seam allowances in opposite directions, the seams should fit tightly against each other, helping you to achieve a perfect match. Press seam allowances where rows were joined.

Sew Easy

If you have a scrap piece of fabric that's perfect for your quilt but too small for strip piecing, simply assemble the block piece by piece, cutting 2½-inch squares. Sew the squares into A and B segments, as shown, pressing the seams toward the darkest fabric. Join the segments to complete the block.

ADDING THE BORDERS

Step 1. Refer to page 242 in "Quiltmaking Basics" for complete details on adding borders with mitered corners. To determine the correct length to make the side borders, measure the quilt top vertically through the center. To this measurement add two times the finished width of the border (6 inches × 2) plus approximately 5 inches. This is the length you need to make the two side borders. In the same manner, measure the quilt top horizontally through the center, and calculate the length of the top and bottom borders.

Step 2. Sew the 6-inch-wide plaid border strips together end to end to make four long borders, then trim them to the exact length needed. For the twin-size quilt, you'll need two strips each for the top and bottom borders and two and a half strips each for the side borders. The double- and queen-size quilts require two and a half strips for each border.

Step 3. Pin and sew the four borders to the quilt top, matching the midpoint of each border to the midpoint of the side to which it's being added. Refer to "Quiltmaking Basics" on page 242 for complete instructions for adding mitered borders to your quilt. When preparing the miters, be sure to carefully match up the plaid in adjacent borders.

QUILTING AND FINISHING

Step 1. Mark the quilt top for quilting. The quilt shown was quilted with a continuous design of fanlike curves, their arches beginning in the upper left corner and continuing diagonally across and down the quilt.

Step 2. Regardless of which quilt size you've chosen to make, the backing will have to be pieced. To make the most efficient use of the yardage, piece the twin-size back with the seams running vertically and the double- and queen-size backs with the seams running horizontally, as illustrated in **Diagram 6**. To piece the twin-size quilt back, cut the backing fabric crosswise into two equal segments, and trim the selvages.

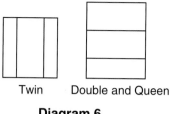

Twin   Double and Queen

Diagram 6

Step 3. Cut one of the segments in half lengthwise, and sew one half to each side of the full-width piece. Press the seams open.

Step 4. To make the backing for the double- and queen-size quilts, cut the backing fabric into three equal segments, and trim the selvages.

Step 5. Sew two of the pieces together along the long side, and press the seam open. Cut a piece approximately 30 inches wide from the third segment. Sew this piece to the joined segment, then press the seam open.

Step 6. Layer the quilt top, batting, and backing, and baste the layers together. Quilt as desired.

Step 7. Make the required length of double-fold binding for your quilt. Refer to page 244 in "Quiltmaking Basics" for complete directions on making and attaching binding. Sew the binding to the quilt using a ¼-inch seam allowance.

SUMMER'S END

Color Plan

Photocopy this page and use it to experiment with color schemes for your quilt.

MY STARS!...THEY'RE PLAID!

Skill Level: *Easy*

114

Betty Alvarez of Marietta, Georgia, whipped up this extravaganza in plaid after being inspired by noted quiltmaker and fabric designer Roberta Horton. Betty's merry mix of madras plaids in vibrant hues makes this star quilt simply twinkle. A randomly pieced border adds a playful final touch — and it's a great way to use up the leftovers from a multi-fabric project.

BEFORE YOU BEGIN

This quilt is a combination of Garden Walk (similar to the traditional 54-40 or Fight block) and Four-in-Nine Patch blocks. Both blocks include 3-inch-square four patch blocks. Quick strip-piecing techniques make it easy to assemble the large quantity of four patches needed. See "Cutting Fabric" on page 223 for general information on rotary cutting.

The light-color triangles for the large and small star backgrounds are cut with templates made from pattern pieces A and B on page 122. When marking fabric, be sure the grain line drawn on the pattern is parallel to the fabric's straight of grain. For more information on making templates, see "Making and Using Templates" on page 224.

CHOOSING FABRICS

This scrap quilt was assembled with a large assortment of colorful woven and madras plaids. To make a quilt similar to the one shown, select as many different fabrics as possible. Like units within each block are identical, but the star blocks each contain three different units (four patches, large star points, and small star points), so each block requires three different plaid fabrics. Try to choose plaids of varying scale, and don't worry too much about color unless you would like to focus on a specific range. Notice in the quilt photograph on the opposite page that darker plaids are used in the outer areas of the quilt, with lighter values placed in blocks near the center. Muslin is used for the background throughout.

Fat quarters are a good choice for this quilt because they are wide and long enough to make several strip sets needed for the four patch units. Fat eighths are also suitable if their longest edge measures 22 inches. Star points can be cut from either fat quarters or fat eighths.

Quilt Sizes		
	Twin	Queen (shown)
Finished Quilt Size	73" × 91"	91" × 109"
Number of Star Blocks	32	50
Number of Alternate Blocks	31	49
Number of Four Patch Units	283	445

Materials		
Fabric	Twin	Queen
Assorted plaids	5½ yards	7 yards
Muslin	5¼ yards	8¼ yards
Backing	5⅝ yards	8⅓ yards
Batting	80" × 98"	98" × 116"
Binding	⅝ yard	⅔ yard

NOTE: *Yardages are based on 44/45-inch-wide fabrics that are at least 42 inches wide after preshrinking.*

Cutting Chart

Fabric	Used For	Strip Width or Piece	Number to Cut Twin	Number to Cut Queen	Second Cut Dimensions	Number to Cut Twin	Number to Cut Queen
Plaids	Four patches	2"	32	50	2" × 21"	63	99
	Large star points	2⅜"	15	23	2⅜" × 4¼"*	128	200
	Small star points	1¼"	8	12	1¼" × 2¼"*	128	200
	Small star centers	1½"	2	2	1½" squares	32	50
	Borders†	2" strips	—	—			
Muslin	Four patches	2"	32	50	2" × 21"	63	99
	Large star background	Template A	128	200			
	Small star background	Template B	128	200			
	Small star corners	1½"	5	8	1½" squares	128	200
	Alternate blocks	3½"	12	18	3½" squares	124	196

* *Cut four identical rectangles for each block.*

† *See Steps 1 and 2 in "Adding the Borders" on page 119.*

The Materials list on page 115 suggests the total plaid yardage required to make this quilt, but as for most scrappy quilts, it may be helpful to think of yardage in terms of the total number of blocks and how many times you plan to repeat a fabric, instead.

To develop a unique color scheme for the quilt, photocopy the **Color Plan** on page 123, and use crayons or colored pencils to test different color arrangements.

CUTTING

All the rotary cutting dimensions and pattern pieces given for this quilt include ¼-inch seam allowances. Cut the number of strips and pieces as described in the Cutting Chart, then follow the directions below for additional cutting information. All strips are cut on the crosswise grain of the fabric.

Note: We recommend that you cut and piece a sample block before cutting all the fabric for your quilt.

For the star points, you will need to make mirror-image triangles. Cut half of the 2⅜ × 4¼-inch plaid rectangles for large star points in half diagonally from the top left to the bottom right, as shown in **Diagram 1A**. Cut the remaining rectangles in half diagonally in the opposite direction, from top right to bottom left, as shown in **1B**. Keep the triangles that you cut from the same fabric paired together.

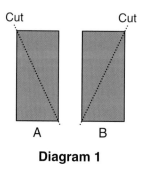

Diagram 1

Repeat the diagonal cutting for the 1¼ × 2¼-inch plaid rectangles for the small star blocks, cutting half in each direction, as shown in the above diagram. Keep the triangles that you cut from the same fabric paired together. For easy assembly of your block later, place a matching 1½-inch square with each set of eight triangles cut from the same plaid fabric.

PIECING THE LARGE STAR BLOCKS

Four-Patch Units

A four patch unit is sewn into each corner of the Star block and at the corners and center of the Alternate block, as shown in the **Block Diagram.** The four patch units within individual blocks are identical, and can be made easily and accurately using a quick-piecing method.

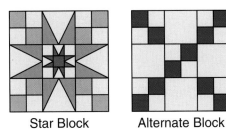

Star Block   Alternate Block

Block Diagram

Step 1. To make the four patch units for the Star blocks, sew a 2 × 21-inch plaid strip to a 2 × 21-inch muslin strip, as shown in **Diagram 2.** Press the seam allowance toward the plaid strip.

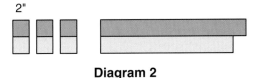

2"

Diagram 2

Step 2. Use your rotary cutting equipment to square up one end of the strip, and cut 2-inch segments from it, as shown in **Diagram 2.**

Step 3. Carefully match the center seams, and sew two segments together, as shown in **Diagram 3.** Press the seam in either direction. Sew the remaining segments together in pairs to make a total of four identical four patch units. Stack together.

Diagram 3

Step 4. Repeat Steps 1 through 3 to assemble the total number of four patch units required for

Sew Easy

When you cut pieces for a quilt block using rotary cutting *and* templates, as in this project, you may notice a variation in the size and fit of your pieces.

Tracing around a template can allow the shape to "grow" due to the width of the pencil line, which can be compounded by cutting along the outside of the drawn line. When you rotary cut, your cutter is positioned snugly against a ruler, which is aligned with the edge of the fabric at a precise measurement. No pencil lines are used.

Don't let the possibility of variation discourage you. It's a situation that can easily be avoided by doing the following things:

• Check your templates for accuracy.

• Use a very narrow pencil line to mark the fabric.

• Be sure to cut all template pieces at the innermost edge of the drawn line.

• As you cut, make sure the pieces match the patterns printed in the book.

• Piece a sample block to make sure all units match correctly. After a while, you will know exactly where to cut to produce accurate results.

your quilt size. Keep each identical set separate from the others if you plan to use like units within each block, as in the quilt shown on page 114.

Star Points

For each Star block, you'll need eight large triangles cut from identical plaid rectangles, four cut along one diagonal, four cut along the opposite diagonal, as shown in **Diagram 1.** While the triangles are cut from the same fabric, it should be a different fabric than you used in the four patch units.

Step 1. Use **Trimming Pattern 1** to trim points, as described in "Sew Easy." Sew a pair of mirror image plaid triangles to either side of a muslin A triangle, as shown in **Diagram 4**. Press the seams toward the plaid triangles.

Diagram 4

Step 2. Repeat, assembling a total of four star point units for each large Star block in your quilt.

— Sew Easy —

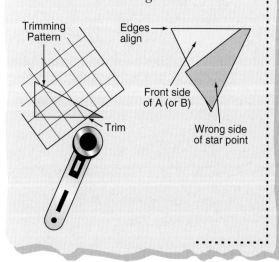

To align your triangles for stitching, trim the tips off the plaid triangles. Since these triangles are not cut at 45-degree angles, the alignment can be a little tricky. Make a paper template of **Trimming Pattern 1** on page 122. Tape it to the underside of a rotary ruler so the trimmed-off tip is flush with the straight edge of the ruler. Align your ruler over the star point triangles, and trim away the excess seam allowance from the triangle's tip with your rotary cutter. You can trim several triangles at a time if you have them carefully layered. **Trimming Pattern 2** is provided for the small star blocks that make up the centers of the large stars.

Trimming Pattern

Edges align

Front side of A (or B)

Trim

Wrong side of star point

Small Star Block

Step 1. Assemble the small Star points in the same manner as you did the large ones. Use plaid triangles cut from the $1\frac{1}{4} \times 2\frac{1}{4}$-inch rectangles. Use **Trimming Pattern 2** to trim the plaid triangle points, as described in "Sew Easy," and attach them to the muslin B triangles.

Step 2. Lay out the components of the block: four star points units, a matching $1\frac{1}{2}$-inch plaid square, and four $1\frac{1}{2}$-inch muslin squares. Sew the pieces together in rows, as shown in **Diagram 5A**. Press the seam allowances in adjoining rows in opposite directions, then sew the rows together, as shown in **5B**. Press the block.

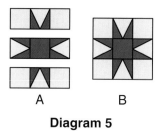

A   B

Diagram 5

Step 3. Repeat Steps 1 and 2 to make the number of small Star blocks for your quilt size.

— Sew Easy —

If you prefer not to work with such small pieces, you can replace the 3-inch Star block with either a $3\frac{1}{2}$-inch (cut size) plaid square or an additional four patch unit made of leftovers from your plaid and muslin strip sets.

ASSEMBLING THE BLOCK

Step 1. Sew the four patch units, star points, and small Star block together in three rows, as shown in **Diagram 6A**. Press the seam allowances toward the large star points, then sew the rows together, as shown in **6B**. Press the block.

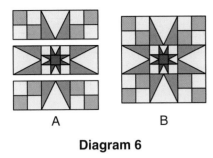

Diagram 6

Step 2. Repeat to complete the total number of large Star blocks required for your quilt size.

PIECING THE ALTERNATE BLOCKS

Step 1. Piece and lay out five identical four patch units and four 3½-inch muslin squares for the block, as shown in **Diagram 7A,** and sew the pieces into three rows. Note that the diagonal line from the lower left corner to the upper right corner is filled with dark patches. This same color layout is used for every Alternate block. Press seams in adjoining rows in opposite directions, then sew the rows together, as shown in **7B.** Press.

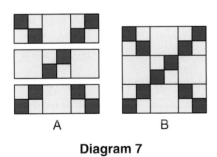

Diagram 7

Step 2. Repeat to make the total number of Alternate blocks required for your quilt size.

⋯⋯Sew Quick⋯⋯

As you sew, use a square rotary ruler or a 3½-inch square template to quickly check the accuracy of all final block components.

ASSEMBLING THE QUILT TOP

Step 1. Arrange the Star and Alternate blocks, as shown in the **Quilt Diagram** on page 121. The heavy line indicates the layout for the twin-size quilt. The queen-size quilt uses 99 blocks. Take care to orient all Alternate blocks as shown in the diagram so you achieve the desired diagonal effect. Rearrange the blocks until the color layout pleases you. Note that in the quilt shown on page 114, darker plaid blocks were placed around the perimeter of the quilt.

Step 2. Sew the blocks in each row together. When possible, press seams in adjoining rows in opposite directions. Sew the rows together, taking care to match all unit intersections. Press the quilt.

ADDING THE BORDERS

The quilt shown has three plaid scrap borders that each finish at 1½ inches wide, giving you a total finished border unit width of 4½ inches. The borders are made by sewing random lengths of plaid scraps end to end with angled seams. The border corners are mitered.

Step 1. To determine the length needed for the borders, measure the quilt top vertically through the center. To this measurement, add two times the finished width of the border unit plus 5 inches (4½ inches × 2 = 9 inches; 9 inches + 5 inches = 14 inches). This is the length you will need to make each of the side borders. Use the same method to calculate strip lengths needed for the top and bottom borders, measuring horizontally through the middle of the quilt.

Step 2. Cut 2-inch-wide strips from all of your plaid scraps. Don't worry if some of your scrap strips are longer than others. Most of the segments in this quilt are approximately 6 to 24 inches long. In fact, if most of your strips are close to the same length, you may want to trim some of them so they are shorter, or cut some in half to make two shorter strips that can be used in different sections of your borders.

Step 3. Stack several strips together, right sides up with left ends aligned, as shown in **Diagram 8A.** Use your rotary ruler to cut a 45-degree angle at the left end of the stack, as shown in **8B.** Align the right ends and make another 45-degree cut through all layers, as shown in **8C.** Cuts should be parallel to each other. Cut approximately half of the 2-inch-wide strips in this fashion. Label them "Right and bottom border strips," and set them aside.

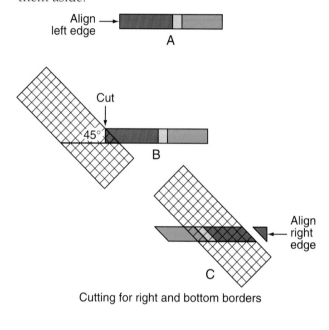

Cutting for right and bottom borders

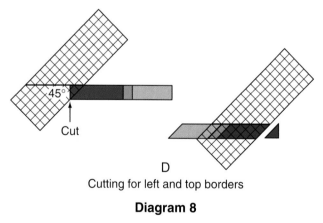

D
Cutting for left and top borders

Diagram 8

Step 4. For the remaining strips, reverse the cutting angle at each end, as shown in **8D.** Label these "Left and top border strips."

Step 5. Sew random-length right border and bottom border strips together end-to-end, as shown in **Diagram 9A,** until you achieve the required length calculated for one of these borders. Repeat, making a total of three border units for the right border and three for the bottom border.

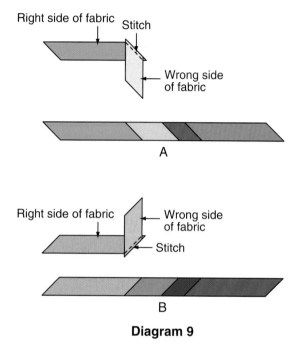

Diagram 9

Step 6. Repeat the process described in Step 5 with the random-length left and top border strips, as shown in **Diagram 9B,** to make three pieced border units for the left border and three for the top border.

Step 7. Working with the right side border units, pin and sew the three units together lengthwise into a new larger unit, making sure the diagonal seams run in the same direction, as shown in **Diagram 10A.** Press the seams toward what will be the inner border. In the same manner, sew the three bottom border units into a single larger unit, pressing the seams toward the outer border.

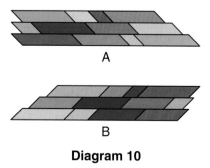

Diagram 10

Step 8. Repeat the process described in Step 7 with the appropriate strips to make the left side and top border units, as shown in **Diagram 10B**.

Step 9. Pin and sew the four border units to the appropriate sides of the quilt top, with the diag-onal seams oriented as shown in the **Quilt Diagram**. Refer to "Mitering Borders" on page 242 for instructions on adding borders with mitered corners. When preparing the miters, be sure to match seams in adjacent borders, as shown in the **Quilt Diagram**.

Quilt Diagram

Quilting and Finishing

Step 1. Mark the top for quilting. Diagonal lines running through the dark squares in the four patches in both Star and Alternate blocks make an easy and effective quilting design. Extend these lines into the border. Quilting ¼ inch from seams in the Star blocks can be "eyeballed" to save time marking.

Step 2. Regardless of which quilt size you've chosen to make, the backing will have to be pieced, as shown in **Diagram 11.** For the twin-size quilt, cut the backing fabric in half and trim the selvages. Cut one piece in half lengthwise, and sew a narrow panel to each side of the full-width piece. Press the seams open.

For the queen-size quilt, cut the backing fabric into three equal segments and trim the selvages. Cut a 38-inch-wide panel from two of the segments, and sew them to each side of the full-width piece. Press the seams open.

Step 3. Layer the backing, batting, and quilt top, and baste the layers together. Hand or machine quilt as desired.

Step 4. Referring to the directions on page 244, make and attach double-fold binding. The binding in the quilt shown finishes at a width of ½ inch. To make binding that finishes this wide, cut your binding strips 2½ inches wide. To calculate the total amount of binding you will need, add up the length of the four sides of the quilt, plus 9 inches.

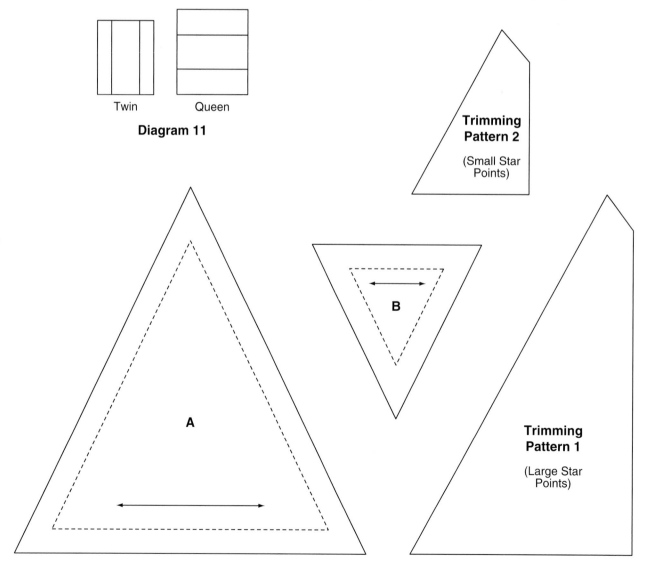

Twin   Queen

Diagram 11

Trimming Pattern 2

(Small Star Points)

B

A

Trimming Pattern 1

(Large Star Points)

MY STARS!...THEY'RE PLAID!

Color Plan

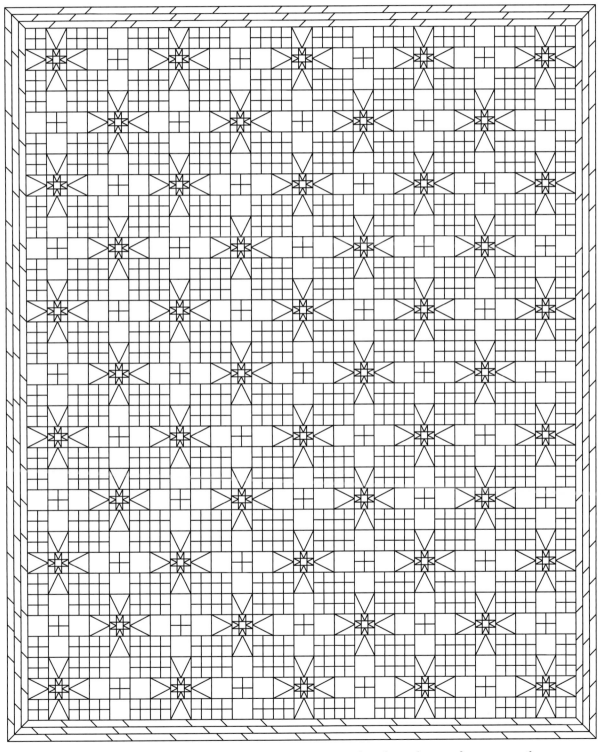

Photocopy this page and use it to experiment with color schemes for your quilt.

CHINESE COINS VARIATION

Skill Level: *Intermediate*

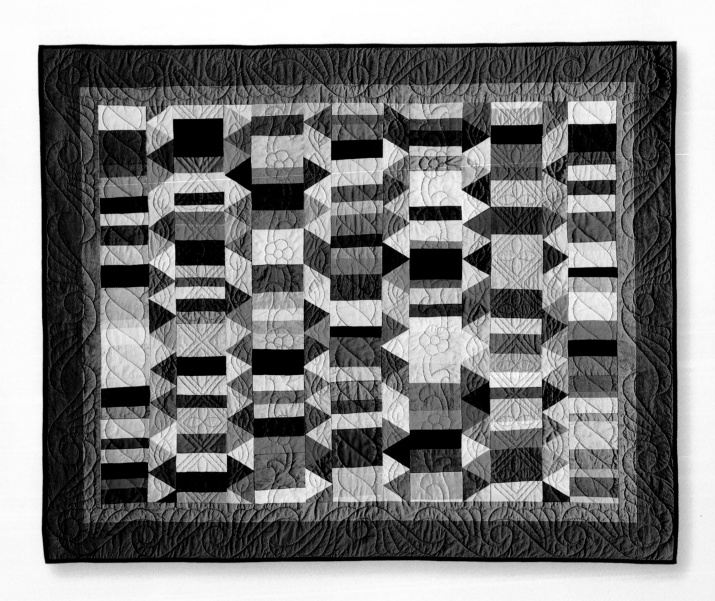

After admiring a similar Amish quilt, Karan Flanscha of Cedar Falls, Iowa, decided this Chinese Coins variation would be the perfect project for trying out her antique treadle sewing machine. She says she gained a greater appreciation for electric sewing machines with built-in lights and had finally mastered "pumping" the treadle by the time she finished piecing the top. Even though Karan's wallhanging was recently completed, it features colors and quilting patterns associated with antique Amish quilts.

Before You Begin

This quilt is a variation of the Chinese Coins pattern, which itself is a variation of the traditional Amish Bars pattern. Here, narrow bars of equilateral triangles are used to separate the bars of stacked "coins." The coins are easily assembled with a strip piecing technique; the triangles are alternated and sewn together to create a narrow bar. To eliminate the need for a triangle-shaped template, the triangles are rotary cut from a fabric strip.

Choosing Fabrics

Collect as many Amish-inspired colors as possible to re-create the scrappy effect of the quilt shown. Be sure to include light, medium, and dark fabrics. The yardages given in the materials chart are a guide and assume that you will choose equally from the three different values. For example, the total yardage required for the assorted colors in the wallhanging is 3 yards. Buy 1/8 yard of 24 different colors, 8 from each color value, to get the most impact. For the larger quilts, quarter-yard cuts of fabric will give you a wide variety of color choices.

In the quilt shown, the inner and outer borders are sewn from fabrics of the same value. Although the colors themselves are entirely different, the two fabrics blend together when viewed from a distance.

To help develop your own unique color scheme for the quilt, photocopy the **Color Plan** on page 131, and use crayons or colored pencils to experiment with different color arrangements.

Quilt Sizes

	Wallhanging (shown)	Twin	Double
Finished Quilt Size	46¾" × 35"	69¾" × 97"	81¼" × 97"
Number of Bars			
Coins	7	11	13
Triangle	6	10	12

Materials

Fabric	Wallhanging	Twin	Double
Assorted lights	1 yard	2¾ yards	3 yards
Assorted mediums	1 yard	2¾ yards	3 yards
Assorted darks	1 yard	2¾ yards	3 yards
Forest green	⅜ yard	¾ yard	⅞ yard
Orchid	¼ yard	½ yard	½ yard
Backing	1⅝ yards	5⅞ yards	7⅝ yards
Batting	52" × 41"	76" × 103"	87" × 103"
Binding	⅜ yard	¾ yard	¾ yard

NOTE: *Yardages are based on 44/45-inch-wide fabrics that are at least 42 inches wide after preshrinking.*

Cutting Chart

Fabric	Used For	Strip Width	Number to Cut		
			Wallhanging	Twin	Double
Assorted lights, mediums, and darks	Equilateral triangles	2¾"	12*	32	38
	Coin bars	1"–3½"	See "Cutting" below		
Forest green	Outer border	3"	4	8	9
Orchid	Inner border	2"	4	8	8

Cut 21-inch-long strips, instead of 42-inch-long strips, to provide more color variety.

CUTTING

All measurements include ¼-inch seam allowances. Referring to the Cutting Chart, cut the required number of strips in the width needed. Cut all strips across the fabric width.

Equilateral triangles are quick-cut from strips of fabric. Triangles used at the ends of bars are cut from rectangles. Stacks of coins are sewn together using quick-piecing techniques, then trimmed to the exact width and length required before the quilt top is assembled.

For the coin bars, cut at least two strips from each of the assorted light, medium, and dark fabrics, varying the strip widths between 1 and 3½ inches wide. When cutting strips, keep in mind that ½ inch of the total width of each strip will be lost in seam allowances. Cut at least three strips from each fabric for the twin size and at least four strips for the double size. Cut each strip into three 14-inch-long pieces.

For the end triangles, cut six 3¼ × 1¾-inch rectangles from various colors for the wallhanging. Cut 10 rectangles for the twin-size and 12 rectangles for the double-size quilt.

ASSEMBLING THE COIN BARS

To obtain the correct length for the coin bars, you will make strip sets 10 and 20 inches wide, then use a combination of both sizes to make the coin bars.

Step 1. Match the edges and sew the assorted color straight-of-grain strips together lengthwise to form the coin bars, as shown in **Diagram 1**. Vary the strip width and color to create a pleasing mixture. Continue sewing strips together until your strip set is approximately 20 inches wide.

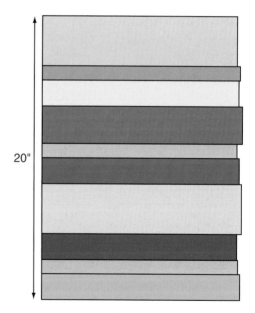

20"

Diagram 1

Step 2. Press all of the seams in one direction. Using a rotary cutter and ruler, square up one side of the pressed set, then cut three 4¼-inch-wide segments from it to form the coin bar segments, as shown in **Diagram 2**.

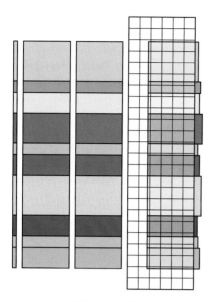

Diagram 2

Step 3. Assemble additional coin bar segments in the same manner as in Steps 1 and 2, making strip sets as follows: For the wallhanging, make seven 10- and seven 20-inch-wide segments. For the twin size, make eleven 10- and forty-four 20-inch-wide segments. For the double size, make thirteen 10- and fifty-two 20-inch-wide segments.

Step 4. For the wallhanging, sew one 10- and one 20-inch segment together along the 4¼-inch edges to create a coin bar (see **Diagram 3**). Repeat to make a total of seven coin bars. Trim each bar to 27 inches. Repeat for the twin and double size, sewing one 10-inch and four 20-inch segments together to create a coin bar. Make 11 coin bars for the twin size and 13 for the double size. Trim the coin bars for both sizes to 89 inches.

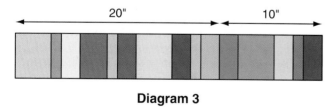

Diagram 3

ASSEMBLING THE TRIANGLE BARS

Step 1. Align the 60-degree angle line on your ruler with the bottom left edge of one equilateral

triangle strip, and make the cut illustrated in **Diagram 4**.

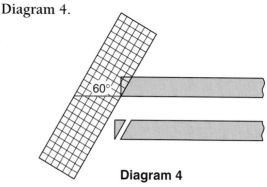

Diagram 4

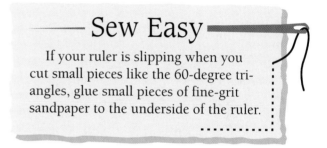

— Sew Easy

If your ruler is slipping when you cut small pieces like the 60-degree triangles, glue small pieces of fine-grit sandpaper to the underside of the ruler.

Step 2. Mark the strip in 3⅛-inch increments, beginning at the lower left edge of the strip, as shown in **Diagram 5**. Cut the triangles as shown, rotating your ruler between cuts so that the 60-degree line is always aligned with either the top or bottom edge of the strip. Cut 132 triangles for the wallhanging, 760 for the twin, and 912 for the double. Sort the triangles by color value.

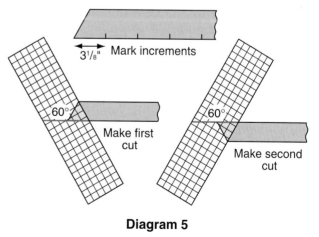

Diagram 5

Step 3. End triangles, or half-equilateral triangles, are used at the top and bottom of the triangle bars. To make an end triangle, cut each 1¾ × 3¼-inch rectangle in half diagonally, as shown in **Diagram 6A.** Keeping the cut rectangles together as a unit, divide the pile in half. Label one half "odd." Flip the remaining half of the cut rectangles over so the cut is in the opposite direction and label them "even."

Note: If you are using a print fabric or a solid fabric that isn't the same color on both sides, cut one half of the rectangles diagonally in one direction, labeling them "odd"; cut the other half of the rectangles in half diagonally in the other direction, labeling them "even," as shown in **Diagram 6B.** Cut a total of 12 end triangles for the wallhanging, 20 for the twin size, and 24 for the double size, making half "odd" triangles and half "even" triangles.

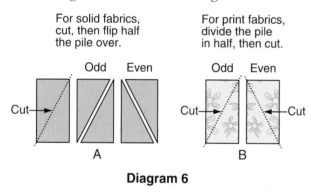

Diagram 6

Step 4. Sew the end triangles and equilateral triangles into bars, alternating fabrics for good contrast. For the wallhanging, sew 22 equilateral triangles together, then add one "odd" end triangle to each end, as shown in **Diagram 7A.** Make six triangle bars, three of which should have "odd" end triangles and three of which should have "even" end triangles, as shown in **7B.** Once the bars are assembled, stack and label them "odd" or "even."

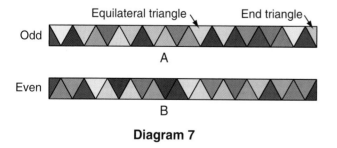

Diagram 7

Both the twin- and double-size quilts have 76 equilateral triangles in each triangle bar. Make 10 triangle bars for the twin size and 12 for the double size. Sew "odd" end triangles to half of the bars and "even" end triangles to the other half. Stack and label the triangle bars "odd" or "even."

ASSEMBLING THE QUILT TOP

Step 1. Arrange the coin bars and the triangle bars into rows side by side, beginning and ending with a coin bar and alternating "odd" and "even" triangle bars. Refer to the **Wallhanging Assembly Diagram** or the **Twin- and Double-Size Assembly Diagram.** Make sure the coin bars are at least as long as the triangle bars. If not, sew an additional 4¼-inch-wide strip of fabric to the top or bottom to increase the length.

Step 2. Pin the bars together lengthwise, matching the top edges. Be sure the equilateral triangle bases are directly across from each other. Sew the seams, then press them toward the coin bars. Trim the coin bars flush with the triangle bars.

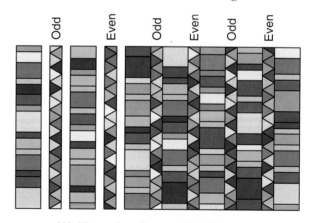

Wallhanging Assembly Diagram

ATTACHING THE BORDERS

Step 1. Attach the top and bottom borders first, referring to the **Wallhanging Diagram** or the **Twin-Size Quilt Diagram** on page 130. Measure the width of the quilt top, taking the measurement through the horizontal center of the quilt. Sew the orchid strips together to make two borders this exact length.

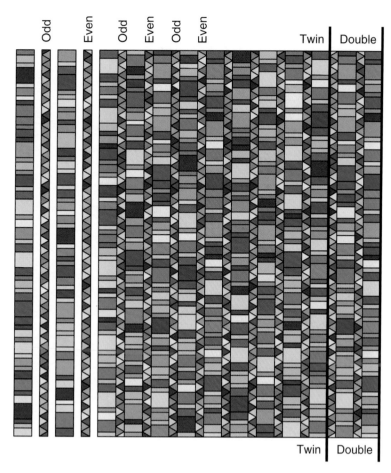

Odd   Even   Odd   Even   Odd   Even   Twin | Double

Twin | Double

Twin- and Double-Size Assembly Diagram

Step 2. Fold one of the strips in half crosswise and crease. Unfold it and position it right side down along the top of the quilt, with the crease at the vertical midpoint. Pin at the midpoint and ends first, then along the length of the entire edge, easing in fullness as necessary. Sew the border to the quilt. Repeat for the bottom border. Press seams toward the borders.

Step 3. Measure the length of the quilt, taking the measurement through the vertical center of the quilt and including the top and bottom borders. Using the orchid strips, piece two border strips this exact length and sew these to the sides of the quilt, in the same manner as in Step 2. Press.

Step 4. In the same manner, prepare and add the outer borders to the quilt, using the 3-inch forest green strips. Attach the top and bottom borders first, and be sure to include the borders when measuring the length of the quilt for the side borders.

QUILTING AND FINISHING

Step 1. Mark the quilt top for quilting. The quilt shown features a thick cable design for the middle and two outer coin bars, a pumpkin seed motif and a simple flower vine for the remaining coin bars, and a leaf design for the triangle bars. The borders were treated as a single unit and feature a stylized swirl that spans the width of both.

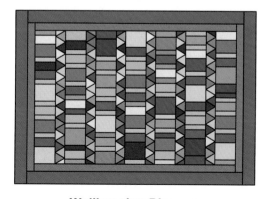

Wallhanging Diagram

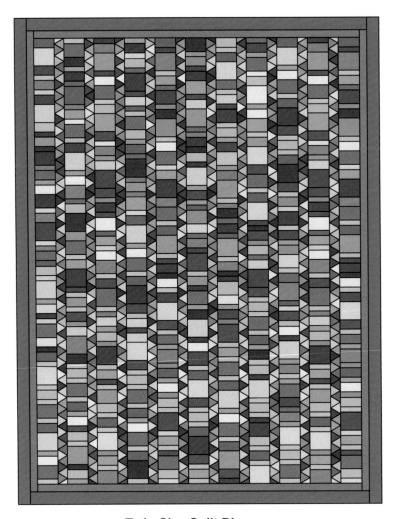

Twin-Size Quilt Diagram

Step 2. If you are making the wallhanging, the backing does not have to be pieced, as shown in **Diagram 8.** For the twin-size quilt, cut the backing fabric crosswise into two equal pieces and trim the selvages. Cut two 18-inch-wide segments from one piece. Sew a narrow segment to each side of the full-width piece, as shown in the diagram. Press the seams open.

Step 3. For the double-size quilt, cut the backing fabric crosswise into three equal pieces, and trim the selvages. Cut 31-inch-wide segments from two of the pieces, then sew one of the narrow segments to each side of the full-width piece as shown in the diagram. Press the seams open.

Step 4. Layer the quilt top, batting, and backing, and baste the layers together. Quilt as desired.

Step 5. Referring to the directions on page 244, make and attach double-fold binding. To calculate the amount of binding needed for the quilt size you are making, add the length of the four sides of the quilt, plus 9 inches.

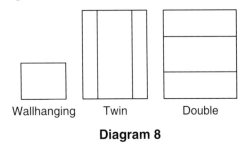

Wallhanging   Twin   Double

Diagram 8

CHINESE COINS VARIATION
Color Plan

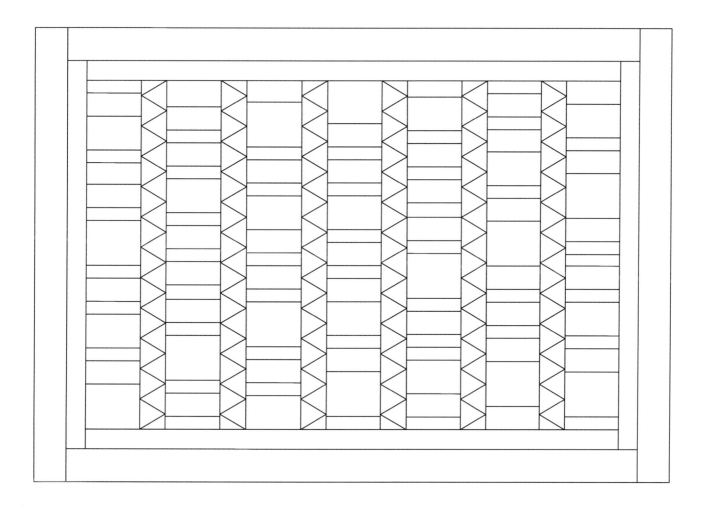

Photocopy this page and use it to experiment with color schemes for your quilt.

Straight Furrows

Skill Level: *Easy*

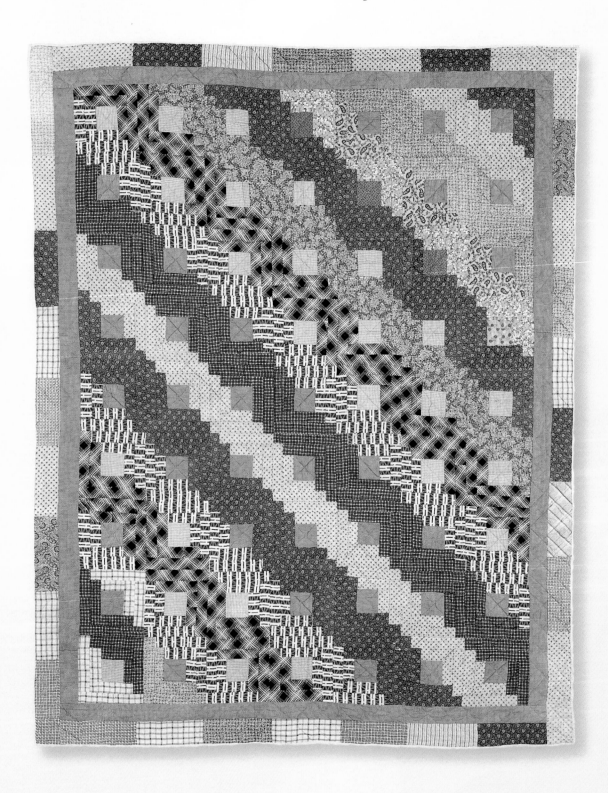

The light and dark rows of this charming 1930s lap-size quilt are reminiscent of the play of light on the furrows of a field freshly plowed and ready for planting. Formerly owned by Marilyn Woodin of Woodin Wheel Antiques in Kalona, Iowa, the quilt was created with warm earth tones, accented with bright blue and green—all contributing to the cozy, homespun feeling of this traditional favorite.

BEFORE YOU BEGIN

The directions for this quilt are written based on using the chain-piecing technique, in which all the logs are cut to length and the blocks are pieced in assembly-line fashion. Since the pieces are fairly large and there are only nine in each block, this is the fastest and most efficient assembly method for this quilt. If you prefer to use the foundation method, prepare a foundation for each block using the pattern on page 139, and refer to page 235 in "Quiltmaking Basics" for piecing instructions.

CHOOSING FABRICS

In this quilt, as with many Log Cabin quilts, color value is more important than the actual colors used, since it's the placement of lights and darks that creates the overall design. Most of the blocks were pieced with light fabrics in log positions 2, 3, 6, and 7 and dark fabrics in log positions 4, 5, 8, and 9. In a few of the blocks, the quiltmaker reversed the light and dark placement, perhaps to add a little interest to the design, or perhaps because the quiltmaker ran out of a particular fabric. The center squares are all medium-value fabrics.

Within the light and dark color scheme, the maker of this quilt used plaids and checks to great effect, including a bold green stripe and busy blue plaid. These fabrics create movement and interest and help to draw the eye over the surface.

If you wish to develop your own unique color scheme, photocopy the **Color Plan** on page

Quilt Sizes

	Lap (shown)	Double	Queen
Finished Quilt Size	63" × 78"	85½" × 100½"	93" × 100½"
Finished Block Size	7½"	7½"	7½"
Number of Blocks	63	120	132

Materials

Fabric	Lap	Double	Queen
Lights	2¼ yards	3¾ yards	4 yards
Darks	2½ yards	4½ yards	4⅞ yards
Medium	1¼ yards	1¼ yards	1¼ yards
Backing	5 yards	8¼ yards	8¾ yards
Batting	69" × 84"	92" × 107"	99" × 107"
Binding	⅝ yard	¾ yard	¾ yard

NOTE: *Yardages are based on 44/45-inch-wide fabrics that are at least 42 inches wide after preshrinking.*

Cutting Chart

| Fabric | Strip Width | Number of Strips | | | Piece | Length* |
		Lap	Double	Queen		
Lights	1¾"*	5	9	10	Log 2	3"
		7	14	15	Log 3	4¼"
		9	18	19	Log 6	5½"
		11	20	22	Log 7	6¾"
	3½"*	4	5	6	Pieced border	9½"
Darks	1¾"*	7	14	15	Log 4	4¼"
		9	18	19	Log 5	5½"
		11	20	22	Log 8	6¾"
		13	24	27	Log 9	8"
	3½"*	4	6	6	Pieced border	9½"
Medium	3"*	5	9	10	Center square	3"
	2¾"*	7	9	9	Inner border	

*NOTE: Add ½" to each strip width if foundation piecing and disregard length measurement.

138, and use crayons or colored pencils to experiment with different color arrangements.

The light and dark yardages given are generous estimates of the total yardage actually used in the quilt. Select four or five fabrics in each value to get the total yardage listed.

CUTTING

All measurements include ¼-inch seam allowances. Referring to the Cutting Chart, cut strips in the width needed, then cut the strips into logs. Cut all strips across the fabric width (crosswise grain). You may find it helpful to pin a number label to each group of logs as you cut them. **Note:** Cut and piece one sample block before cutting all the pieces for the quilt.

PIECING THE FIRST BLOCK

Refer to "Foundation Piecing" on pages 232–238 if you plan to use foundation. Be sure to read the note in the cutting chart before beginning. If assembly-line piecing by adding logs one at a time, piece a sample block first. This will allow you to become acquainted with the technique and

to double-check the accuracy of your seam allowances. Cut enough logs for one sample block, and use the **Block Diagram** as a color sample and a guide to piecing order. The completed block should measure 8 inches square, including seam allowances.

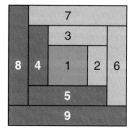

Block Diagram

Step 1. Using a ¼-inch seam allowance, sew a center piece 1 to a light log 2, as shown in **Diagram 1**. Press the seam allowance toward log 2.

Diagram 1

Step 2. Add a light log 3, as shown in **Diagram 2.** The length of log 3 should match the length of the partially sewn unit. If the lengths aren't the same, your ¼-inch seam allowance may need to be adjusted. If log 3 is shorter, your seam allowance may be less than ¼ inch. If log 3 is longer, your seam allowance may be more than ¼ inch. If your seam allowance is accurate, check to be sure you've carefully pressed the seam between pieces 1 and 2.

Diagram 2

Step 3. Continue to add logs in numerical order in a counterclockwise direction. Press seams as you work, always pressing toward the newest log.

PIECING THE REMAINING BLOCKS

Chain piecing can speed up the block assembly process. Instead of making one block from start to finish, perform one step at a time on all the blocks.

Step 1. Stack the light and dark logs near your sewing machine. Keep your sample block handy to use as a guide. Stitch a log 2 to a center piece 1 as described. Without removing the stitched pair from the sewing machine or lifting the presser foot, insert and sew a second pair. Continue sewing until all center sections are pieced. See **Diagram 3.**

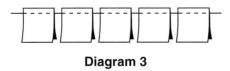

Diagram 3

Step 2. Cut the stitched segments apart. Press each seam allowance toward log 2. In the same manner, add the remaining logs to the blocks until you have completed all the blocks.

ASSEMBLING THE QUILT TOP

Step 1. Using a design wall or flat surface, lay out your blocks in a pleasing arrangement. Use the photo on page 132, the **Lap-Size Quilt Diagram**

······· Sew Quick ·······

When chain piecing, you might find it easier to work in groups of blocks rather than working on all of the quilt's blocks at one time. You'll still save lots of time using the chain-piecing method, but piecing a dozen blocks at a time from start to finish will give you a sense of accomplishment and let you see some real progress.

on page 136, or your own color drawing as a guide. The quilt diagram illustrates the layout of the lap-size quilt, which has 9 rows of 7 blocks each. The layout for the other two quilts is essentially the same: The double quilt has 12 rows of 10 blocks each and the queen-size quilt has 12 rows of 11 blocks each.

Step 2. When you are pleased with the arrangement, sew the blocks into rows, pressing the seams in opposite directions from row to row.

Step 3. Sew the rows together, carefully matching seams where blocks meet. If you've pressed the seam allowances in opposite directions, the seams should fit tightly against each other.

ADDING THE INNER BORDER

The procedure for adding borders is the same for all three quilt sizes. Prepare the strips first, then add them to the quilt according to the directions below.

Step 1. For the lap-size quilt, sew four 2¾-inch inner border strips together in pairs, making two long side borders. For the top and bottom borders, cut a fifth strip in half crosswise, and sew one half each to the two remaining border strips.

Step 2. For the double and queen-size quilts, sew eight of the 2¾-inch inner border strips together in pairs. Cut the remaining strip in half crosswise, and sew one half each to two of the long border strips.

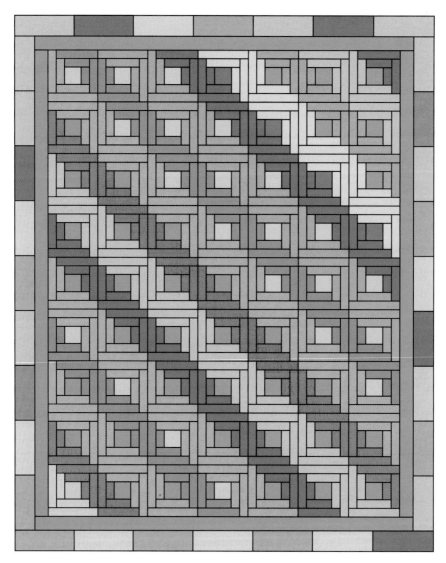

Lap-Size Quilt Diagram

Step 3. Once the border strips are prepared, measure the quilt from top to bottom, taking the measurement through the vertical center of the quilt, not at the sides. Cut the two longest strips to this length.

Step 4. Fold one strip in half crosswise and crease. Unfold it and position it right side down along one side of the quilt top, with the crease at the horizontal midpoint. Pin at the midpoint and ends first, then along the length of the entire side, easing in fullness if necessary. Sew the border to the quilt top using a ¼-inch seam allowance. Press the seam allowance toward the border. Repeat on the opposite side.

Step 5. Measure the width of the quilt, taking the measurement through the horizontal center of the quilt and including the side borders. Cut the remaining two border strips to this length.

Step 6. In the same manner as for the side borders, position and pin one strip to one end of the quilt top. Stitch and press the seam toward the border. Repeat on the opposite end.

ADDING THE PIECED BORDER

The outer border in the quilt shown is pieced with 9-inch-long segments of the same fabrics used in the blocks. Lay out and piece the four long border strips first, then add them to the quilt sides and then to the top and bottom.

Step 1. For the lap-size quilt, lay out four dark and four light segments for each side border, and four dark and three light segments for each top and bottom border.

Step 2. For the double quilt, lay out six dark and five light strips for each side border, and five dark and five light strips for each top and bottom border.

Step 3. For the queen-size quilt, lay out six dark and six light strips for each side border, and five dark and five light strips for each top and bottom border.

Step 4. When you are pleased with the arrangement, sew the strips together end to end, using accurate ¼-inch seam allowances.

Step 5. In the same manner as for the inner border, measure the length of the quilt, trim the strips to length, and stitch the side borders to the quilt. Repeat for the top and bottom pieced borders.

QUILTING AND FINISHING

Step 1. Mark the quilt top for quilting. The antique quilt shown has a 1-inch diagonal grid quilted over the whole surface.

— Sew Easy —

The lengths of the borders on the double and queen-size quilts are not evenly divisible by nine, so part of a segment will be trimmed off when you cut the border strips to length. If you prefer to have full segments at the ends of the borders, you can take the excess length from one or more of the segments in the middle of the border. Open up the seam, trim the segments (remember to allow for seam allowance), and resew the seam. Be careful not to trim too much or the border will not fit.

Step 2. Regardless of which quilt size you've chosen to make, the backing will have to be pieced. To make the most efficient use of the yardage, piece the back for the lap-size quilt with the seams running vertically across the quilt. For the double and queen-size quilts, piece the back with the seams running horizontally. **Diagram 4** illustrates the three quilt backs.

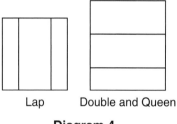

Lap   Double and Queen

Diagram 4

Step 3. For the lap quilt, divide the backing fabric crosswise into two equal pieces (each approximately 90 inches long), and trim the selvages. Divide one of the pieces in half lengthwise, and sew one half to each side of the full-width piece. Press the seams open.

Step 4. The backings for the double and the queen-size quilts are the same length, but two different widths. Begin by dividing the backing fabric into three equal pieces (approximately 99 inches each for the double and 105 inches each for the queen) and trimming the selvages. The pieced backing should measure approximately 112 inches long. Sew two of the pieces together along the long side and press the seam open. Measure the width of this piece and subtract that number from 112. The result is the amount that must be added from the third piece. Cut the piece and add it to the larger joined piece. Press the seams open.

Step 5. Layer the backing, batting, and quilt top, then baste. Quilt as desired.

Step 6. Referring to the directions on page 244 in "Quiltmaking Basics," make and attach double-fold binding. To calculate the amount of binding needed for the quilt size you are making, add up the length of the four sides of the quilt and add 9 inches. The total is the approximate number of inches of binding you will need.

Straight Furrows

Color Plan

Photocopy this page and use it to experiment with color schemes for your quilt.

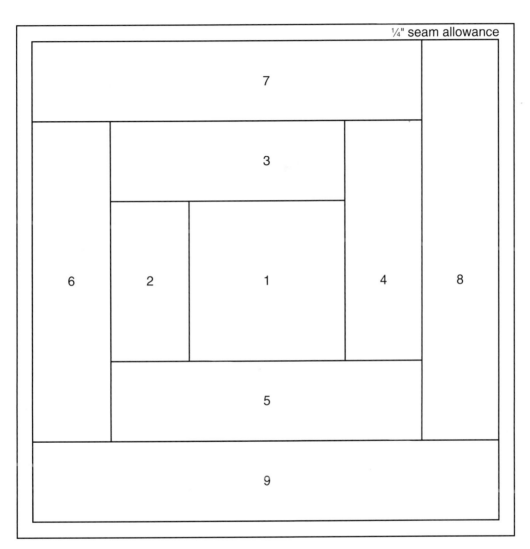

Block Pattern

Pattern shown is the mirror image of the finished block.
Note: Pattern is reduced. Enlarge it 150 percent before tracing.

SISTER'S CHOICE

Skill Level: *Intermediate*

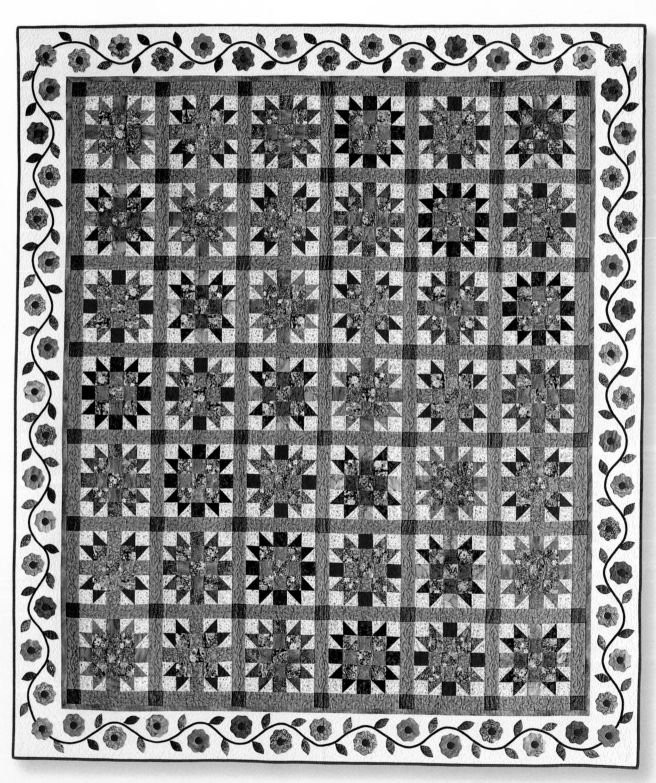

The lovely Sister's Choice is a first cousin to the typical Star block, with its eight sparkling points and radiant image. This "garden-fresh" version is a true group effort, designed and assembled by Beverly Rogers. Members of the Kingwood (Texas) Area Quilt Guild stitched the jewel-tone blocks, and Dori Hawks added the crowning touch with her masterful machine quilting.

BEFORE YOU BEGIN

We've given this quilt an intermediate rating primarily because of the scope of the project and the appliqué border. Actually, the construction techniques are simple enough for a confident beginner to handle easily.

With the exception of a few appliqué pieces that require you to make and use templates, the entire quilt can be rotary cut. An efficient strip-piecing technique is included for you to use to construct the nine-patch centers for the Sister's Choice blocks, and the triangle squares are made using another quick-cutting, quick-piecing method that we describe for you.

Border vines are made from long bias strips, and you'll love the simple process and terrific results of freezer paper appliqué for preparing and stitching the flowers and leaves.

Refer to "Quiltmaking Basics" starting on page 221 for specific information and tips on rotary cutting, quick piecing, freezer paper appliqué, and a variety of other techniques that will help you as you work on this project.

Quilt Sizes

	Twin	Queen (shown)
Finished Quilt Size	65" × 89"	89" × 101"
Finished Block Size	10"	10"
Number of Blocks	24	42
Total Number of Nine Patches	24	42
Number of Triangle-Square Units*	192	336

You will need eight identical units for each block.

Materials

Fabric	Twin	Queen
White-on-white print	1⅔ yards	2⅛ yards
Assorted dark and bright jewel-tone prints (total)	1⅜ yards	2⅛ yards
Medium blue subtle print	1¼ yards	1⅞ yards
Light floral print	1⅛ yards	1⅞ yards
Assorted medium prints (total)	⅞ yard	1¼ yards
Royal blue solid or subtle print*	⅞ yard	1 yard
Dark green subtle print	¾ yard	⅞ yard
Dark green floral print	⅔ yard	1⅛ yards
Orchid batik print	⅓ yard	½ yard
Medium-dark green print	¼ yard	⅓ yard
Assorted green scraps (total)†	¼ yard	¼ yard
Backing	5½ yards	9 yards
Batting	72" × 96"	96" × 108"

NOTE: *Yardages are based on 44/45-inch-wide fabrics that are at least 42 inches wide after preshrinking.*

* Includes binding.

† You may have enough leftovers from other greens to eliminate this yardage.

CHOOSING FABRICS

The fabrics in this quilt suggest a garden in the riot of full bloom. While these quiltmakers have used just six different block colorations and arranged them in diagonal rows, the interesting mix of fabrics suggests a much scrappier quilt. In fact, to simplify construction, we are suggesting that you follow a similar color scheme, but take a somewhat more scrappy approach.

Refer to the quilt photo on page 140 and the **Block Diagram**. To achieve a look similar to the quilt shown, begin with a light background print. You'll want to choose an airy, open floral—not too busy—with lots of white space. This print will be used for the light triangle points (B) and the background squares (D) of each block, unifying all of the other prints.

Each block has a nine-patch center square (Unit A) composed of two fabrics. Choose a single dark green floral to appear in every block. Then select five or six medium-value floral fabrics in blue,

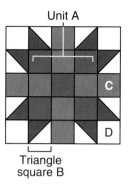

Block Diagram

green, pink, purple, or other "garden" colors, so that you'll have a variety of different nine-patch units.

To complete each block, select a different jewel-tone color for the dark triangle points (B) and for the perimeter squares (C). Deep reds, teals, greens, purples, fuchsias, and electric blues all make wonderful choices. Focus on subtle, "reads-as-solid" or medium-scale floral prints for these shapes.

Carry the garden motif a step further by selecting a medium blue subtle print for the sashing

Fabric	Used For	Strip Width	Number to Cut Twin	Number to Cut Queen	Second Cut Dimensions	Number to Cut Twin	Number to Cut Queen
White-on-white print	Outer border	7"	8	10			
Batik	Inner border	1¼"	8	10			
Medium blue print	Sashing	2½"	15	25	2½" × 10½"	58	97
Medium dark green print	Corner squares	2½"	3	4	2½" squares	35	56
Light floral print	Triangle squares (B)	2⅞"	7	12	2⅞" squares	96	168
	D	2½"	6	11	2½" squares	96	168
Assorted medium prints	Nine patches	2½"	7	12			
Dark green floral print	Nine patches	2½"	8	15			
Assorted dark jewel-tone prints	Triangle squares (B)	2⅞"	7	12	2⅞" squares	96	168
	C	2½"	6	11	2½" squares	96	168
Dark green print	Vines	27" × 27"	1	—			
		30" × 30"	—	1			

Cutting Chart

strips and a rich green print for the corner squares. Add a narrow inner border of orchid batik, perhaps borrowed from one of the blocks. Finish with an elegant white-on-white outer border. White makes the perfect contrast to the appliqué floral motifs, which are cut from leftover scraps of fabric used elsewhere in the quilt.

To develop your color scheme, photocopy the **Color Plan** on page 149, and use colored pencils or crayons to experiment with different color arrangements.

CUTTING

All measurements include ¼-inch seam allowances. No templates are required for the pieces in these blocks, since every piece can be rotary cut. For easy reference, however, a letter identification is given for each pattern piece or unit in the **Block Diagram**.

Use templates to cut pieces for the appliqué flowers and leaves. Make templates for appliqué pieces X, Y, and Z from the patterns on page 148. Refer to page 239 for information on making and using freezer paper templates for appliqué.

Refer to the Cutting Charts and cut the required number of strips and pieces in the sizes needed. Cut all strips across the width of the fabric (crosswise grain). If you are working with scraps and do not have the full 42-inch width of fabric, be certain that your shorter strips total the full number of 42-inch strips required.

Note: We suggest that you cut and piece a sample block before cutting all of your fabric.

─── Sew Easy ───

As you select the various fabrics for this quilt, keep in mind that a fabric may serve "double duty" by altering its position within the block. For example, a fabric used for the B triangle squares in one block might be used for the C perimeter squares in another.

Appliqué Cutting Chart

Fabric	Used For	Number to Cut Twin	Number to Cut Queen
Assorted medium and dark jewel-tone prints	Flowers (X)	48	60
Royal blue solid or print	Flower centers (Y)	48	60
Assorted green scraps	Leaves (Z)	88	112

ASSEMBLING THE BLOCK COMPONENTS

Refer to the Quilt Sizes chart on page 141 to determine the required number of nine-patch units and triangle squares for the quilt you are making.

Piecing the Nine-Patch Units

The Sister's Choice block has a nine-patch unit (A) at its center. Each nine patch is made up of 2½-inch-wide strips cut from contrasting fabrics. The dark green floral strips remain consistent, but you'll want lots of combinations with the coordinating medium print strips. Before you begin to assemble the nine-patch units, you may wish to cut some of the strips into matching shorter lengths so that they can be mixed for greater variety.

Step 1. Sew a 2½-inch-wide dark green floral strip to each side of a 2½-inch-wide medium print strip to make a strip set, as shown in **Diagram 1.** Press the seams toward the green strips. This will be Strip Set 1.

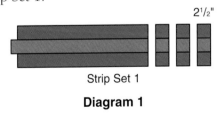

2½"

Strip Set 1

Diagram 1

Step 2. Square up one end of Strip Set 1, then cut it into 2½-inch segments, as shown.

Step 3. Sew a 2½-inch-wide strip of the same or a coordinating medium print to each side of a 2½-inch-wide green floral strip to make a strip set, as shown in **Diagram 2**. Press seam allowances toward the green strip. This will be Strip Set 2.

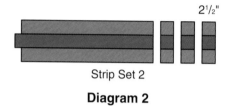

Strip Set 2

Diagram 2

Step 4. Square up one end of Strip Set 2, then cut it into 2½-inch segments.

Step 5. Continue making strip sets and cutting segments until you have made 48 Strip Set 1 segments for the twin-size or 84 segments for the queen-size quilt. Similarly, make 24 or 42 Strip Set 2 segments for the twin and queen, respectively.

Step 6. Matching seams carefully, sew identical Strip Set 1 segments to the top and bottom of a Strip Set 2 segment, as shown in **Diagram 3**. You may select a Strip Set 2 segment made with the same or a different print, depending on how scrappy you want your blocks. Place the segments in proper order, as shown, so the green floral is placed consistently in each unit. Press seam allowances away from the center segment.

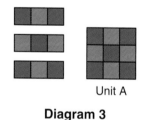

Unit A

Diagram 3

Step 7. Repeat to make the required number of nine-patch units for your quilt, as shown in the Quilt Sizes chart on page 141.

Piecing the Triangle-Square Units

We recommend that you use quick-piecing Method 2 on page 226 to make the triangle squares for this quilt. This method saves steps and is easy and accurate, while still allowing you to use a variety of fabrics for the triangle squares.

Refer to the Quilt Sizes chart and make the required number of triangle squares for your quilt using Method 2. Pair four 2⅞-inch light floral squares with four identical 2⅞-inch jewel-tone squares to yield the eight identical triangle squares needed for each block.

PIECING THE SISTER'S CHOICE BLOCKS

Step 1. Select one nine-patch center (Unit A), eight identical triangle squares, four identical C squares, and four background D squares. Sew a triangle square to each side of a C square, as shown in **Diagram 4A**. Press seam allowances away from the triangle squares. Make four of these strips.

Step 2. Sew two of the strips to opposite sides of the nine patch, as shown in **4B**. Press seam allowances toward the nine patch.

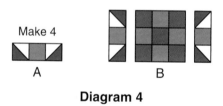

Make 4

A   B

Diagram 4

Step 3. Sew a background D square to each end of the remaining two strips, as shown in **Diagram 5A**. Press seam allowances toward the D squares.

Step 4. To complete the block, sew a strip to the top and bottom edges, as shown in **5B**. Press the block carefully.

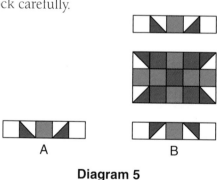

A   B

Diagram 5

Step 5. Repeat Steps 1 through 4 to assemble the required number of blocks for the size quilt you are making.

ASSEMBLING THE QUILT

Step 1. Use a design wall or other flat surface to arrange the blocks, sashing strips, and corner squares, as shown in the **Assembly Diagram.** The twin-size quilt has six horizontal rows of four blocks each. The queen-size quilt has seven horizontal rows of six blocks each.

Step 2. Sew the blocks, sashing strips, and corner squares in horizontal rows, as shown. Press all seams toward the blue sashing strips.

Step 3. Sew the rows together, matching seams carefully. Press the quilt.

ADDING THE MITERED BORDERS

This quilt has two mitered borders. The narrow batik and wide white border strips are sewn together first and are added to the quilt top as a single unit.

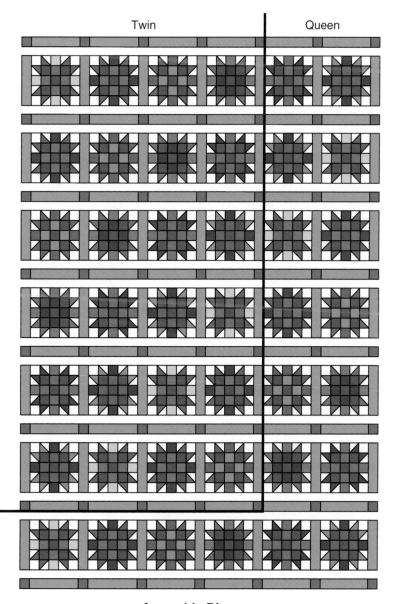

Twin   Queen

Assembly Diagram

Step 1. To determine the correct length for the side borders, measure the quilt top vertically through the center. To this measurement, add two times the finished width of both borders ($7^{1}/_{4} \times 2$ inches = $14^{1}/_{2}$ inches, plus 5 inches = $19^{1}/_{2}$ inches). This is the length you will need to make all the side border strips. In the same manner, measure the quilt top horizontally through the center, and calculate the lengths of the top and the bottom borders.

Step 2. Regardless of the size quilt you are making, you will need to sew some of the border strips together end to end to achieve the required length. For the twin-size quilt, fold two each of the batik and the white border strips into thirds. Trim off $^{1}/_{3}$ of each strip at the fold. Sew one full strip and a $^{1}/_{3}$ strip segment together for the top and the bottom borders. Sew one full strip and a remaining $^{2}/_{3}$ strip segment together for each of the side borders. Trim each of the border strips to the required lengths.

For the queen-size quilt, cut two each of the batik and the white border strips in half. For each border, sew two full strips and one half strip together, then trim to the required lengths.

Step 3. Beginning with the side border strips, pin and sew a batik and a white border strip together lengthwise to form a single side border unit. Press the seam toward the batik strip. Make two of these side border units. In the same manner, pin and sew the top and bottom border strips into units.

Step 4. Fold each border unit to find its midpoint, and crease. Sew the four border units to the appropriate sides of the quilt top, positioning the narrow batik border closest to the quilt top, as shown in the **Quilt Diagram**. Match and pin the midpoints and then follow the directions on page 242 for mitering borders.

Preparing Pieces for Appliqué

Use your preferred method to prepare all flowers (X), flower centers (Y), and leaves (Z) for appliqué. Refer to page 239 for information on an easy freezer paper method of appliqué.

Making the Vines

Since they curve so gracefully, we recommend that you use bias strips to make the vines for the borders of your quilt. Refer to the instructions on page 240 for information on preparing bias strips. For either quilt, cut the bias strips $1^{1}/_{8}$ inches wide. Then fold, press, and sew the strips as instructed. To avoid overlapping edges, sew strips together end to end to achieve the required lengths before folding and pressing. You will need approximately 360 inches of vine for the twin-size quilt, and 450 inches for the queen-size quilt.

······· Sew Quick·······

If you prefer to work with shorter lengths of bias vine, you can divide the single long piece into four shorter segments. For the twin-size quilt, you'll need approximately 75 inches of vine for both the top and the bottom borders and approximately 105 inches for each of the sides. For the queen-size quilt, you'll need approximately 105 inches for both the top and the bottom borders and approximately 120 inches for each of the sides. There's no need to worry about the raw edges where the segments meet—they'll be covered at each corner by an appliqué flower.

Appliquéing the Outer Border

Step 1. Refer to the **Quilt Diagram** and position a prepared bias strip vine on each outer border, turning the corners as shown. Pin or baste the vines in place, then use your preferred method to appliqué the vine in place. Refer to "Appliqué Basics" on page 238 for more information.

Twin   Queen

Quilt Diagram

Step 2. Position flowers along the vine, as shown in the **Quilt Diagram.** For the twin-size quilt, place 9 flowers on the top and the bottom borders and 13 flowers on each side border. For the queen-size quilt, place 13 flowers on the top and bottom borders and 15 flowers on each side border. Center a flower over the intersection of vines at each corner of the quilt. Pin or baste in place. Pin or baste a royal blue Y circle in the center of each flower. Use your preferred method to appliqué all flowers and flower centers.

Step 3. Position leaves along the vine as shown in the **Quilt Diagram**. For the twin-size quilt, place 18 leaves (in groups of two) on the top and bottom borders, and 26 leaves on each side border. For the queen-size quilt, place 26 leaves (in groups of two) on the top and bottom borders, and 30 leaves on each side border. Pin or baste the leaves in place, then appliqué using your preferred method.

Quilting and Finishing

Step 1. Mark the top for quilting. The quilt shown has been machine quilted. An Orange Peel motif softens the angular lines of each pieced block. A continuous vine and leaf motif is quilted in the sashing strips. All of the flower and leaf appliqués are outlined, and the background of the white border is stipple quilted.

Step 2. Regardless of which quilt size you've chosen to make, the backing will need to be pieced. For the twin-size quilt, cut the backing fabric in half crosswise and trim the selvages. Cut two 18-inch-wide panels from the entire length of one piece. Sew a narrow panel to each side of the full-width piece, as shown in **Diagram 6.** The seams will run parallel to the sides of the quilt. Press the seams open.

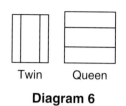

Twin   Queen

Diagram 6

For the queen-size quilt, divide the backing fabric crosswise into three equal pieces and trim the selvages. Cut a 33-inch-wide panel from the entire length of two of the pieces. Sew one of the narrower panels to each side of the full-width piece, as shown. The seams will run parallel to the top edge of the quilt. Press the seams open.

Step 3. Layer the backing, batting, and quilt top, and baste the layers together. Quilt by hand or machine, adding additional quilting of your choice as desired.

Step 4. Referring to the directions on page 244 in "Quiltmaking Basics," use the remaining royal blue fabric to make and attach double-fold binding to finish at a width of 1/4 inch. To calculate the amount of binding you will need, add up the length of the four sides of the quilt plus 9 inches. The total is the approximate number of inches of binding you will need.

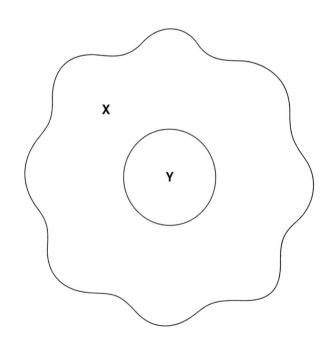

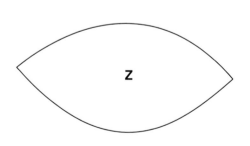

SISTER'S CHOICE

Color Plan

Photocopy this page and use it to experiment with color schemes for your quilt.

FEED SACK WEDDING RING

Skill Level: *Intermediate*

*T*rue to the spirit of the late 1920s, when the Wedding Ring pattern was developed, this delightful example is made from recycled garments and feed sacks. Bertha Rush, the owner of this colorful double-size bed quilt, pointed out that one of her favorite childhood dresses has been preserved in the rings of this quilt. Her grandmother stitched this quilt (along with six others for Bertha's brothers and sisters) in the 1940s, and it was hand quilted by a group of her friends.

BEFORE YOU BEGIN

A large assortment of print fabrics were used to piece the arcs in this traditional quilt, while solid green and pink pieces at their tips complete the rings. In a scrappy quilt like this, color is not as important as variety, so use the yardage requirement for the prints as a guide only—the more prints, the better.

The quilt shown was made primarily with the green-tipped arcs arranged vertically and the pink-tipped arcs arranged horizontally. However, the quiltmaker made a few alterations to this plan along the top row and bottom right corner. To simplify the directions and to avoid the confusion of altering a few of your arcs, we have provided directions that call for all green-tipped arcs to be positioned vertically and all pink-tipped arcs to run horizontally. If you'd like to make your quilt exactly like the quilt in the photograph, you will need 47 green-tipped arc/melon units, 41 pink-tipped arc/melon units, and 9 arc/melon units with one green

and one pink tip. Refer to the photograph for the layout.

CHOOSING FABRICS

Many prints in this Wedding Ring quilt were cut from fabric sacks, a recycling method women used in a more frugal

part of this century. Making a replica of this quilt is easy, since an ever-increasing choice of reproduction fabrics is offered at many quilt shops. Period prints are often sold in fat quarters or fat eighths, providing a perfect opportunity to build your scrap collection.

Quilt Sizes		
	Wallhanging	**Double (shown)**
Finished Quilt Size	43½" × 43½"	83½" × 96½"
Finished Ring Diameter	18"	18"
Number of Rings	9	42
Number of Pieced Arcs	48	194

Materials		
Fabric	**Wallhanging**	**Double**
Muslin	1¼ yards	6¾ yards
Assorted prints	1 yard	6 yards
Green solid	¼ yard	¾ yard
Pink solid	¼ yard	¾ yard
Backing	3 yards	7⅝ yards
Batting	50" × 50"	87" × 100"
Binding	½ yard	⅞ yard

NOTE: *Yardages are based on 44/45-inch-wide fabrics that are at least 42 inches wide after preshrinking.*

151

Cutting Chart

Fabric	Used For	Piece	Number of Pieces	
			Wallhanging	Double
Muslin	Background	A	9	42
	Melons	B	24	97
Assorted prints	Outer wedges of arcs	C	48	194
	Outer wedges of arcs	C reverse	48	194
	Inner wedges of arcs	D	96	776
Green	Connecting wedges	E	24	97
Pink	Connecting wedges	E	24	97

CUTTING

All pattern pieces include ¼-inch seam allowances. Referring to the Cutting Chart, trace and cut the required number of pieces for your quilt size. See page 224 in "Quiltmaking Basics" for information about constructing and using templates.

Note: Cut and piece one sample ring before cutting all of the fabric for the quilt.

PIECING THE ARCS

Step 1. Use chain piecing, an assembly line method that will help speed up the sewing process, to sew pairs of D pieces together. When all of the D pieces have been sewn into pairs, use chain piecing again to link the sewn pairs into units containing four D pieces each, as shown in **Diagram 1**. For more information on chain, or assembly line, piecing, refer to page 225 in "Quiltmaking Basics."

Diagram 1

Step 2. Stack the C and C reverse pieces in separate piles near your sewing machine. Use chain piecing to sew a C piece to the left side of each

Sew Easy

You'll want your rings to have a scrappy look, so mix up the fabrics. Toss all of the D pieces in a bag and shake it up. Then reach in and pull out two pieces and stitch them together. Your quilt will have a scrappier look if you ignore color and value and sew the pieces together as they come out of the bag.

partial arc assembled in Step 1. Next, sew a C reverse piece to the right side of each arc. See **Diagram 2**. Gently press all seams in the same direction, taking care not to stretch the fabric.

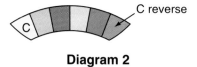

Diagram 2

Step 3. Sew a pieced arc to one side of each B melon, as shown in **Diagram 3**, matching the middle seam of the arc with the midpoint of the melon. For more information about sewing curved seams, see page 229. Press the seam away from the melon. You will use half of the pieced arcs for this step.

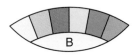

Diagram 3

Step 4. Sew a green E piece to each end of 49 (12 for wallhanging) of the remaining pieced arcs. Press the seams toward the green pieces. Sew the pink E pieces to the remaining 48 (12) arcs. Press the seams away from the pink pieces. See **Diagram 4.**

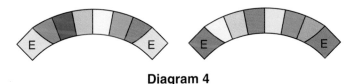

Diagram 4

Step 5. Sew the arcs from Step 4 to the melons, matching the middle seam of the arcs to the midpoint of the melons. Press the seams toward the arcs. You will have two types of arc/melon units—49 with green tips and 48 with pink tips for the double or 12 each for the wallhanging, as shown in **Diagram 5.**

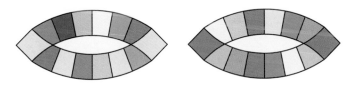

Diagram 5

ASSEMBLING THE QUILT TOP

Step 1. Lay out the completed arc/melon units and background pieces on a design wall or other flat surface.

Important: Note that all arc/melon units with green E pieces are positioned vertically within the quilt top and all arc/melon units with pink E pieces are positioned horizontally.

Step 2. Sew the arc units to the background A pieces in horizontal rows, as shown in the **Partial Assembly Diagram**, leaving ¼ inch open at the beginning and end of each seam and backstitching. If you are making the wallhanging, your layout will only be three rings wide. Refer to page 231 for more details about assembling the rings into rows.

Step 3. Sew the rows together, starting and stopping ¼ inch from the end of each arc and backstitching. Press the completed quilt top. Refer to the **Double-Size Quilt Diagram** on page 154 to see all the rows assembled.

QUILTING AND FINISHING

Step 1. Mark the quilt top for quilting. The quilt shown was quilted in the ditch around all the rings, and the background was quilted with a floral motif.

Step 2. Regardless of which quilt size you've chosen to make, the backing will have to be pieced.

Partial Assembly Diagram

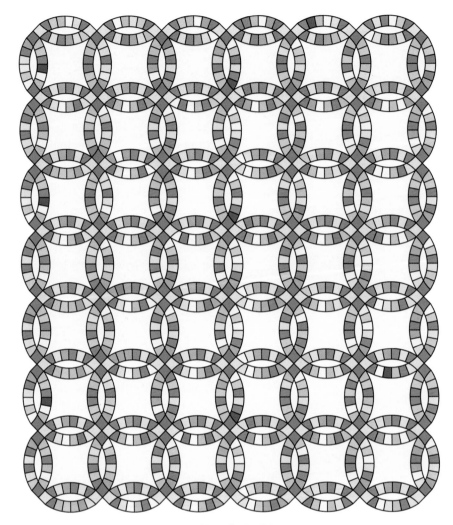

Double-Size Quilt Diagram

For the wallhanging, cut the backing fabric cross-wise into two equal lengths, and trim the selvages. Cut a 36-inch-wide lengthwise panel from one piece and a 16-inch-wide lengthwise panel from the remaining piece. Sew the two panels together, as shown in **Diagram 6.** Press the seam open.

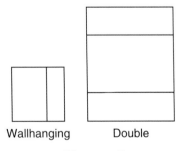

Wallhanging   Double

Diagram 6

Step 3. For the double quilt, cut the backing fabric into three equal lengths, and trim the selvages. Cut a 30-inch-wide panel from two of the segments, then sew one of these panels to each side of the full-width piece, as shown. Press the seams open.

Step 4. Layer the backing, batting, and quilt top, and baste. Quilt as desired.

Step 5. Use a narrow bias binding to bind the quilt, since a narrower binding will be easier to attach around the curves. Refer to the instructions on pages 244–246 for information about making bias binding, calculating the amount needed, and applying it around curves.

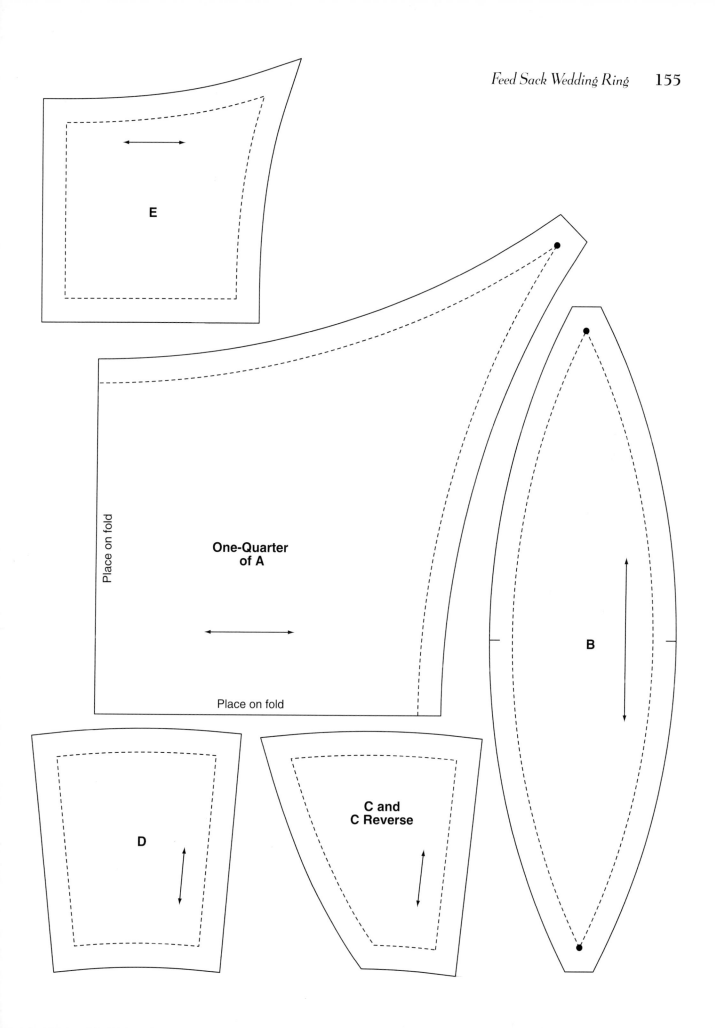

E

Place on fold

One-Quarter of A

Place on fold

B

C and C Reverse

D

81 Patch

Skill Level: *Easy*

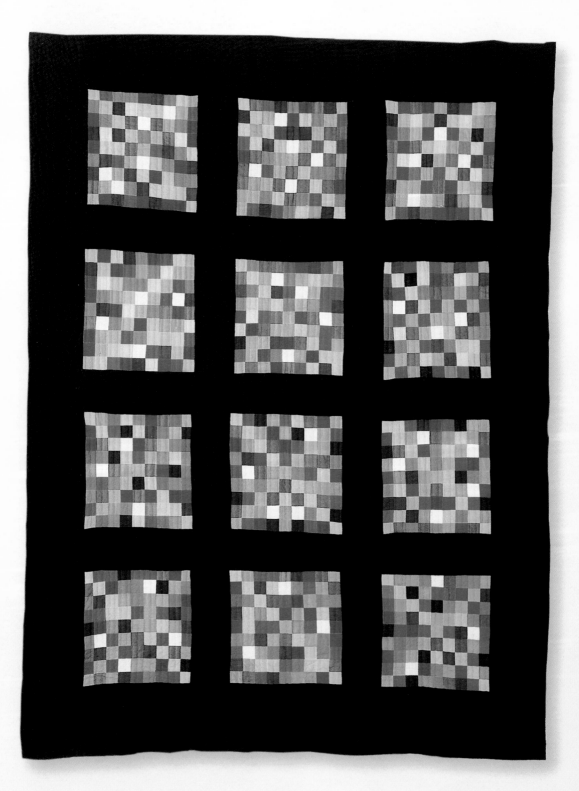

The jewel-tone fabrics in this antique quilt sparkle like sunbeams through a stained glass window. From the collection of Shelly Zegart, the twin-size, 81 Patch design was pieced during the 1930s in the Amish community of Holmes County, Ohio. While the quiltmaker is unknown, there's no doubt that she dug deep into her scrap bag to find the crisp, brilliant solids for the multicolor blocks.

BEFORE YOU BEGIN

Each block in this quilt contains eighty-one 1½-inch finished squares. The 81 Patch blocks are joined by sashing strips, then finished with a wide border. All of the components of this quilt are cut and assembled using quick-cutting and quick-piecing techniques. The directions for the blocks are written based on using an easy strip-piecing method. Strips of fabric are sewn together into strip sets, and the strip sets are then cut apart and resewn into blocks. For information on rotary cutting, see page 223.

CHOOSING FABRICS

Subtle yet sparkling, the colors of the squares that crisscross through each block remain the same from block to block. From the top right corner to the lower left corner, you'll find medium blue squares. Medium pink squares are used on the opposite diagonal, stopping only for the blue square at the block's center. All other colors are placed randomly within the block.

To re-create the quilt shown, choose a medium pink solid for the squares of one diagonal and a medium blue solid for the other. Select an assortment of light to dark solids for the remaining squares in the block. The majority of fabrics in the quilt are of a medium value, with lights and darks sprinkled throughout. The quick-piecing instructions are written to allow the use of smaller

yardages of fabric for the 81 Patch blocks. Purchasing fat quarters (18 × 22 inches) or fat eighths (11 × 18 inches) is a good way to increase the number of different colors used without investing in a tremendous amount of fabric.

To help develop your own unique color scheme for the

Quilt Sizes

	Twin (shown)	Queen	King
Finished Quilt Size	67" × 85½"	85½" × 104"	104" × 104"
Finished Block Size	13½"	13½"	13½"
Finished Square Size	1½"	1½"	1½"
Number of Blocks	12	20	25

Materials

Fabric	Twin	Queen	King
Black	2⅞ yards	4¼ yards	5 yards
Assorted mediums	2 yards	2⅜ yards	2⅜ yards
Assorted darks	1 yard	1¼ yards	1⅜ yards
Assorted lights	1 yard	1¼ yards	1⅜ yards
Medium blue	½ yard	⅝ yard	⅞ yard
Medium pink	½ yard	⅝ yard	⅝ yard
Backing	5¼ yards	7¾ yards	9⅜ yards
Batting	73" × 91"	91" × 110"	110" × 110"
Binding	⅝ yard	¾ yard	⅞ yard

NOTE: *Yardages are based on 44/45-inch-wide fabrics that are at least 42 inches wide after preshrinking.*

Cutting Chart

Fabric	Used For	Strip Width	Number to Cut		
			Twin	Queen	King
Black	Horizontal sashing	5½"	3	6	7
	Vertical sashing	5½"	4	7	9
	Border	8¼"	7	9	10
Assorted mediums	Strip Sets*	2"	25	30	41
Assorted darks	Strip Sets*	2"	13	18	22
Assorted lights	Strip Sets*	2"	13	18	22
Medium blue	Strip Sets*	2"	7	9	12
Medium pink	Strip Sets*	2"	6	8	10

Double the number you cut if you're using fat quarters or fat eighths of fabric instead of 42-inch-wide fabric.

quilt, photocopy the **Color Plan** on page 163, and use crayons or colored pencils to experiment with different color arrangements.

CUTTING

All measurements include ¼-inch seam allowances. Referring to the Cutting Chart, cut the required number of strips in the width needed. Cut all strips across the fabric width. When you have cut the number of strips listed in the Cutting Chart, refer to the following instructions to cut the individual pieces.

• If you are using 42-inch-wide fabric, cut the 2-inch strips in half so they are approximately 21 inches long.

• If you are using fat quarters or fat eighths, cut the strips across the width of the fabric (11- or 22-inch measurement), not along the length of the fabric (9- or 18-inch measurement).

• For the horizontal sashing, cut the 5½-inch strips into 5½ × 14-inch rectangles.

ASSEMBLING THE BLOCKS

Each block in this quilt is assembled using a combination of five different strip sets. Strip Sets 1 through 5 are assembled in rows first, then strip

sets 1 through 4 are added in the reverse order and turned 180 degrees to continue the medium pink and medium blue diagonal design, as shown in the **Block Diagram.**

Strip Set 1
Strip Set 2
Strip Set 3
Strip Set 4
Strip Set 5

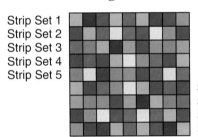

Strip Set 4 turned 180°
Strip Set 3 turned 180°
Strip Set 2 turned 180°
Strip Set 1 turned 180°

Block Diagram

The following charts show how many of each strip set to make and how many segments to cut from each strip set for each quilt size.

	Number of 21-inch Strip Sets to Piece		
	Twin	Queen	King
Strip Set 1	3	4	5
Strip Set 2	3	4	5
Strip Set 3	3	4	5
Strip Set 4	3	4	5
Strip Set 5	2	2	3

Number of Segments to Cut			
	Twin	Queen	King
Strip Set 1	24	40	50
Strip Set 2	24	40	50
Strip Set 3	24	40	50
Strip Set 4	24	40	50
Strip Set 5	12	20	25

Step 1. Sort the strips cut for the blocks, keeping the medium pink and medium blue strips separate. Sort the remaining strips into piles of lights, mediums, and darks.

Step 2. Make strip set 1 by sewing nine strips together lengthwise, beginning with a medium pink strip and ending with a medium blue strip, as shown in **Diagram 1**. Choose other strips from your assortment of colors and values. Position strips so all adjoining fabrics are of a different value or color. Your strip ends may be uneven due to shrinkage after prewashing. Press the seams in the direction of the arrow in the diagram.

Square off one end of each strip set.

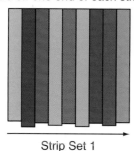

Strip Set 1

Diagram 1

········Sew Quick········

Save time when cutting quantities of strips by placing a piece of masking tape on the wrong side of your rotary ruler at the needed measurement line. You won't waste precious seconds scanning the ruler because the edge of the masking tape is an instantly recognizable guide.

Step 3. Use your rotary equipment to square up one end of the strip set, then cut as many 2-inch-wide segments from it as you can, as shown in **Diagram 2**. Set the cut strips aside. Duplicate strip set 1 until you have the total number required for your quilt size. For better color variety, use a different combination of fabrics for the assorted strips in each Strip Set 1, but keep the medium pink and medium blue strips in the same position. If it is necessary to use the same fabrics for each block, vary their positions in each set.

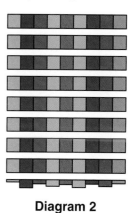

Diagram 2

— Sew Easy —

Use gray thread whenever you're sewing fabrics of different colors. It blends nicely with lights, mediums, and darks, and it saves you time by eliminating the need to change your spool every time you join a new fabric color.

Step 4. Make Strip Sets 2 through 5 in the same manner, paying close attention to the position of medium pink and medium blue strips, as shown in **Diagram 3** on page 160. Choose and arrange all of the other colors randomly. Press the seams in each set in the direction of the arrow in the diagram. Cut the assembled sets into 2-inch-wide segments and repeat until you have the number of segments required for your quilt. Stack segments in piles by strip set number and label them.

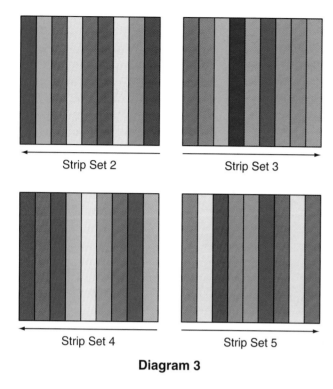

Strip Set 2   Strip Set 3

Strip Set 4   Strip Set 5

Diagram 3

Step 5. Select two 2-inch-wide segments each from Strip Sets 1 through 4, and one segment from Strip Set 5. Referring to the **Block Diagram** on page 158, position the strip sets together to form a block. Sew the rows together, taking care to match the seams.

ASSEMBLING THE QUILT TOP

Step 1. Use a flat surface to arrange the blocks, short horizontal sashing strips, and long vertical sashing strips, as shown in the **Assembly Diagram.** The twin-size quilt has three vertical rows of four blocks each. The queen-size quilt has four vertical rows of five blocks each. The king-size quilt has five vertical rows of five blocks each.

Step 2. Sew together the columns of blocks and short sashing strips. To add a sashing strip, fold it in half crosswise and crease. Unfold it and position it right side down along the bottom of the first block, matching the crease to the vertical center of the block. Pin at the midpoint and ends, and place additional pins along the

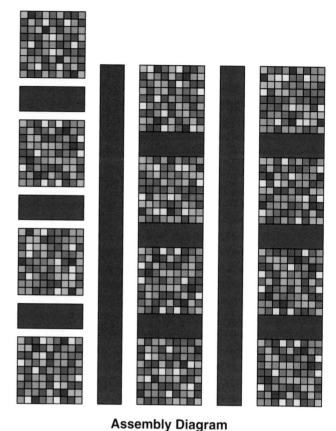

Assembly Diagram

width, easing in fullness as necessary. Sew the sashing to the block. Press the seam toward the sashing. Repeat for all of the blocks and sashing strips.

Step 3. Sew the vertical sashing to the columns. Fold the first long sashing strip in half crosswise and crease. Repeat for the first column of blocks. Match the midpoints, pinning at the center and ends first, then along the length of the entire sashing, easing in fullness as necessary. Sew the sashing strips to the blocks, taking care to align them so that your 81 Patch blocks align on both sides of a vertical sashing strip. Press the seam toward the sashing. Repeat for all remaining rows of blocks and vertical sashing strips.

ATTACHING THE BORDERS

Step 1. Attach the top and bottom borders first. Measure the width of the quilt top, taking the measurement through the horizontal center of the quilt, rather than along the edges. Sew the 8¼-inch black strips together end to end to make two borders this exact length.

Step 2. Fold one strip in half crosswise and crease. Unfold it and position it right side down along the top of the quilt, with the crease at the vertical midpoint. Pin at the midpoint and ends first, then along the length of the entire edge, easing in fullness as necessary. Sew the border to the quilt. Repeat for the bottom border. Press seams toward the borders.

Step 3. Measure the length of the quilt top, taking the measurement through the vertical center of the quilt and including the top and bottom borders. Using the remaining black strips, piece two border strips this exact length and sew these to the sides of the quilt, referring to Step 2. Press seams toward the borders.

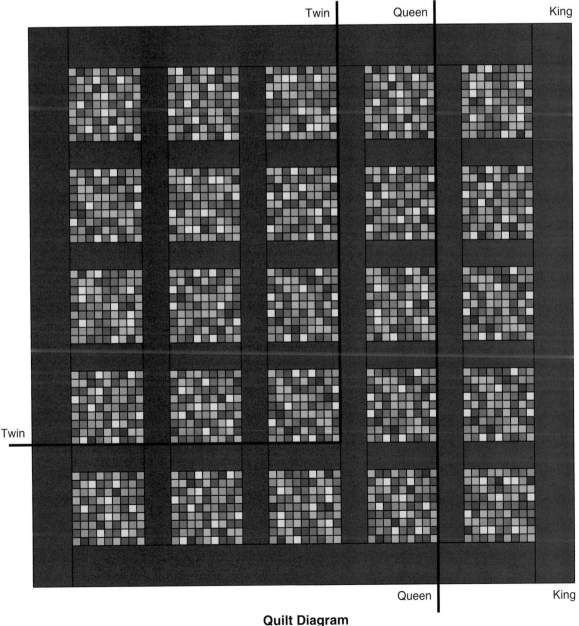

Quilt Diagram

QUILTING AND FINISHING

Step 1. Mark the quilt top for quilting. The quilt shown on page 156 features a cable motif in the border and cross-hatching in the black sashing. Vertical lines were quilted in the ditch in each block.

Step 2. To make the backing for the twin-size quilt, cut the backing fabric in half crosswise and trim the selvages. Cut two 16-inch-wide segments from the entire length of one of the pieces, and sew one segment to each side of the full-width piece, as shown in **Diagram 4.** Press the seams open.

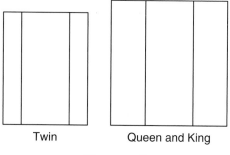

Twin   Queen and King

Diagram 4

Step 3. To make the backing for the queen-size quilt, cut the backing fabric crosswise into three equal pieces and trim the selvages. Cut a 26-inch-wide segment from the entire length of two of the pieces. Sew one segment to each side of the full-width piece, as shown in the diagram. Press the seams open.

Step 4. To make the backing for the king-size quilt, cut the backing fabric crosswise into three equal pieces and trim the selvages. Cut a 35-inch-wide segment from the entire length of two of the pieces. Sew one segment to each side of the full-width piece, as shown in the diagram. Press the seams open.

Step 5. Layer the quilt top, batting, and backing, and baste the layers together. Quilt as desired.

Step 6. Referring to the directions on page 244, make and attach double-fold binding. To calculate the amount of binding needed for the quilt size you are making, add the length of the four sides of the quilt, plus 9 inches.

81 Patch

Color Plan

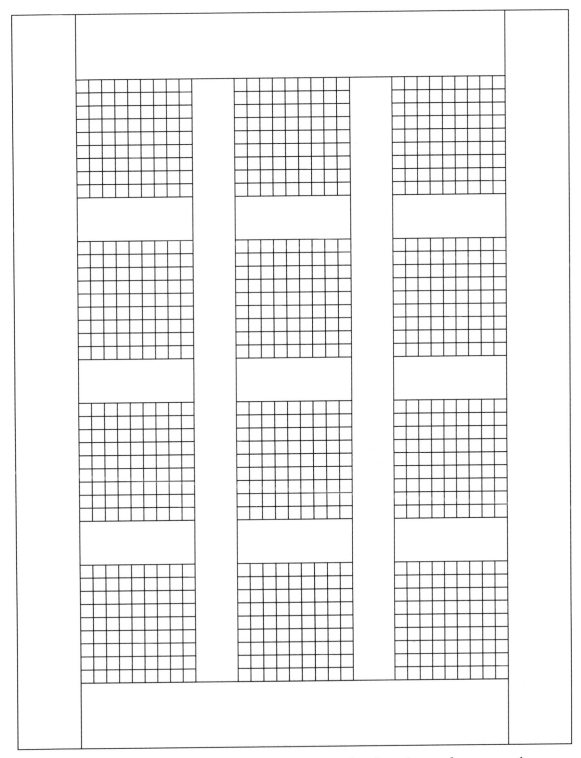

Photocopy this page and use it to experiment with color schemes for your quilt.

163

MY CABIN
MADE OF LOGS

Skill Level: *Intermediate*

Quiltmaker Jane Graff developed the perfect recipe when she created this queen-size beauty that mixes two beloved designs—Schoolhouse and Log Cabin—to create a spectacular set. A popular homespun color scheme, a pieced border that makes efficient use of leftovers, plus favorite techniques like rotary cutting and strip piecing make this a quiltmaker's dream!

BEFORE YOU BEGIN

Although this design requires eight different block variations to achieve its clever barn raising setting, the construction of the quilt is actually quite easy. Just read the instructions carefully and refer often to the visuals provided, especially the photo, the **Schoolhouse Block Diagram** on page 167, the **Assembly Diagram** on page 170, and the **Quilt Diagram** on page 171. The latter will be particularly helpful as you position the various blocks to achieve the desired overall effect.

Two size variations are given: a generously sized queen (as shown in the photograph) and a twin size. The twin size simply eliminates the outer ring of blocks, so the overall barn raising effect is not disturbed.

With the exception of a few simple shapes that require templates, all of the pieces are strips that can be rotary cut. A simple strip-piecing technique is provided for making the pieced border and parts of the Schoolhouse block, while chain piecing makes quick work of the Log Cabin blocks.

Quilt Sizes

	Twin	Queen (shown)
Finished Quilt Size	70½" × 70½"	90½" × 90½"
Finished Block Size		
Overall	10"	10"
Schoolhouse	4"	4"
Number of Blocks	36	36
Red Schoolhouses	18	32
Blue Schoolhouses	18	32
Variations 1, 4, 6, and 7	5 each	8 each
Variations 2, 3, 5, and 8	4 each	8 each

Materials

Fabric	Twin	Queen
Dark brown plaid	1⅞ yards	2⅛ yards
Tan solid	⅝ yard	⅞ yard
Assorted red prints	⅝ yard	⅞ yard
Assorted blue prints	⅝ yard	⅞ yard
Assorted light plaids, checks, and stripes	1⅞ yards	3¼ yards
Dark blue plaids, checks, and stripes	1⅛ yards	1⅞ yards
Dark red plaids, checks, and stripes	1⅛ yards	1⅞ yards
Backing	1¼ yards	8 yards
Batting	77" × 77"	97" × 97"

NOTE: *Yardages are based on 44/45-inch-wide fabrics that are at least 42 inches wide after preshrinking.*

Cutting Chart

Fabric	Used For	Strip Width or Piece	Number to Cut Twin	Number to Cut Queen	Second Cut Dimensions	Number to Cut Twin	Number to Cut Queen
Dark brown plaid	Inner borders	2½"	8	9			
	Outer borders	2½"	8	10			
Tan solids	Unit 2	2"	1	1			
	Unit 3	1"	2	4			
	Unit 1	1"	1	2			
	H	1"	3	5	1" × 3"	36	64
	B	Template B	36	64			
	D	Template D	36	64			
	D reverse	Template D	36	64			
Assorted red and blue prints*	Unit 2	1"	1	2			
	Unit 3	1"	2	2			
	Unit 1	1"	2	4			
	E	1"	2	4	1" × 2"	18	32 each
	F	1"	3	4	1" × 2"	18	32 each
	G	1"	2	2	1" × 2½"	18	32 each
	A	Template A	18	32			
	C	Template C	18	32			
Assorted light plaids and stripes	Pieced border	1½"	5	7			
Assorted red and blue plaids and stripes	Pieced border	1½"	5	7			

From the assorted red and blue prints, you will need to cut the quantity of strips or pieces listed from each of the prints (18 for twin or 32 for queen).

Fabric	Used For	Strip Width or Piece	Number to Cut Twin	Number to Cut Queen
Assorted light plaids and stripes	Logs	1½"	36	64
Assorted dark red plaids and stripes	Logs	1½"	22	37
Assorted dark blue plaids and stripes	Logs	1½"	22	37

Then, from the 1½" strips, cut the following pieces:

Fabric	Used For	Length of Log	Twin	Queen	Fabric	Used For	Length of Log	Twin	Queen
Assorted light plaids and stripes	Log 1	4½"	36	64	Assorted dark red and dark blue plaids and stripes	Log 3	5½"	18	32
	Log 2	5½"	36	64		Log 4	6½"	18	32
	Log 5	6½"	36	64		Log 7	7½"	18	32
	Log 6	7½"	36	64		Log 8	8½"	18	32
	Log 9	8½"	36	64		Log 11	9½"	18	32
	Log 10	9½"	36	64		Log 12	10½"	18	32

NOTE: *The "Number of Logs" is the total number to cut from each color group, not from each plaid.*

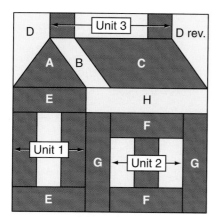

Schoolhouse Block Diagram

Before you begin, read through "Set-In Seams" in "Quiltmaking Basics," beginning on page 227, for more information about assembling the basic Schoolhouse block and for more details on set-in piecing techniques.

CHOOSING FABRICS

This quilt lends itself to all kinds of fabric and color schemes. You can follow this quiltmaker's lead and use warm country reds, blues, beiges, and browns. As alternatives, consider rich reds and greens for a special holiday heirloom, soft pastels for a cabin in springtime look, or rainbow brights to please a child. You can make all of the Log Cabin blocks from the same six fabrics or utilize your scrap bag to make each block different.

The success of a Log Cabin design depends upon careful placement of light and dark fabrics. If you are working with a multitude of different fabrics, presort them into lights and darks. The lights don't need to be super light, just relatively lighter than the darks you pair them with.

To help develop your own unique color scheme for the quilt, photocopy the **Color Plan** on page 173, and use crayons or colored pencils to experiment with different color arrangements.

CUTTING

All of the measurements include ¼-inch seam allowances. Refer to the Cutting Chart and cut the required number of strips in the sizes

needed. Cut all strips across the fabric width (crosswise grain).

Make templates for pieces A, B, C, and D, using the full-size pattern pieces on page 172. Refer to page 224 for complete details on making and using templates. The Cutting Chart indicates how many of each piece to cut with each template. Place the B, C, and D templates right side up on the wrong side of the fabric to cut those pieces. Turn the D template over to cut the D reverse pieces. The A pattern is symmetrical, so it can be placed faceup or facedown.

Note: Cut and piece one sample block before cutting all the fabric for the quilt.

PIECING THE SCHOOLHOUSE BLOCKS

Refer to the **Schoolhouse Block Diagram** as you assemble each Schoolhouse block. Each pattern piece is identified by letter, and strip-pieced units are numbered. Refer to the Quilt Sizes chart on page 165 to determine the number of red and blue Schoolhouse blocks you will need for the quilt size you are making.

The Blue Schoolhouses

Step 1. Sew a 1-inch-wide blue strip to either side of a 1-inch-wide tan strip to form a strip set, as shown in **Diagram 1.** Press the seams toward the blue strips. Using a rotary cutter and ruler, square up one end of the strip set and cut 2-inch-wide segments from it, as shown. Label these segments Unit 1. Continue making strip sets and cutting them into segments until you have assembled one blue Unit 1 segment for each blue Schoolhouse block in your quilt.

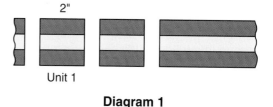

Diagram 1

Step 2. Sew a blue E along the top and bottom of each Unit 1, as shown in **Diagram 2** on page 168. Press the seams toward E. Set these units aside.

Unit 1

Diagram 2

Step 3. Sew a 1-inch tan strip to each side of a 1-inch blue strip. See **Diagram 3**. Press the seams toward the blue strip. Cut 1½-inch segments, as described in Step 1 on page 167. Continue making strip sets and cutting them into segments until you have one Unit 2 for each blue Schoolhouse block.

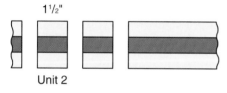

Unit 2

Diagram 3

Step 4. Sew a blue F along the top and bottom edges of each Unit 2, as shown in **Diagram 4**. Press the seams toward F. Then sew a blue G piece to each side of the unit, as shown. Press the seams toward G. Finally, add a tan H piece to the top of the unit, and press seams toward the blue fabric.

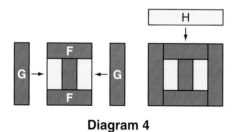

Diagram 4

Step 5. Join the two units, as shown in **Diagram 5**, to complete the base of the house. Press the seams toward Unit 2 and set aside.

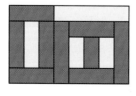

Diagram 5

Step 6. Sew a blue A piece, a tan B piece, and a blue C piece in sequence, as shown in **Diagram 6**. Press the seams toward the blue pieces. Stitch this roof unit to the top edge of the base of the house, as shown. Press the seams and set aside.

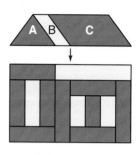

Diagram 6

Step 7. Sew a 1-inch-wide blue strip to either side of a 2-inch-wide tan strip to form a Unit 3 strip set, as shown in **Diagram 7**. Press the seams toward the blue strips. Cut 1-inch-wide segments. Continue making strip sets and cutting them into segments until you have one blue Unit 3 for each blue Schoolhouse block.

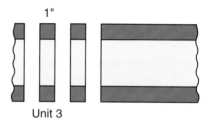

Unit 3

Diagram 7

Step 8. Sew a Unit 3 to the top edge of the house, as shown in **Diagram 8**. Begin and end stitching ¼ inch from the raw edges, as indicated by the dots. Press the seams toward the house.

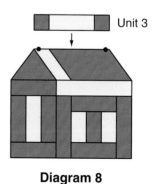

Unit 3

Diagram 8

Step 9. Set in the D and D reverse pieces, as shown in **Diagram 9**. For each piece, begin stitching ¼ inch from the raw edge at the base of the chimney (shown as dots on the diagram), and stitch outward in the direction indicated by the arrows. Press the seams toward the roof. Refer to page 227 for additional information on set-in seams.

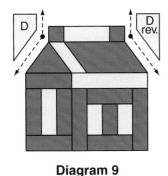

Diagram 9

The Red Schoolhouses

To construct the red Schoolhouse blocks, repeat Steps 1 through 9 under "The Blue Schoolhouses" on page 167, substituting red strips and pieces for the blue ones. Continue using tan pieces as directed for the blue Schoolhouse blocks.

COMPLETING THE LOG CABIN BLOCKS

There are eight block variations in this quilt. Each is pieced using the traditional log cabin method, with a light half and a dark half. Blocks 2, 4, 6, and 8 have a red schoolhouse as the center square. These blocks use blue strips for logs 3, 4, 11, and 12 and red strips for logs 7 and 8. All of the rest of the logs are light. Blocks 1, 3, 5, and 7 have a blue schoolhouse in the center. These blocks use red strips for logs 3, 4, 11, and 12 and blue strips for logs 7 and 8. The rest of the logs are light.

The only other difference between the blocks is where you start piecing with log 1. Use the labels on the **Log Cabin Blocks Diagram** for guidance in positioning log 1 and for the piecing order. Once log 1 has been sewn in place, the sewing procedure remains exactly the same for each variation.

Step 1. Attach each log by placing it right side down on top of the Schoolhouse block, aligning

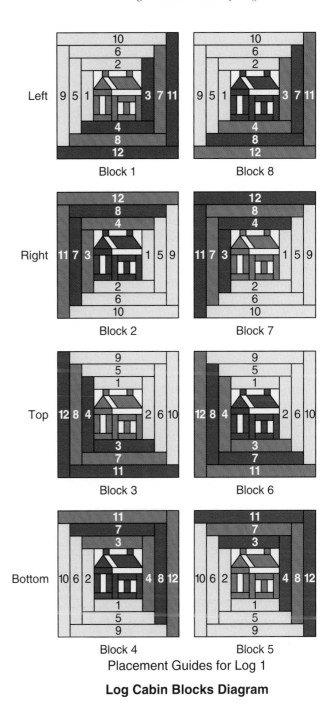

Log Cabin Blocks Diagram

the raw edges with the block edge to which it will be sewn. Press each seam away from the house before the next log is attached.

Step 2. Continue working your way around the block clockwise, adding logs in numerical order, as shown in **Diagram 10** on page 170. Refer to the Quilt Sizes chart on page 165 for the number of each block variation you will need for your quilt size.

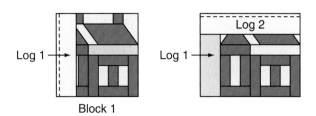

Diagram 10

ASSEMBLING THE QUILT TOP

Step 1. Refer to the **Assembly Diagram** to lay out the quilt blocks. The twin-size quilt has six rows of six blocks each; the queen size has eight rows of eight blocks each. The **Assembly Diagram** is number coded to indicate which block variation should appear in each position in the quilt top. The heavy line inside the last ring of blocks indicates the layout for the twin-size quilt, while all of the blocks are required for the queen-size quilt. Refer to the photograph on page 164 for additional assistance.

Step 2. Sew the blocks together in horizontal rows, pressing the seams in opposite directions from row to row.

Step 3. Sew the rows together, carefully matching seams. Press as desired.

1	2	1	2	5	6	5	6
2	1	2	1	6	5	6	5
1	2	1	2	5	6	5	6
2	1	2	1	6	5	6	5
3	4	3	4	7	8	7	8
4	3	4	3	8	7	8	7
3	4	3	4	7	8	7	8
4	3	4	3	8	7	8	7

Assembly Diagram

Chain piecing is a real time-saver for constructing Log Cabin blocks. Pin and stack all like units that must be joined, such as the center Schoolhouse block and log 1. Begin sewing as usual, but do not backstitch or clip the thread between units. Continue to feed the units one after the other. Clip the connecting threads only after all of the units have been sewn. Press the seam allowances before proceeding to the next step. This method can be used to add each successive log to the blocks.

MAKING THE PIECED BORDER

Step 1. Make strip sets by sewing together pairs of 1½-inch-wide light plaids and stripes and assorted red and blue plaids and stripes. Press all seams toward the darker fabrics. See **Diagram 11**.

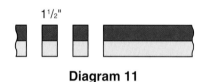

Diagram 11

Step 2. Using your rotary cutter and ruler, square up one end of a strip set and cut as many 1½-inch-wide segments as possible from it, as shown. Continue making and cutting strip sets until you have made 65 segments for the twin-size quilt or 85 segments for the queen size.

Step 3. Join the border units into strips, as shown in **Diagram 12**, alternating dark and light squares and mixing the fabrics as the strips are pieced. Press the seams toward the darker squares. For the twin size, you will need two strips of 32 units each for the side borders and two strips of 33 units each for the top and bottom borders. For the queen size, you will need two borders of 42 units each and two borders of 43 units each.

Quilt Diagram

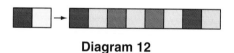

Diagram 12

ADDING THE BORDERS

Refer to the **Quilt Diagram** as you assemble and attach the three borders to the quilt. The heavy line in the interior of the **Quilt Diagram** indicates the size of the twin-size quilt before borders are added.

Step 1. For either size quilt, you will need to piece the inner plaid borders to achieve the necessary length. For the twin-size quilt, sew four 2½-inch-wide dark plaid strips into pairs to form two long borders for the top and bottom of the quilt. Press the seams as desired. Cut one of the re-maining 2½-inch-wide dark brown plaid strips in half, and sew one half to each of the remaining two strips to make the side borders.

For the queen-size quilt, sew the eight 2½-inch-wide dark brown plaid strips together into pairs to form four long border strips.

Step 2. Measure the quilt from top to bottom, taking the measurement through the center of the quilt, not along the sides. Trim the inner plaid side border strips to this length.

Step 3. Fold one trimmed side border in half crosswise and crease. Unfold it and position it right side down along one side of the quilt, with the crease at the quilt's horizontal midpoint. Pin at the midpoint and ends first, then along the length of the entire side, easing in fullness if necessary.

Sew the border to the quilt top, using a ¼-inch seam allowance. Press the seams toward the border. Repeat on the opposite side.

Step 4. Measure the width of the quilt, taking the measurement through the center of the quilt, including the side borders. Trim the top and bottom inner plaid borders to this length. Add the top and bottom borders to the quilt in the same manner as for the side borders.

Step 5. Position and pin a side pieced border strip to one side of the quilt top. Match the midpoints and ends first, and ease in fullness if necessary. Sew the border to the quilt, using a ¼-inch seam allowance. Press the seams toward the dark plaid border. Repeat on the opposite side. In the same manner, add the remaining pieced border strips to the top and bottom edges of the quilt.

Step 6. For either size quilt, piece the outer plaid borders to achieve the necessary length. For the twin-size quilt, join the eight 2½-inch-wide dark brown plaid strips into pairs to form four long border strips. For the queen size, join eight of the 2½-inch-wide dark brown plaid strips in pairs to form four long border strips. Cut the remaining two strips in half, and sew a half to each border.

Step 7. Attach the outer borders in the same manner as the inner borders. Add the side borders first, followed by the top and bottom borders.

QUILTING AND FINISHING

Step 1. Mark the quilt top for quilting. In the quilt shown, the house in each block is quilted in the ditch. The balance of the quilt is quilted in a crosshatch pattern of diagonal lines spaced ¾ inch apart.

Step 2. Regardless of which size quilt you're making, you'll need to piece the backing. For the twin-size quilt, cut the backing fabric in half crosswise, and trim the selvages. Cut one piece in half lengthwise and sew one half to each side of the full-width piece. Press the seams away from the center panel.

For the queen-size quilt, cut the backing fabric crosswise into three equal pieces, and trim the selvages. Sew the three pieces together along the long edges, pressing the seams away from the center panel. For either quilt, the backing seams will run parallel to the sides of the quilt. For more information on pieced quilt backs, see page 243.

Step 3. Layer the backing, batting, and quilt top, and baste. Quilt all marked designs, adding any additional quilting as desired.

Step 4. Referring to page 244, make and attach double-fold bias binding using the remaining dark plaid fabric. For the twin size, you will need approximately 290 inches of binding; for the queen size, you will need approximately 370 inches.

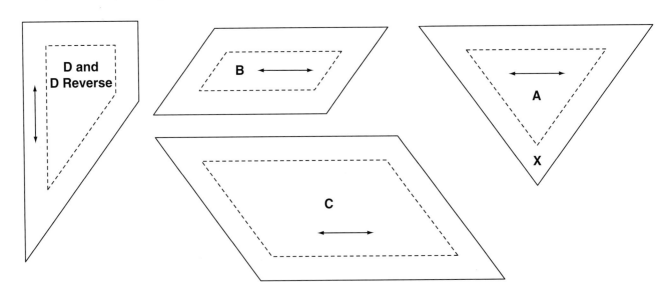

MY CABIN
MADE OF LOGS
Color Plan

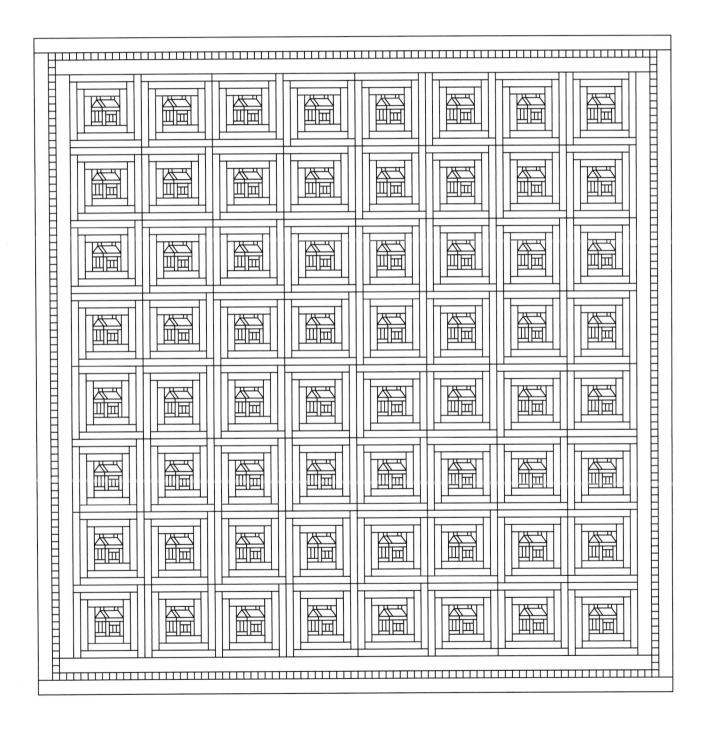

Photocopy this page and use it to experiment with color schemes for your quilt.

Scrap Baskets with Nine-Patch Sashing

Skill Level: *Intermediate*

This new quilt is fashioned in the traditional Grape Basket pattern. While this quilt has the look of a scrap quilt, quiltmaker Wilma Sestric of Ballwin, Missouri, used a controlled palette of blues, burgundies, roses, peaches, and browns. You could expand upon the number of colors and patterns with successful results since the Nine-Patch sashing unifies the quilt with its secondary design.

BEFORE YOU BEGIN

Each basket handle requires several triangle squares. Directions are given for cutting triangles from squares to make the number needed of each scrap fabric. If you choose to make all of your baskets from either the same or a limited number of print fabrics, the grid technique explained on page 225 will help you to construct triangle squares more quickly than you could using traditional methods. Use a $2^7/8$-inch grid. Also note that the bias edge of the setting triangles will be the outside edge of your quilt. Handle these triangles carefully to avoid stretching them out of shape.

CHOOSING FABRICS

What could be more fun than raiding a scrap basket to make this delightful quilt? Mixing and matching colors and prints, darks and lights, and old and new fabrics can spark your imagination. If you don't have a scrap stash, buy lots of fat quarters in a wide variety of shades and patterns.

Of course, you can make this basket pattern in a limited color palette, too. Choose one color for the background, one for the baskets, and another for the sashing strips and Nine-Patch blocks. To help you create your own color scheme, photocopy the **Color Plan** on page 181, and use crayons or colored pencils to experiment with different color arrangements.

Quilt Sizes

	Double (shown)	Queen
Finished Quilt Size	$81^1/8" \times 98^1/2"$	$98^1/2" \times 98^1/2"$
Finished Block Size		
Basket	10"	10"
Nine Patch	$2^1/4"$	$2^1/4"$
Number of Blocks		
Basket	32	41
Nine Patch	49	60

Materials

Fabric	Double	Queen
Assorted prints	Approx. 12" × 13" of 32 prints *or* $1^3/4$ yards total	Approx. 12" × 13" of 41 prints *or* $2^1/4$ yards total
Muslin	$6^1/2$ yards	$7^3/4$ yards
Blue print	$1^3/8$ yards	$1^5/8$ yards
Backing	$7^5/8$ yards	$8^5/8$ yards
Batting	88" × 105"	105" × 105"
Binding	$3/4$ yard	$3/4$ yard

NOTE: *Yardages are based on 44/45-inch-wide fabrics that are at least 42 inches wide after preshrinking.*

Cutting Chart				
Fabric	Used For	Strip Width	Number of Strips	
			Double	Queen
Assorted prints	Basket handles	2⅞"	1 of each	1 of each
	Basket feet	2⅞"	1 of each	1 of each
	Baskets	6⅞"	1 of each	1 of each
Muslin	Basket handles	2⅞"	8	11
	Basket background	6⅞"	3	4
	Basket sides	2½"	11	14
	Bottom triangles	4⅞"	2	3
	Sashing strips	1¼"	40	50
	Nine-Patch blocks	1¼"	6	8
	Setting triangles	18⅝"	2	2
	Corner triangles	15⅜"	1	1
	Outer border	4"	8	8
Blue print	Sashing strips	1¼"	20	25
	Nine-Patch blocks	1¼"	8	10
	Inner border	1¼"	8	8

NOTE: *Strip widths are assumed to be 42 inches except for the assorted print fabrics for the baskets, which are assumed to be 12 inches wide based on the fabric requirement given in the Materials chart on page 175.*

CUTTING

All pieces are cut using rotary-cutting techniques. Refer to the Cutting Chart and cut the required number of strips in the width needed. Cut all strips across the fabric width. From these strips, subcut the individual pieces according to the instructions provided here. All measurements include ¼-inch seam allowances.

• For the basket handles, cut the 2⅞-inch-wide assorted print and muslin strips into 2⅞-inch squares. Cut the squares in half diagonally, as shown in **Diagram 1**.

• For the basket feet, cut the 2⅞-inch print strips into 2⅞-inch squares. Cut the squares in half diagonally.

• For the baskets, cut one 6⅞-inch square from each print. Cut the square in half diagonally. You need one triangle per basket.

• For the basket background, cut the 6⅞-inch muslin strips into 6⅞-inch squares. You need 16 squares for the double size and 21 squares for the

queen size; cut all squares in half diagonally.

• For the basket sides, cut the 2½-inch-wide muslin strips into 2½ × 6½-inch rectangles. Cut two for each block.

• For the bottom triangles of the basket blocks, cut the 4⅞-inch-wide muslin strips into 4⅞-inch squares. Cut 16 for the double-size quilt and 21 for the queen size. Cut the squares in half diagonally.

• For the side setting triangles, cut the 18⅝-inch-wide muslin strips into two 18⅝-inch squares. Cut the squares diagonally both ways, as shown in **Diagram 1**.

• For the corner setting triangles, cut two 15⅜-inch squares from the 15⅜-inch muslin strips. Cut each square in half diagonally.

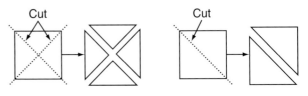

Diagram 1

PIECING THE BASKET BLOCKS

Step 1. Seven identical triangle squares are needed to complete the handle of each basket. Use four $2\frac{7}{8}$-inch squares from the assorted prints and four from muslin. Draw a diagonal line on one side of each muslin square, then pair each square with its print counterpart, with right sides together. Match edges of pairs carefully, then sew a seam $\frac{1}{4}$ inch from each side of the drawn line. After sewing the seams, cut the squares in half on the drawn line. Press the seam in each resulting triangle square toward the blue fabric. See **Diagram 2.**

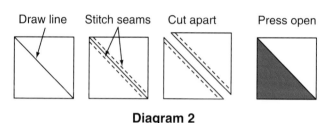

Diagram 2

This method produces eight triangle squares, one more than you need for each basket. If you are repeating print fabrics, just use the extra in another block. If you are not repeating fabrics, sew only one seam on one pair. When cut apart, you will have one triangle square plus a muslin and print $2\frac{7}{8}$-inch triangle. The print triangle can be used to make the foot of the basket.

Step 2. Sew the triangle squares together into two units, referring to **Diagram 3** for placement. Press the seams toward the print fabric.

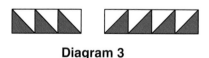

Diagram 3

Step 3. Each block requires two $6\frac{7}{8}$-inch triangles—one muslin and one print. Sew the short triangle-square unit to the muslin triangle, as shown in **Diagram 4.** Press the seam toward the muslin. Then sew the longer triangle-square unit to the muslin triangle as shown, matching seams where the triangle squares meet. Press.

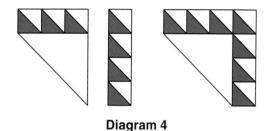

Diagram 4

Step 4. Sew the print triangle to the bottom of unit, as shown in **Diagram 5.** Press the seam toward the print triangle.

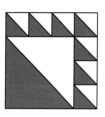

Diagram 5

Step 5. Sew a $2\frac{7}{8}$-inch print triangle to one end of two $2\frac{1}{2} \times 6\frac{1}{2}$-inch muslin rectangles, as shown in **Diagram 6.**

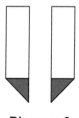

Diagram 6

Step 6. Sew the rectangle units to the partially assembled basket, as shown in **Diagram 7.** Press the seams toward the print fabric. (If seams are too bulky, press them toward the muslin.)

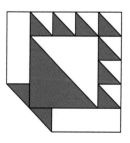

Diagram 7

Step 7. Sew a 4⁷⁄₈-inch muslin triangle to the bottom of the basket, as shown in the **Block Diagram,** completing the block. Press the seam toward the print fabric. Repeat to make the number of basket blocks required for your quilt.

Block Diagram

MAKING THE SASHING STRIPS

Step 1. Refer to the cutting chart for the number of 1¼ × 42-inch strips of muslin and blue print fabric required for your quilt. Pin and sew a muslin strip to each side of a blue print strip, as shown in **Diagram 8.** Press the seams toward the blue strip.

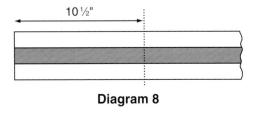

Diagram 8

Step 2. Square up one end of a set, then cut as many 10½-inch segments as possible from the long strip set. Make 80 sashing strips for the double-size quilt and 100 for the queen-size quilt.

PIECING THE NINE-PATCH BLOCKS

The Nine-Patch blocks can be assembled quickly using strip-piecing techniques. The dark portions of sashing, the inner border, and the binding are all sewn from the same fabric.

Step 1. Pin and sew a blue print Nine-Patch strip to either side of a muslin Nine-Patch strip to make strip set A, as shown in **Diagram 9.** Press the seams toward the print strips. Square up one end of the strip set, then cut as many 1¼-inch segments from it as possible.

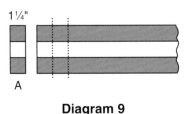

Diagram 9

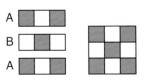

Sew Easy

If your strips ripple when making the sashing strips and Nine-Patch blocks, start sewing the third strip at the end where your first seam stopped. Match edges carefully and pin strips before sewing. If you still have distortion problems, shorten the length of your strip units to about 22 inches, since shorter lengths are somewhat easier to handle.

Step 2. Pin and sew a muslin Nine-Patch strip to either side of a blue print Nine-Patch strip to make strip set B. Press seams toward the blue strip. This strip set will look just like the strip sets you made for the sashing strips (see **Diagram 8**). Square up one end of the strip set, then cut as many 1¼-inch segments from it as possible.

Step 3. Sew an A segment to the top and bottom of a B segment, as shown in **Diagram 10,** matching seams carefully. Repeat until you have assembled 49 Nine-Patch blocks for the double size and 60 Nine-Patch blocks for the queen size.

A
B
A

Diagram 10

Sew Quick

If you have leftover pieces from the sashing strips that weren't quite 10½ inches long, you can use them for the Nine-Patch blocks. Simply cut 1¼-inch B segments from each leftover strip set.

ASSEMBLING THE QUILT TOP

Step 1. Use a design wall or flat surface to lay out the basket blocks, setting triangles, sashing strips, and Nine-Patch blocks in diagonal rows. The double-size quilt is shown in the **Assembly Diagram.** For the queen-size quilt, your layout will be one block wider.

Step 2. Sew the rows of basket blocks and sashing strips together exactly as shown, pressing seams toward the sashing strips. Notice that one diagonal row has a sashing strip sewn to

Assembly Diagram

the top and bottom of the basket row. These rows must be sewn together as a unit before the setting triangles will fit. Sew the remaining rows of sashing strips and Nine-Patch blocks together, pressing seams toward the sashing strips.

Step 3. Sew the side setting triangles to the ends of the basket block rows. Sew all rows together. Sew the corner setting triangles on last. Press.

Note: The larger quilt is assembled in much the same manner; however, some rows will contain a different number of blocks.

ADDING THE BORDERS

The quilt has a narrow blue print inner border and a wider muslin outer border, as shown in the **Quilt Diagram** on page 180. You will sew the border strips for each side together first, then add them to the quilt top as a single unit, mitering the corners. See page 242 in "Quiltmaking Basics" for details on adding borders with mitered corners.

Step 1. To determine the correct length for the side borders, measure the quilt top vertically through the center. To this measurement add two times the finished width of the double border (3½ inches + 1 inch = 4½ inches) plus 5 inches. This is the length you need to make the two side borders. In the same manner, measure the quilt top horizontally through the center, then calculate the length of the top and bottom borders.

Step 2. Sew the print border strips together end to end until you've achieved the required lengths for each border. Repeat with the muslin border strips. Be sure to keep the side border strips separate from the top and bottom border strips if you're making the double-size quilt. For the queen-size quilt, the border lengths will be the same for the sides, top, and bottom.

Step 3. Working with the side border strips first, pin and sew the long strips together length-wise into two units. Press seams toward the outer border. In the same manner, pin and sew the top and bottom border strips together into two units. Press seams toward the outer border.

Step 4. Pin and sew the four border units to the quilt top, carefully lining up the matching strips in adjacent borders.

QUILTING AND FINISHING

Step 1. Mark the top for quilting, if desired.

Step 2. Regardless of which quilt size you've chosen to make, the backing will have to be pieced. **Diagram 11** illustrates the layout for either the double- or queen-size quilt back. For either quilt, divide the backing fabric crosswise into three equal pieces, and trim the selvages. Sew the three pieces together along the long sides, and press the seams open.

Diagram 11

Step 3. Layer the quilt top, batting, and backing, and baste the layers together. Quilt as desired.

Step 4. Referring to the directions on page 244 in "Quiltmaking Basics," make and attach double-fold binding with a finished width of ¹/₂ inch. Add the length of the four sides of the quilt plus 9 inches. The total is the approximate number of inches of binding you will need.

Quilt Diagram

SCRAP BASKETS WITH NINE-PATCH SASHING

Color Plan

Photocopy this page and use it to experiment with color schemes for your quilt.

SCRAP HALF LOG CABIN

Skill Level: *Easy*

Deep, rich jewel tones fairly sparkle in this fast and fun twin-size scrap quilt by Sharyn Craig of El Cajon, California. A pieced border adds new interest to the traditional Straight Furrows setting. The blocks, called Half Log Cabin or Off-Center Log Cabin, are built out from a corner square rather than a center square. Like traditional Log Cabin blocks, they're extremely versatile and can be arranged in a variety of settings.

Before You Begin

The directions for this quilt are written based on using a unique piecing method developed by quiltmaker Sharyn Craig. It is a form of chain piecing, but instead of sewing all matching units at one time, you sew together varying stages of up to four blocks at a time. Once the first block is completed, you can produce blocks at a rate of about four to eight an hour, and each one will be different. The technique makes sewing this scrappy Log Cabin quilt fun and easy. Since the method may be a bit different from others you have used, we suggest you read through the instructions a few times before beginning.

Quilt Sizes

	Crib	Twin (shown)	Queen
Finished Quilt Size	44½" × 60"	73" × 95½"	89½" × 104½"
Finished Block Size	7½"	7½"	7½"
Number of Blocks	24	88	120

Materials

Fabric	Crib	Twin	Queen
Dark fabrics	1½ yards	4¼ yards	5½ yards
Light fabrics	½ yard	2⅜ yards	3 yards
Light border fabric	1½ yards	1⅝ yards	2⅛ yards
Backing	3 yards	5½ yards	8½ yards
Batting	48" × 64"	77" × 100"	94" × 109"
Binding	½ yard	⅝ yard	½ yard

NOTE: *Yardages are based on 44/45-inch-wide fabrics that are at least 42 inches wide after preshrinking.*

Choosing Fabrics

The yardage requirements for light and dark logs is an approximation of the amounts actually used in the blocks. For a successful scrap quilt, variety is important, so you will likely start out with more yardage than indicated, but not all of it will be used.

Long strips of fabric are required for this method of block assembly. If you purchase new fabrics, select regular yardage cuts, not fat quarters. For best results, choose fabrics with lots of contrast. Including a few medium-value fabrics will add interest, but most of the fabrics should be either dark or light.

You can vary the look of the quilt by controlling the use of one or more of the fabrics. For example, you might use a single fabric for all of the light logs. Or you might reverse the positions of the light and dark fabrics—start with a light square instead of a dark one, and the resulting quilt will have a lighter overall effect.

To help develop your own unique color scheme for the quilt, photocopy the **Color Plan** on page 191, and use crayons or colored pencils to experiment with different color arrangements.

CUTTING

All measurements include ¼-inch seam allowances. Referring to the Cutting Chart, cut the strips and squares needed for which quilt size you are making. Cut one or two strips from each fabric to begin with. The total number of strips you use from each piece will depend on the number of different fabrics you've chosen to work with. Cut all strips across the fabric width (crosswise grain). Accurate cutting is critical to this piecing technique, so measure and cut all strips carefully.

Cutting Chart

	Crib				
Fabric	2" Strips	2¾" Strips	4" Squares	3⅜" Squares	6¼" Squares
Darks	16		38		
Lights	11				
Light borders		5		8	17

	Twin				
Fabric	2" Strips	2¾" Strips	4" Squares	3⅜" Squares	6¼" Squares
Darks	57		64		
Lights	39				
Light borders	8			8	30

	Queen				
Fabric	2" Strips	2¾" Strips	4" Squares	3⅜" Squares	6¼" Squares
Darks	75		74		
Lights	51				
Light borders		9		8	35

········· Sew Quick ·········

You can increase your fabric choices by using the wrong side of some fabrics. Many medium and dark fabrics make good light fabrics when flipped over. Generally, quilters do not have as many light-value fabrics as they do medium and dark values, so using the wrong side is very helpful.

PIECING THE BLOCKS

Step 1. Sort the fabric strips into a light pile and a dark pile, and trim the selvage from one end of each strip, squaring up that end. Don't worry about color placement as you assemble blocks; just think of the fabrics in terms of light and dark. A fabric that doesn't look quite right in a single block won't even be noticeable when the quilt is assembled. There are four basic steps to assembling the blocks:

1. **Sew** the units to a strip.
2. **Cut** the units apart.
3. **Press** the seam allowance.
4. **Stack** the sewn units on top of each other.

These four steps are the key to this piecing system. Follow them carefully when assembling the blocks. The numbers on the **Block Diagram** show the order in which strips are added. In the quilt shown, the odd numbers are dark strips and the even numbers are light strips.

Step 2. Pick up a dark strip. Use your rotary cutter to cut a 2-inch square from the trimmed end, then set the remainder of the strip aside. (Begin all steps with the trimmed, squared-up end of the strips.)

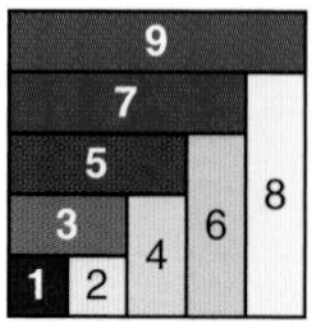

Block Diagram

Step 3. Pick up a light strip. Position it right side up in front of you. Position the dark 2-inch square right side down on top of your light strip. Sew them together, as shown in **Diagram 1A,** using a ¼-inch seam allowance.

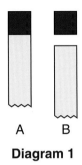

Diagram 1

Step 4. Cut the light strip at the bottom edge of the dark 2-inch square, as shown in **1B.** The resulting sewn piece, containing a dark and a light portion, is called a unit.

Step 5. Press the seam allowance toward the newest fabric, in this case the light.

Step 6. Position the pressed unit, right side down, on your sewing table, as shown in **Diagram 2.** Pay close attention to the placement of the light and dark portions.

Step 7. Pick up a dark strip of fabric. Make sure it's different from the one you used to start the block. Position it right side up at the machine.

Sew Easy

Here's a pressing technique that will help prevent stretching and distorting the unit. Place the unopened unit on the ironing board with the newest fabric on top and the sewn edge away from you. Press with the iron to "set" the stitches. Lift the top piece to open up the unit. Set the iron on the portion nearest you, then glide it gently toward the new fabric to direct the seam allowance toward the newest fabric.

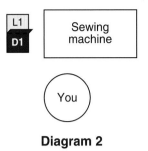

Diagram 2

Pick up the sewn unit and place it right side down directly on top of your new dark strip. Be careful not to change the position of your sewn unit; the newest (light) strip should still be positioned at the top, as shown in **Diagram 3.** Align the top edge of the sewn unit with the trimmed end of the dark strip.

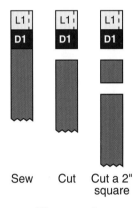

Diagram 3

Step 8. Sew the pieces together along the right-hand edge, using a ¼-inch seam allowance. Cut the dark strip at the bottom edge of the unit, as shown in the diagram. Press the seam allowance toward the newest strip.

Step 9. Cut a 2-inch square from the end of the dark strip. This new square is the start of your second block. From this point on, every time you add a new dark fabric to your blocks, you will cut a 2-inch starter square from it.

Step 10. Position the pieced unit and the new dark square right side down, as illustrated in **Diagram 4** on page 186, with the newest dark fabric (D2) in the bottom position. Stack the new starter square on top of the unit as shown, placing it on the strip of fabric it matches. You will not sew the extra square to the unit—stacking the units in this way will help you remember fabric position, which will become increasingly important as blocks are assembled.

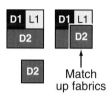

Diagram 4

Step 11. Place a new light strip right side up at the sewing machine. Pick up the stack and position the two units on the new light strip, as shown in **Diagram 5.** Make sure both units are aligned with the right-hand edge of the new light strip.

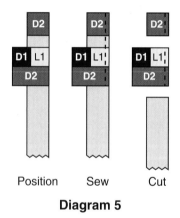

Position   Sew   Cut

Diagram 5

Step 12. Sew the pieces together using a ¼-inch seam allowance. Cut the light strip at the bottom edge of the unit, then cut the units apart, as shown in **Diagram 5.** Press the seam allowance toward the newest strip. You now have partial units for two blocks. **Diagram 6** shows the partial units (right side down).

Stacking the units correctly is the most important step for accurate block assembly. Always fol-

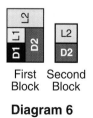

First   Second
Block   Block

Diagram 6

low this rule: If the last fabric added was a *light* fabric, stack the units with that new light fabric in the *top* position (away from you). If the last fabric added was a *dark* fabric, stack the units with that new dark fabric in the *bottom* position (toward you).

Step 13. Stack the two units, as shown in **Diagram 7,** making sure the newest light fabric (L2) pieces are matched up and in the top position.

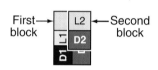

Diagram 7

Step 14. Place a new dark strip right side up at the sewing machine. Pick up the stack and position the two units right side down on the new dark strip, as shown in **Diagram 8.** Make sure both units are aligned with the right-hand edge of the new dark strip. Sew the pieces together using a ¼-inch seam allowance. Cut the dark strip at the bottom edge of the unit, then cut the units apart, as shown in the diagram. Press the seam allowance toward the newest strip.

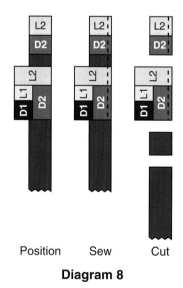

Position   Sew   Cut

Diagram 8

Step 15. Cut a new 2-inch square from the dark strip. You now have partial units for three blocks. See **Diagram 9** (shown right side down).

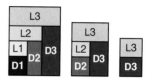
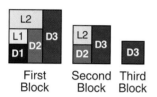

Diagram 9

Step 16. Stack the units, matching fabrics. The last fabric added was dark (D3), so stack the units with that fabric in the bottom position, as shown in **Diagram 10**.

Diagram 10

Step 17. Place a new light strip right side up at the sewing machine. Position the stacked units right side down on the new strip, as shown in **Diagram 11**. Make sure the units are aligned with the right-hand edge of the new light strip.

Diagram 11

Step 18. Sew, cut the units apart, and press as described. The three units should now look like those in **Diagram 12** (shown right side down).

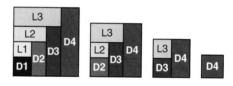

Diagram 12

Step 19. Stack the units, matching like fabrics as before. The last fabric added was light (L3); place it in the top position. Put a new dark strip in place at the sewing machine and position the units right side down on top of it, keeping them in correct position.

Step 20. Sew, cut, and press. Cut an extra 2-inch square. You now have units for four Half Log Cabin blocks. See **Diagram 13** (shown right side down).

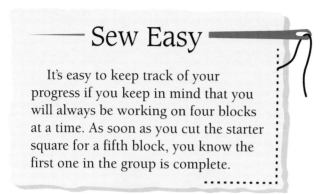

Diagram 13

Step 21. In the same manner, add another light strip, then another dark strip. With the addition of this dark strip, you will complete the first block and begin the fifth block.

Look at the completed block, the three unfinished units, and the newest 2-inch square, shown right side down in **Diagram 14**. Even though some of the fabrics repeat, their position in each block varies. As you continue making blocks and then arranging them with others into a setting, the repetition won't be obvious. The end result will be a true scrap quilt, with randomly placed fabrics.

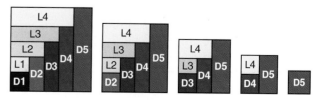

Diagram 14

Step 22. Continue adding strips in this manner until you have completed the required number of blocks for your chosen quilt size.

ASSEMBLING THE QUILT TOP

Step 1. Use a design wall or flat surface to arrange your blocks into a pleasing design. Use the photo on page 182, the **Twin-Size Quilt Diagram**, or your own shaded drawing as a guide to block placement. The quilt diagram illustrates the layout of the twin-size quilt, which consists of 11 rows with 8 blocks in each row. Except for the number of blocks, the layout for the other two sizes is the same. The crib quilt is arranged in 6 rows with 4 blocks in each row, and the queen-size quilt consists of 12 rows with 10 blocks in each row.

Step 2. When you are satisfied with the layout, sew the blocks into rows, as shown by the dark horizontal lines in the **Twin-Size Quilt Diagram**, pressing the seam allowances in opposite directions from row to row.

Step 3. Sew the rows together, carefully matching seams where blocks meet. If you've pressed the seam allowances in opposite directions, the seams should fit tightly against each other, helping you achieve a perfect match. Press the seams where rows were joined.

MAKING THE PIECED BORDER

Step 1. Cut the 3⅜-inch light fabric squares in half diagonally, as shown in **Diagram 15A**, producing two triangles per square. Cut the 6¼-inch light fabric squares diagonally both ways, as shown in **15B**, producing four triangles per square. Keep the resulting triangles in separate stacks to avoid confusion.

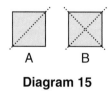

Diagram 15

Step 2. Sew a small triangle (from a 3⅜-inch square) to two sides of a 4-inch dark square, as shown in **Diagram 16A**. Press the seams toward the dark square. Add a large triangle (from a 6¼-inch square) to the unit, as shown in **16B**. Press. Make a total of eight of these units and set them aside for now; they will form the ends of the borders.

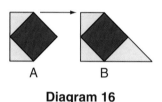

A   B

Diagram 16

Step 3. Sew a large triangle from a 6¼-inch square to two sides of the remaining 4-inch dark squares, as shown in **Diagram 17**. Press the seams toward the dark squares.

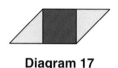

Diagram 17

Step 4. To assemble the side borders, sew the Step 3 units together, as shown in **Diagram 18**. Continue adding units until the strip reaches the required length. For the crib quilt, join 8 units; for the twin-size quilt, sew together 15 units; for the queen-size quilt, join 17 units. Repeat, making a second strip containing the same number of units.

Diagram 18

Step 5. Referring to **Diagram 19**, sew a Step 2 unit to each end of each side border strip. The side borders are now complete.

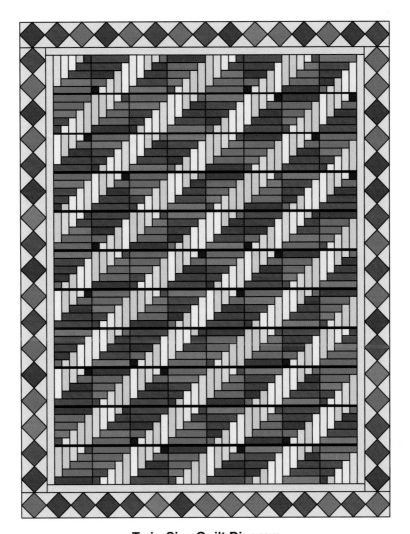

Twin-Size Quilt Diagram

Diagram 19

Step 6. To make the top and bottom borders, sew Step 3 units together as described previously. For the crib quilt, join 7 units for each strip; for the twin-size quilt, join 13 units for each; for the queen-size quilt, sew together 16 units for each strip.

Step 7. Sew a Step 2 unit to each end of each border strip to complete the top and bottom borders.

ADDING THE BORDERS

The procedure for adding the borders to the quilt is the same regardless of which quilt size you've chosen to make. However, the narrow inner border is prepared differently for each of the three sizes.

Step 1. For the crib quilt, cut one 2¾-inch-wide border strip in half crosswise, and sew one half each to two of the remaining strips. You will have two long borders and two shorter borders. For the twin-size quilt, sew the 2-inch-wide border strips together in pairs, making four long borders of equal length. For the queen-size quilt, sew the 2¾-inch-wide border strips together in pairs, then divide the remaining strip in half crosswise and sew one half each to two of the long strips.

Step 2. Measure the quilt from top to bottom, taking the measurement through the vertical center of the quilt, not at the sides. Cut the two longest border strips to this length.

Step 3. Fold one strip in half crosswise and crease. Unfold it and position it right side down along one side of the quilt top, with the crease at the horizontal midpoint. Pin at the midpoint and ends first, then along the length of the entire side, easing in fullness if necessary. Sew the border to the quilt using a ¼-inch seam allowance. Press the seam allowance toward the border. Repeat on the opposite side.

Step 4. Measure the width of the quilt, taking the measurement through the horizontal center of the quilt and including the side borders. Cut the remaining two border strips to this length.

Step 5. In the same manner as for the side borders, position and pin a strip along one end of the quilt top, easing in fullness if necessary. Stitch, using a ¼-inch seam allowance. Press the seam toward the border. Repeat on the opposite end.

Step 6. Determine the midpoint of the side pieced borders, pin in position, and stitch them to the quilt.

Step 7. Determine the midpoint of the top and bottom pieced borders, and add them to the quilt in the same manner. The completed quilt top should look like the one shown in the **Twin-Size Quilt Diagram.**

QUILTING AND FINISHING

Step 1. Mark the quilt top for quilting. The quilt shown in the photo was machine quilted in an allover meandering pattern.

Step 2. Regardless of which quilt size you've chosen to make, the backing will have to be pieced. To make the most efficient use of yardage, piece the back for the crib and queen-size quilts

with the seams running horizontally across the quilt. For the twin-size quilt, piece the back with the seams running vertically. **Diagram 20** illustrates the three quilt backs. Begin by trimming the selvages and dividing the yardage into equal pieces. For the crib and twin sizes, you need two equal pieces. For the queen size, divide the yardage into three equal pieces.

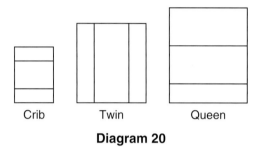

Diagram 20

Step 3. For the crib quilt, divide one of the backing pieces in half lengthwise, and sew one narrow piece to each side of the full-width piece. Press the seams open. Layer the backing, batting, and quilt top, making sure the seams of the backing run horizontally across the quilt.

Step 4. For the twin-size quilt, divide one of the pieces in half lengthwise, and sew one narrow piece to each side of the full-width piece. Press the seams open. Layer the backing, batting, and quilt top.

Step 5. The queen-size backing should be at least 96 × 111 inches. Sew two full-width pieces together and measure their width. Subtract that figure from 111 inches to determine the width you need to cut from the third strip. Cut the strip and sew it to the joined section. Press the seams open. Layer the backing, batting, and quilt top, making sure the seams of the backing run horizontally across the quilt.

Step 6. Baste the layers together. Quilt as desired.

Step 7. Referring to the directions on page 244 in "Quiltmaking Basics," make and attach double-fold binding. To calculate the amount of binding needed for which quilt size you are making, add up the length of the four sides of the quilt and add 9 inches. The total is the approximate number of inches of binding you will need.

SCRAP HALF LOG CABIN

Color Plan

Photocopy this page and use it to experiment with color schemes for your quilt.

JOB'S TEARS

Skill Level: *Intermediate*

Quiltmakers and teachers Susan Aylsworth Bushnell and Suzzy Chalfant Payne made this Job's Tears quilt when they were researching quilt patterns with a biblical reference for their book Creative American Quilting Inspired by the Bible. While the pattern is not technically a Double Wedding Ring, it is closely related. This quilt pattern is also known by other names, among them Slave Chain, Texas Tears, and Rocky Road to Kansas. Job's Tears requires sewing curves and setting in seams as do most of the other quilts in this book. However, you may find it a bit easier to construct since you can use standard straight line assembly, rather than continuing with more curved sewing, once the blocks are made.

BEFORE YOU BEGIN

Each 16-inch Job's Tears block is composed of four 8-inch quarter blocks. Each of these quarter blocks is assembled in the same way. Then four quarter- blocks are positioned to form a complete block, as shown in the **Block Diagram** on page 194.

You will need to make templates from pattern pieces A, B, C, D, E, F, and G on pages 198–201. For information on making and using templates, see page 224.

CHOOSING FABRICS

The C pentagons are all from the same small-scale dark blue print. Since four pentagons meet to form links for the rings, their uniformity ties the rings together. Select the fabric for these pieces carefully, since the octagon formed when the C pieces are joined together is fairly large. You want

a fabric that won't overpower your quilt or fade into the background.

The curved A strips are cut from assorted medium- to

dark-value prints of varying colors. The yardage requirement for these strips is estimated. For a scrappy quilt such as this, you will likely begin with

Quilt Sizes		
	Double (shown)	King
Finished Quilt Size	82½" × 98½"	114½" × 114½"
Finished Block Size	16"	16"
Number of Blocks	20	36

Materials		
Fabric	Double	King
Muslin	7¾ yards	12¾ yards
Dark blue print	¾ yard	1½ yards
Assorted prints	3½ yards	5¾ yards
Blue print	¾ yard	1⅛ yards
Rose print	½ yard	⅝ yard
Backing	7¾ yards	10 yards
Batting	90" × 106"	120" × 120"
Binding	¾ yard	1 yard

NOTE: *Yardages are based on 44/45-inch-wide fabrics that are at least 42 inches wide after preshrinking.*

Cutting Chart

Fabric	Used For	Piece	Number of Pieces	
			Double	King
Muslin	Melons	B	80	144
	Background crescents	D	160	288
	Middle border	5" strips	7	10
Dark blue print	Pentagons	C	160	288
Assorted prints	Curved strips	A	160	288
	Center fan blades	E	4	4
	Inner fan blades	F	4	4
	Inner fan blades	F reverse	4	4
	Outer fan blades	G	4	4
	Outer fan blades	G reverse	4	4
Blue print	Outer border	3½" strips	7	10
Rose print	Inner border	2" strips	7	10

more actual yardage but have leftover pieces for your next scrap project. The fan blades in the corners are assembled from the same assortment of prints used in the curved strips.

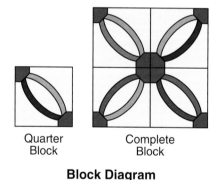

Quarter
Block

Complete
Block

Block Diagram

CUTTING

All measurements include ¼-inch seam allowances. Referring to the Cutting Chart, cut the required number of pieces for your quilt size.

Note: Cut and piece one sample block before cutting all of the fabric for the quilt.

PIECING THE BLOCKS

Step 1. With right sides together, pin a curved A strip to a B melon, matching centers. Sew the pieces together with the curved strip on top, as shown in **Diagram 1**. Ease the strip's edge to fit the melon. Press the seam toward the strip.

Step 2. In the same manner, sew a curved strip to the opposite side of the melon, as shown in **Diagram 2**, and press the seam toward the strip.

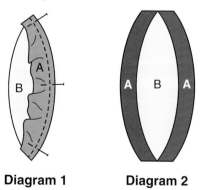

Diagram 1   **Diagram 2**

Step 3. With right sides together, align a C pentagon with one end of a melon unit, matching the straight edges. The point of the melon unit will extend slightly beyond the aligned edge. With the melon unit on top, sew the pieces together, beginning and ending your seam ¼ inch from either side of the melon unit's outer edges. Your seam should cross the intersection where the curved pieces were sewn to the melon, as shown in **Diagram 3A.** Repeat on the opposite end of the melon. Press the seams toward the pentagons to complete the melon/pentagon unit, as shown in **3B.**

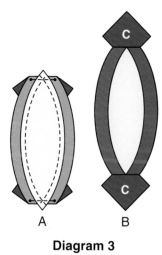

Diagram 3

Step 4. To attach a D crescent piece to the melon/pentagon unit, match a short side of the pentagon to the narrow end of a crescent and pin the pieces. Referring to **Diagram 4,** set in seam 1. Begin stitching ¼ inch from the inside corner and stitch to the end of the pieces, as indicated by the directional arrow. For details on setting in seams, see page 227.

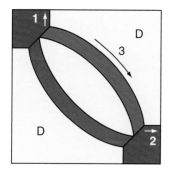

Diagram 4

Step 5. Match the pentagon at the opposite end of the melon unit with the opposite narrow end of

the crescent, as shown, and pin the seams together. Sew seam 2 following the direction of the arrow, beginning the seam ¼ inch from the inside corner of the pentagon.

Step 6. With the crescent piece on top, sew the crescent to the melon unit along the curved strip, easing in seam 3 to fit. Sew in the direction of the arrow, starting and stopping stitching ¼ inch from each end of the crescent.

Step 7. Add a second D crescent to the opposite side of the melon unit in the same manner, completing a quarter block. Press all seams.

Step 8. Repeat Steps 1 through 7 to make three more quarter blocks. Lay out four quarter blocks, as shown in the **Block Diagram,** and sew them together, matching pentagon seams carefully.

Step 9. Repeat, making the number of complete blocks required for your quilt size.

ASSEMBLING THE QUILT TOP

Step 1. Using a design wall or other flat surface, lay out the blocks in rows, as shown in the **Double-Size Assembly Diagram** on page 196, until you are pleased with the color arrangement. As shown, the double size has five vertical rows of four blocks each. For the king-size quilt, you will have six vertical rows of six blocks each. Press seams in adjoining rows in opposite directions.

Step 2. Sew the rows together, matching seams carefully. Press all seams.

ATTACHING THE BORDERS

Three borders are used in this quilt, with a large pieced fan radiating outward from each corner.

Step 1. Sew an F and F reverse piece to either side of the E center piece, as shown in **Diagram 5** on page 26. Then sew a G piece to the F piece and a G reverse piece to the F reverse piece, as shown. Press all seams in one direction. Repeat, making three more fan units.

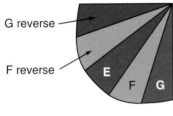

Diagram 5

Step 2. The border strips for each side of the quilt are sewn together, then added to the quilt as a single unit. To make the top and bottom borders, measure the width of the quilt top, taking the measurement through the horizontal center of the quilt rather than along the edge. Piece the rose border strips end to end, then from the long border strip, cut two strips to the measured length. Repeat with the muslin and blue strips.

— Sew Easy —

If you find that there is a lot of bulk at the point where all of the fan pieces intersect, trim the seam allowances a bit to reduce the amount of fabric.

Step 3. Pin and sew an outer blue border strip to a muslin border strip. Pin and sew a rose inner border strip to the opposite side of the muslin strip, referring to **Diagram 6**. Press the seams toward the dark borders. Repeat with remaining three strips to make the border for the other end of the quilt.

Diagram 6

Step 4. To make the side borders, measure the length of the quilt top, taking the measurement through the vertical center of the quilt rather than

Double-Size Assembly Diagram

along the sides. Piece like-color strips together to achieve two strips of the necessary length as you did for the top and bottom borders.

Step 5. Sew the strips together into two border units as you did with top and bottom borders. See **Diagram 6**.

Step 6. Sew a completed fan to each end of the side borders, as shown in **Diagram 7**.

Diagram 7

Step 7. Fold the completed top border in half crosswise and crease. Unfold it and position it right side down along the top edge of the quilt, with the crease at the vertical midpoint. Pin at the midpoint and ends first, then along the length of

Double-Size Quilt Diagram

the entire end, easing in fullness if necessary. Sew the border to the quilt top using a ¼-inch seam allowance. Press the seam toward the border. Repeat on the opposite end of the quilt.

Step 8. Fold a completed side border unit in half crosswise and crease. Unfold it and position it right side down along one side of the quilt, with the crease at the horizontal midpoint. Pin at the midpoint and ends first, then along the length of the entire side, easing in fullness if necessary and matching seams where the fan edge meets the inner rose border at the top and bottom of the quilt. Sew the border to the quilt using a ¼-inch seam allowance. Press the seam toward the border.

Repeat on the opposite side of the quilt. See the **Double-Size Quilt Diagram.**

QUILTING AND FINISHING

Step 1. Mark the quilt top for quilting. The quilt shown has a combination of cross-hatching and outline quilting. Teardrops were quilted in the borders and the muslin crescents.

Step 2. Regardless of which quilt size you've chosen to make, the backing will have to be pieced. To make the backing for the double-size quilt, cut the backing fabric crosswise into three

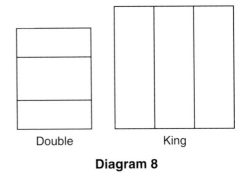

Double   King

Diagram 8

Sew Easy

To quickly and easily mark quilting lines, try a hera. Sold in most quilt shops, this plastic tool fits in the palm of your hand. By pressing the curved edge along the fabric, you create an indentation in the fabric that serves as a quilting guide. Once you're done stitching, there are no lines to erase!

equal lengths, and trim the selvages. Cut a 33-inch-wide panel from two of the pieces, then sew one of these to each side of the full-width piece, as shown in **Diagram 8.** For the king-size quilt, cut the backing fabric crosswise into three equal lengths, and trim the selvages. Sew the three panels together lengthwise, as shown. Press the seams open.

Step 3. Layer the backing, batting, and quilt top, and baste. Quilt as desired.

Step 4. Make and attach double-fold binding, referring to the directions on page 244 in "Quiltmaking Basics" for more information. To calculate the amount of binding needed for your quilt size, add the length of the four sides of the quilt plus 9 inches. The total is the approximate number of inches of binding you will need.

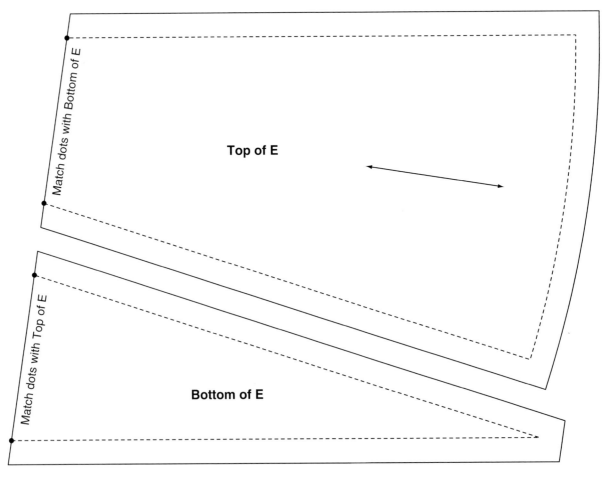

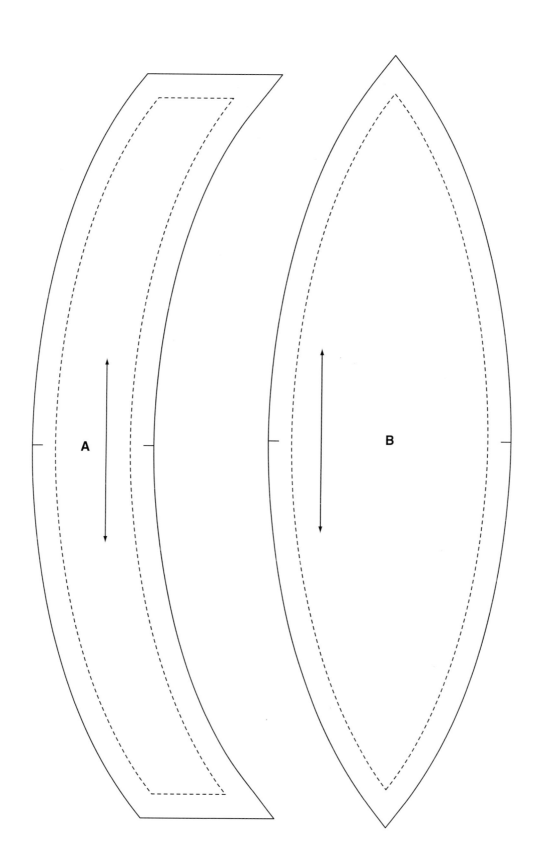

A

B

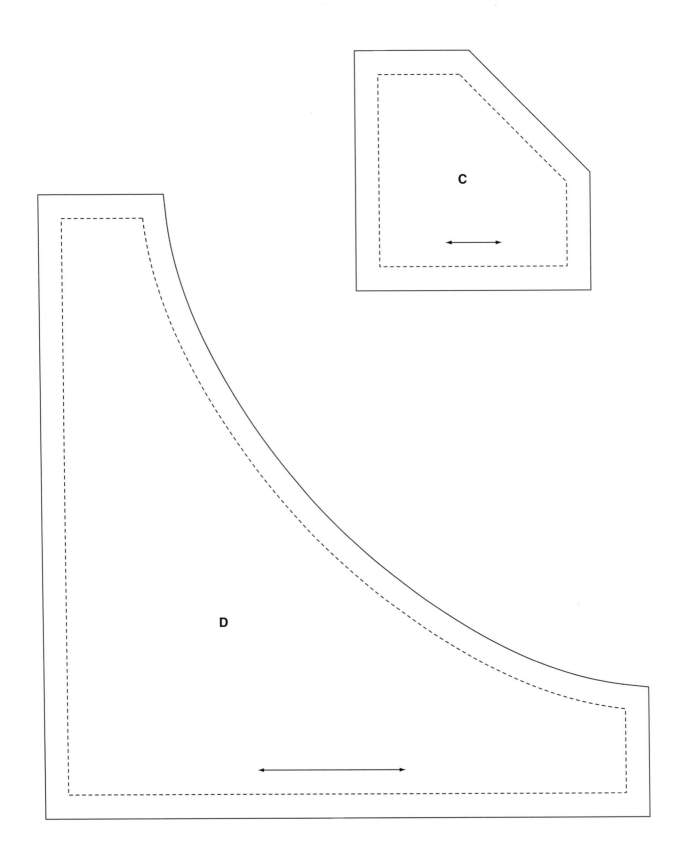

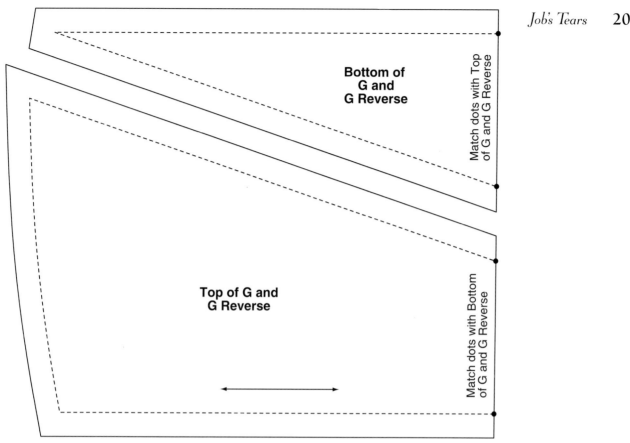

Bottom of
G and
G Reverse

Match dots with Top
of G and G Reverse

Top of G and
G Reverse

Match dots with Bottom
of G and G Reverse

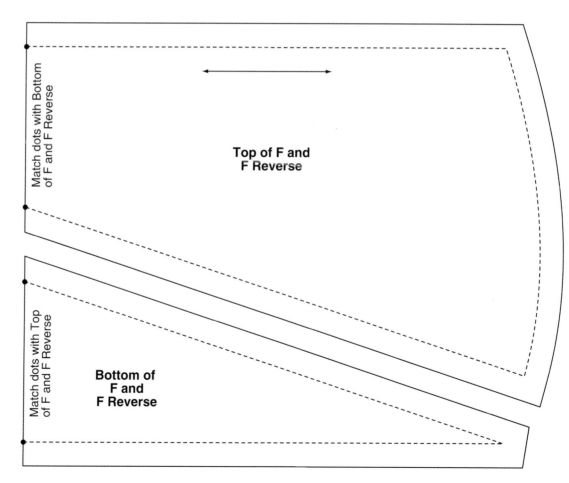

Match dots with Bottom
of F and F Reverse

Top of F and
F Reverse

Match dots with Top
of F and F Reverse

Bottom of
F and
F Reverse

SUNSHINE AND SHADOW

Skill Level: *Easy*

The classic setting of this quilt, made by Bettina Havig as a gift to Joyce Gross, emphasizes the half-light, half-dark division of the Log Cabin blocks. In this version, 3½-inch blocks make a simple crib quilt. As with many Log Cabin settings, the size of the quilt can be varied by changing the block size or the number of blocks.

BEFORE YOU BEGIN

The directions for this quilt are written based on using the foundation technique, which makes it easier to work with the small pieces in the wallhanging and crib quilt. The larger pieces in the twin-size quilt make it possible to use either the foundation method or the chain-piecing technique. Read the general construction directions in "Piecing a Block," beginning on page 235, to become familiar with the foundation technique. Prepare a foundation for each block using one of the patterns on pages 209–210. The 7-inch block pattern has been reduced; enlarge it 150 percent before tracing. If you prefer to use the chain-piecing technique, see page 225 for details.

CHOOSING FABRICS

In the quilt shown, red center squares and a red border are a perfect complement to the predominantly blue scrap fabrics, creating a warm, homespun feeling. But the fabric colors used in this scrappy quilt are not as important as their value, the term indicating how light or dark a color is. Select a group of light fabrics with the same basic value and a group of dark fabrics with the same basic value.

To help develop your own unique color scheme for the quilt, make several photocopies of the **Color Plan** on page 211, and use crayons, colored pencils, or markers to experiment with different color arrangements.

Light and dark yardages given are generous estimates of the total yardage actually used in the quilt. Since small amounts of many fabrics are a key ingredient for a successful scrap quilt, you will likely begin with more yardage than indicated but not use all of it.

Quilt Sizes

	Wallhanging	Crib (shown)	Twin
Finished Quilt Size	30½" × 30½"	37½" × 44½"	65½" × 79½"
Finished Block Size	3½"	3½"	7"
Number of Blocks	36	80	80

Materials

Fabric	Wallhanging	Crib	Twin
Dark prints	¾ yard	1⅜ yards	3¼ yards
Light prints	¾ yard	1¼ yards	2½ yards
Dark brown print	⅝ yard	¾ yard	1 yard
Red	⅜ yard	½ yard	¾ yard
Backing	1¼ yards	1½ yards	5 yards
Batting (optional)	36" × 36"	43" × 50"	71" × 85"
Binding	⅜ yard	½ yard	¾ yard
Foundation material	½ yard	⅞ yard	3¾ yards

NOTE: *Yardages are based on 44/45-inch-wide fabrics that are at least 42 inches wide after preshrinking.*

Cutting Chart

Fabric	Piece	Wallhanging		Crib		Twin	
		Strip Width	Number of Strips	Strip Width	Number of Strips	Strip Width	Number of Strips
Dark prints	Logs	1¼"	15	1¼"	33	1¾"	60
Light prints	Logs	1¼"	12	1¼"	26	1¾"	46
Dark brown print	Outer border	4"	4	4"	5	4"	8
Red	1 (center)	1"	1	1"	2	1½"	3
	Inner border	1¾"	4	1¾"	5	1¾"	8

CUTTING

Referring to the Cutting Chart, cut the number of strips needed. Cut all strips across the fabric width (crosswise grain). **Note:** Cut and sew one sample block before cutting all the pieces for the quilt.

Measurements for the borders include ¼-inch seam allowances. The cut sizes listed for the logs are slightly wider than the finished log size plus ¼-inch seam allowances. With the foundation method, it's easier to work with slightly wider strips. You may wish to decrease the width in ⅛-inch increments as you become more familiar with the technique, but don't cut pieces less than 1 inch wide for the wallhanging and crib quilt or less than 1½ inches wide for the twin quilt.

The number of dark and light strips needed for logs is estimated based on using full-width yardage. If you are using scraps, the number of strips needed will vary.

MAKING THE FOUNDATIONS

Step 1. Make a template by tracing one of the block patterns on pages 209–210.

Step 2. Following the instructions on page 234, transfer the pattern to your chosen foundation material. Make sure the marked lines are visible from the back side when you hold the foundation up to the light. Use the **Block Diagram** as a color guide and a reference for piecing order. Cut out the foundations, leaving a bit of extra material on all sides.

Sew Easy

If you have chosen to use the chain-piecing method without a foundation, you'll need to cut the logs to length before sewing them. Refer to the chart below to cut the strips into logs.

Even if you are using the foundation method, this list is useful as a guideline to determine whether a particular scrap of fabric is large enough. With the foundation method, of course, it is not necessary to precut the fabric to these sizes.

Log Number	Log Size	
	Wallhanging and Crib	Twin
1, 2	1" × 1"	1½" × 1½"
3, 4	1" × 1½"	1½" × 2½"
5, 6	1" × 2"	1½" × 3½"
7, 8	1" × 2½"	1½" × 4½"
9, 10	1" × 3"	1½" × 5½"
11, 12	1" × 3½"	1½" × 6½"
13	1" × 4"	1½" × 7½"

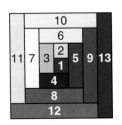

Block Diagram

PIECING THE BLOCKS

Make a sample block before cutting fabric for the entire quilt. If you experience problems while assembling the block, increase the strip width. Using strips that are slightly wider than necessary can be a real time-saver since not as much precision is needed when positioning them for sewing. Reevaluate your work often. You may find that strip width can be decreased again once you are more familiar with the method.

Step 1. Cut the centers of the blocks from the red strips. For the wallhanging and crib quilt, cut the 1-inch strips into 1-inch squares. For the twin-size quilt, cut the 1½-inch strips into 1½-inch squares.

Step 2. Place a red center square right side up on the back side of a foundation, covering the area of piece 1, as shown in **Diagram 1.** Secure with tape, a bit of glue stick, or a pin.

Hold the foundation up to the light with the back side away from you. You should be able to see a shadow of the center square through the foundation. Check to make sure it extends past all lines surrounding piece 1. If it doesn't, reposition the square and check again.

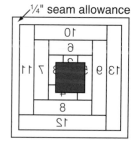

Reverse side of foundation

Diagram 1

Step 3. Select a light fabric for log 2. Place the strip right side down on top of the center square, aligning the top and left edges, as shown in **Diagram 2A.** (The strip will completely cover the red square.) Holding the fabric in position, flip the foundation to its front side and sew on the line separating pieces 1 and 2, as shown in **2B.** Begin and end the line of stitches approximately ⅛ inch on either side of the line.

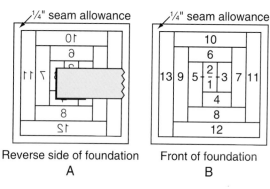

Sew Easy

Your first piece of fabric is always positioned right side up. All remaining pieces are positioned right side down for sewing.

Reverse side of foundation
A

Front of foundation
B

Diagram 2

Step 4. Remove the foundation from the machine and flip it over to the back side. If you used tape to secure the center square, remove it now. Cut away the excess tail of fabric (cut just past the end of stitches, as shown in **Diagram 3A**). Trim the seam allowance if necessary to reduce bulk. Flip piece 2 into a right-side-up position, finger pressing it into place. See **3B.** Hold the foundation up to the light with the back side away from you. Check to make sure the shadow of piece 2 overlaps all unsewn lines around its perimeter.

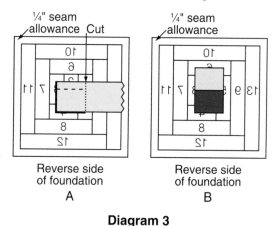

Reverse side of foundation
A

Reverse side of foundation
B

Diagram 3

Step 5. Select a light fabric for log 3, and position it right side down on log 2, as shown in

Diagram 4A. Holding the strip in place, flip the foundation over and sew on the line separating pieces 1 and 2 from 3, again beginning and ending approximately ⅛ inch on either side of the line. Remove from the machine, trim the tail, and flip piece 3 into a right-side-up position, finger pressing it into place, as shown in **4B.** If necessary, trim excess bulk from the seam allowances.

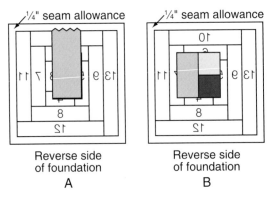

Diagram 4

The front of your foundation should now look like **Diagram 5.** Notice that the seam lines intersect each other. This crisscrossing of lines will continue, helping to stabilize your seams.

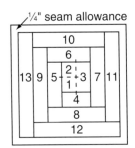

Diagram 5

Step 6. Continue to add pieces in numerical order, trimming seams to reduce bulk and finger pressing each piece open as you work. When adding pieces 10 through 13, make sure their edges will extend past the perimeter of the marked seam allowance when flipped right side up after sewing. After the last piece is sewn, press the block with a warm iron. Cut on the outermost line of the foundation.

Step 7. Repeat Steps 2 through 6, making the required number of blocks for your chosen quilt size.

ASSEMBLING THE QUILT TOP

Step 1. Use a design wall or flat surface to arrange your blocks into a pleasing design. Use the photo on page 202, one of the quilt diagrams (shown on the opposite page and page 208), or your own color drawing as a guide to block placement.

Step 2. When you are satisfied with the layout, sew the blocks into four-block units. First sew the blocks together in pairs, as shown in **Diagram 6,** pressing the seams in opposite directions. If you are using removable foundations, tear away the portion surrounding the seam allowances where blocks are joined.

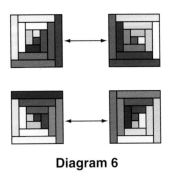

Diagram 6

Note: Permanent foundations create additional bulk in the seam allowance. If seams are too bulky to press to one side, it may be necessary to press them open. Be sure to match and pin pressed-open seams carefully when rows are joined.

Step 3. Referring to **Diagram 7,** sew the pairs together into a four-block unit.

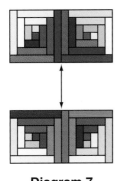

Diagram 7

Step 4. Repeat with the remaining blocks, making a total of 9 four-block units for the wallhanging or 20 four-block units for the crib and twin quilts. Be sure to place each sewn unit back into its proper position in your quilt layout.

Step 5. Sew the units into rows, as shown in **Diagram 8.** Make a total of three rows for the wallhanging or five rows for the crib and twin quilts.

Diagram 8

Step 6. Referring to the quilt diagrams on this page and page 208, sew the rows together, carefully matching seams. Tear away any remaining removable foundation material from the seam allowances.

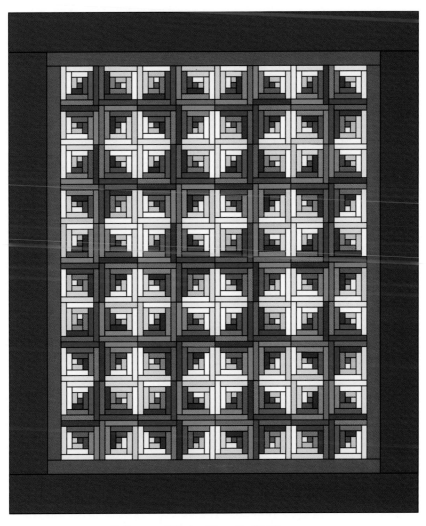

Crib- and Twin-Size Quilt Diagram

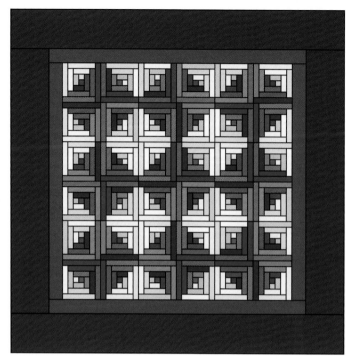

Wallhanging Diagram

ADDING THE BORDERS

The procedure for adding the borders is the same regardless of the quilt size you are making. For both the crib and twin quilts, however, you must first make long border strips.

Step 1. For the crib quilt, cut one of the red border strips in half, and sew one half each to two red border strips. You will have two long borders and two short borders. Repeat with the brown outer border strips. For the twin quilt, simply sew the border strips together in pairs. You will have four long red inner borders and four long dark brown outer borders.

Step 2. Measure the length of the quilt top, taking the measurement through the vertical center of the quilt rather than along the sides. Cut two 1¾-inch red border strips to the measured length.

Step 3. Fold one strip in half crosswise. Unfold it and position it right side down along one side of the quilt top, with the crease at the horizontal midpoint. Pin at the midpoint and ends first, then along the length of the entire side, easing in full-

ness if necessary. Sew the border to the quilt top using a ¼-inch seam allowance. Press the seam allowance toward the border. Repeat on the opposite side.

Step 4. Measure the width of the quilt, taking the measurement through the horizontal center of the quilt rather than along the edge. Cut the remaining two red border strips to this length.

Step 5. In the same manner as for the side borders, position and pin a strip along one end of the quilt top, easing in fullness if necessary. Stitch, using a ¼-inch seam allowance, and press the seam toward the border. Repeat on the opposite end of the quilt top.

Step 6. In the same manner as for the inner borders, add the dark brown outer border strips to the four sides of the quilt top.

QUILTING AND FINISHING

Step 1. Mark the quilt top for quilting. A fan design, sometimes called Baptist Fan, was used in the borders of this quilt. An X was quilted in the red center of each block. The logs were quilted lengthwise down the center, with lines intersecting and turning at the edges to create a series of squares.

Step 2. If you are making the twin-size quilt, you will have to piece the backing. Divide the 5-yard piece of fabric in half crosswise and trim the selvages. Cut one of the pieces in half lengthwise, and sew one half to each side of the full-width piece. Press the seams open.

Step 3. Layer the top, batting (if used), and backing. Baste the layers together.

Step 4. Quilt as desired.

Step 5. Referring to the directions on page 244 in "Quiltmaking Basics," make and attach double-fold binding. To calculate the amount of binding needed for the quilt size you are making, add up the length of the four sides of the quilt and add 9 inches. The total is the approximate number of inches of binding you will need.

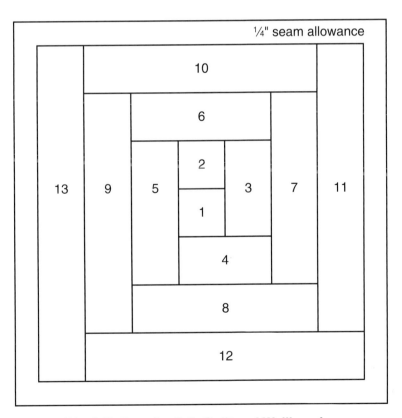

Block Pattern for Crib Quilt and Wallhanging

Pattern shown is the mirror image of the finished block.

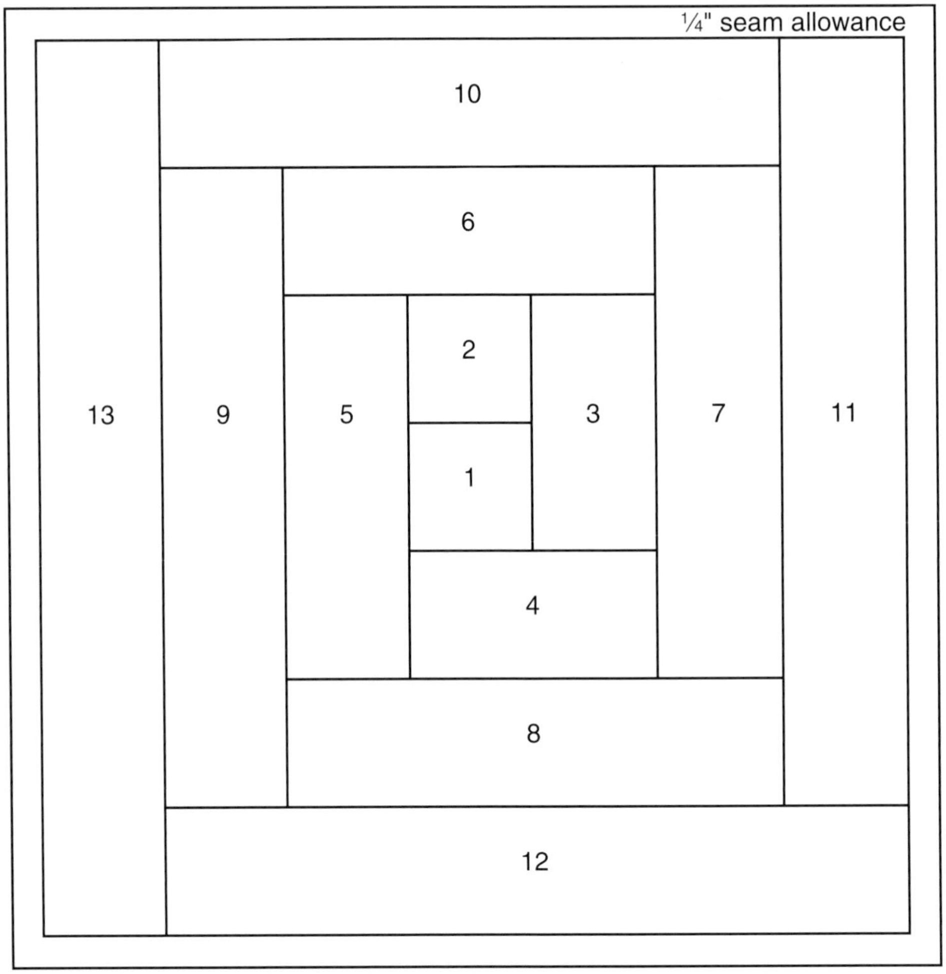

¼" seam allowance

10

6

2

13   9   5   3   7   11

1

4

8

12

Block Pattern for Twin Quilt

Pattern shown is the mirror image of the finished block.
Note: Pattern is reduced. Enlarge it 150 percent before tracing.

SUNSHINE AND SHADOW

Color Plan

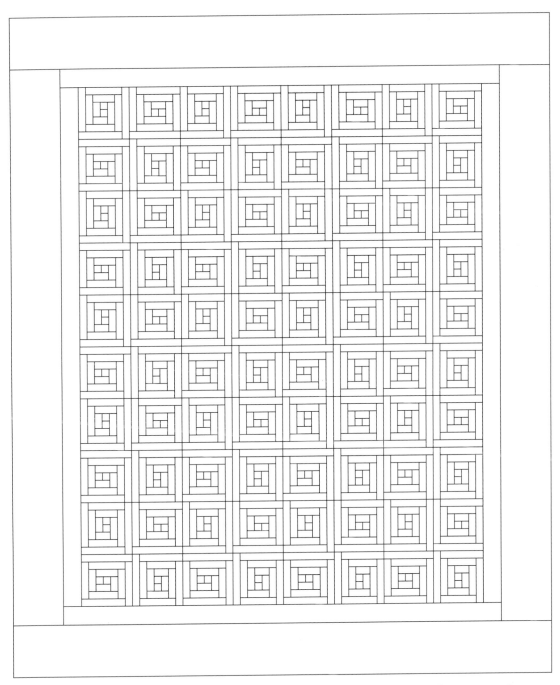

Photocopy this page and use it to experiment with color schemes for your quilt.

DOTS AND DASHES

Skill Level: *Intermediate*

The basic Nine-Patch block teams up with a traditional Rail-Fence block in this vibrant lap-size quilt. An assortment of red fabrics works together to unify the scraps and create terrific energy in this quilt by Sharyn Craig of El Cajon, California. The border is easy to piece using extra Rail-Fence blocks.

BEFORE YOU BEGIN

The directions for this quilt are written based on using an easy strip-piecing technique for making the Nine-Patch blocks. Strips of fabric are sewn together into strip sets. The strip sets are then cut apart and resewn into blocks. The Rail-Fence blocks are even easier to construct: Simply sew strips into sets, then cut the strip sets apart. No further sewing is necessary. Read through the general construction directions beginning on page 143, for further details on strip piecing.

The outer pieced border is simply Rail-Fence blocks sewn together into long strips.

CHOOSING FABRICS

The Nine-Patch blocks in this quilt appear to be totally scrappy, but they are actually all made from the same strip sets. Flipping the segments within the blocks or turning the completed blocks in different directions adds to the illusion that many different fabrics were used. Choose four different red prints and five different light solids or prints to make these strip sets. The inner border is pieced from these same four reds, plus one or two more for variety.

The Rail-Fence blocks also are not as totally scrappy as they seem. Most of the fabric combinations appear at least four or five times and are used in both the inner quilt and the outer border. For best results, combine a wide variety of prints and solids in different values to get the total yardage required. Using full-width yardage will make construction faster and easier.

To help develop your own unique color scheme for the quilt, photocopy the **Color Plan** on page 219, and use crayons or colored pencils to experiment with different color combinations.

Quilt Sizes

	Lap (shown)	Queen
Finished Quilt Size	50¼" × 63"	83¾" × 105"
Finished Block Size	4½"	7½"
Number of Blocks		
Nine Patch	18	18
Rail Fence	96	96

Materials

Fabric	Lap	Queen
Assorted darks	1½ yards	3⅝ yards
Assorted lights	1⅛ yards	2¾ yards
Cream	1¼ yards	2 yards
Red prints	¾ yard	2 yards
Backing	3½ yards	8 yards
Batting	56" × 69"	90" × 111"
Binding	½ yard	¾ yard

NOTE: Yardages are based on 44/45-inch-wide fabrics that are at least 42 inches wide after preshrinking.

Cutting Chart

Fabric	Used For	Lap		Queen	
		Strip Width	Number of Strips	Strip Width	Number of Strips
Assorted darks	Strip sets	2"	24	3"	40
Assorted lights	Strip sets	2"	17	3"	30
Cream	Setting squares	5"	3	8"	4
	Side setting triangles	7⅝"	2	11⅞"	2
	Corner setting triangles	4⅛"	1	6¼"	1
Red prints	Inner border	2"	5	3"	9
	Strip sets	2"	4	3"	8

CUTTING

All measurements include ¼-inch seam allowances. Referring to the Cutting Chart, cut the required number of strips in the width needed. Cut all strips across the fabric width (crosswise grain). The number of strips called for in the Cutting Chart assumes that you will be cutting full-width (at least 42-inch-wide) fabric. If you use fat quarters or scraps, the number of strips required will vary.

The side setting triangles and corner setting triangles are cut from squares. To make the side setting triangles, cut the 7⅝-inch-wide strips into 7⅝-inch squares (11⅞-inch strips and squares for the queen size). Cut each square diagonally both ways to get four triangles, as shown in **Diagram 1A.** To make the corner setting triangles, cut the 4⅛-inch-wide strip into 4⅛-inch squares (6¼-inch strips and squares for the queen size). Cut each square in half diagonally to get two triangles, as shown in **1B.** Cutting the triangles from squares in this way puts the straight grain of the fabric on the outside edge of the quilt, where it's needed for stability.

Note: Cut and piece one sample block before cutting all the fabric for the quilt.

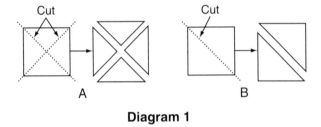

Diagram 1

PIECING THE BLOCKS

This quilt is made up of two different pieced blocks, as shown in the **Block Diagram.** Solid setting squares, side setting triangles, and corner setting triangles complete the inner quilt.

Both the Nine-Patch blocks and the Rail-Fence blocks are assembled using easy strip-piecing techniques. Additional Rail-Fence blocks are used to make the outer pieced border.

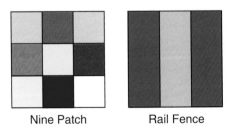

Nine Patch   Rail Fence

Block Diagram

Piecing the Nine-Patch Blocks

Each Nine-Patch block requires two different segment variations, as shown in **Diagram 2**. There are two A segments and one B segment in each block.

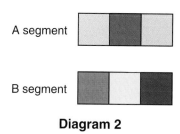

Diagram 2

Step 1. The blocks are assembled using a strip-piecing technique. Refer to the Cutting Chart to determine the total number of strips required to make the Nine-Patch blocks for your quilt. Be sure to cut strips in the correct width for the quilt size you are making. Cut the correct number of red and light strips from an assortment of fabrics.

Step 2. To make the A segments, use a ¼-inch seam to sew a light strip to each side of a red strip, as shown in **Diagram 3A**. Press the seams toward the red strip.

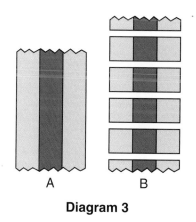

Diagram 3

Step 3. Using a rotary cutter and ruler, square up one end of the strip set. See page 223 in "Quiltmaking Basics" for complete details on rotary cutting. Cut segments from the strip set, as shown in **3B**. For the lap-size quilt, cut 2-inch-wide segments; for the queen-size quilt, cut

3-inch-wide segments. Continue making strip sets and cutting them into segments until you have assembled the required number of A segments needed for your quilt. You need two A segments for each Nine-Patch block in your quilt.

Step 4. To make the B segments, sew a different red print strip to each side of a light strip, as shown in **Diagram 4A**. Press the seams toward the red print strips.

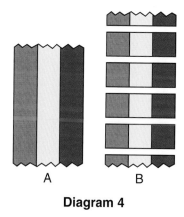

Diagram 4

Step 5. Using a rotary cutter and ruler, square up one end of the strip set. Cut segments from the strip set, as shown in **4B**. For the lap-size quilt, cut 2-inch-wide segments; for the queen-size quilt, cut 3-inch-wide segments. Continue making strip sets and cutting them into segments until you have assembled the required number of B segments needed for the quilt size you are making. You need one B segment for each Nine-Patch block in your quilt.

Step 6. Sew two A segments and one B segment together, as shown in **Diagram 5** on page 216, matching seams carefully. To keep the blocks as scrappy looking as possible, alter the fabric placement by flipping some segments end for end before joining them. Since the seam allowances on the segments are pressed in opposite directions, the intersections should fit together tightly. Stitch, using a ¼-inch seam allowance. Press. Repeat until you have assembled the required number of blocks for your quilt.

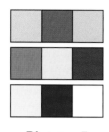

Diagram 5

Piecing the Rail-Fence Blocks

The scrappy Rail-Fence blocks can also be assembled by strip piecing. Each block is sewn from two dark strips and one light strip.

Step 1. Sew a different dark strip to each side of a light strip, as shown in **Diagram 6A**. Press the seams toward the dark strips.

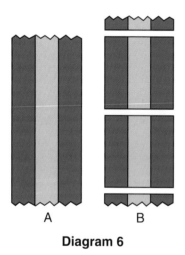

A   B

Diagram 6

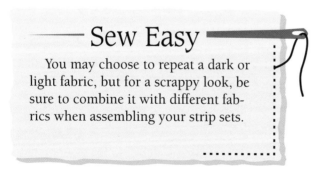

— Sew Easy —

You may choose to repeat a dark or light fabric, but for a scrappy look, be sure to combine it with different fabrics when assembling your strip sets.

Step 2. Using a rotary cutter and ruler, square up one end of the strip set. Cut segments from the strip set, as shown in **6B**. Cut 5-inch segments for the lap-size quilt and 8-inch segments for the queen-size quilt. Continue making strip sets and cutting them into segments until you have the required number of Rail-Fence blocks for your quilt.

Assembling the Quilt Top

Step 1. The blocks in this quilt are set on point. Use a design wall or flat surface to arrange blocks and side setting triangles in diagonal rows, as shown in the **Assembly Diagram.** The diagram illustrates the lap-size quilt. Except for the number of blocks, the layout for the queen-size quilt is the same.

Step 2. When you are satisfied with the layout, sew the blocks into rows. Press the seams in each row in the same direction. Press seams in adjoining rows in opposite directions. Sew the rows together, matching seams carefully. Press.

Step 3. Add the corner triangles. The triangles are slightly oversize and need to be trimmed after they are added. Press the seams toward the triangles, then use your rotary cutter to trim the triangles and square up the corners. Be sure to trim ¼ inch beyond the edge of the blocks, leaving the seam allowance intact.

Adding the Inner Border

Step 1. The inner border is pieced from the same red fabrics used for the blocks. You can use one fabric on all four sides of the quilt, use a different fabric on each side, or use several different fabrics on each side. Piece together red strips to make two long borders. Measure the length of the quilt top, taking the measurement through the vertical center of the quilt rather than along the sides. Trim strips to the exact measured length.

Step 2. Fold one strip in half crosswise and crease. Unfold it and position it right side down along one side of the quilt top, with the crease at the horizontal midpoint. Pin at the midpoint and ends first, then along the length of the entire side,

Assembly Diagram

easing in fullness if necessary. Sew the border to the quilt top using a ¼-inch seam allowance. Repeat on the opposite side of the quilt.

Step 3. Piece together red strips to make two long borders. Measure the width of the quilt top, taking the measurement through the horizontal center of the quilt and including the side borders. Trim the strips to the exact measured length.

Step 4. Fold one strip in half crosswise and crease. Unfold it and position it right side down along one end of the quilt top, matching the crease to the vertical midpoint. Pin at the midpoint and ends first, then across the entire width of the quilt top, easing in fullness if necessary. Stitch, using a ¼-inch seam allowance. Repeat on the opposite end of the quilt top.

ADDING THE OUTER BORDER

Step 1. The outer pieced border is made up of Rail-Fence blocks. Place the quilt top on a design

wall or other flat surface, then position the blocks for the pieced border around the quilt top. Move the blocks around until you are satisfied with the arrangement.

Note: In the quilt shown in the **Quilt Diagram** on page 218 and in the photo on page 212, the orientation is changed for two of the blocks in the border. This does not change the manner in which the borders are pieced and added; simply remember to turn one block at one end of the top and bottom borders.

Step 2. Measure the length of the quilt top in the same manner as for the inner border. Join Rail-Fence blocks until you have a side border strip of the required length. It may be necessary to add or remove individual strips to make the border fit. Press all the seams in the same direction. Repeat to make a second side border strip.

Step 3. Pin and sew a border to one side of your quilt as you did with the inner border, easing in fullness as necessary. Repeat on the opposite side of the quilt.

Step 4. Measure the width of the quilt top in the same manner as for the inner border. Sew Rail-Fence blocks together until you have obtained the measured length. If needed, add or remove individual strips to make the border fit. Press the seams in one direction. Repeat to make a second strip.

Step 5. In the same manner as for the inner border, pin and sew a pieced strip to one end of your quilt, easing in fullness as necessary. Repeat on the opposite end of the quilt.

QUILTING AND FINISHING

Step 1. Mark the top for quilting. The quilt shown has a 1-inch horizontal and vertical grid stitched in the inner quilt and a 2-inch diagonal grid stitched in the borders.

Step 2. Regardless of which quilt size you are making, the backing will have to be pieced. For both sizes, you'll make the most efficient use of the yardage by running the seams horizontally across the quilt. **Diagram 7** illustrates the two quilt backs. To make the backing for the lap-size quilt, cut the yardage in half crosswise, and trim the selvages. Cut one of the pieces in half lengthwise and sew one half to each side of the full-width piece. Press the seams open.

Step 3. To make the backing for the queen-size quilt, cut the backing fabric crosswise into three equal pieces, and trim the selvages. Sew the three pieces together along the long sides and press the seams open.

Step 4. Layer the quilt top, batting, and backing; baste the layers together. Quilt as desired.

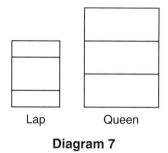

Lap   Queen

Diagram 7

Step 5. Referring to the directions on page 244 in "Quiltmaking Basics," make and attach double-fold binding. To calculate the amount of binding needed for the quilt size you are making, add up the length of the four sides of the quilt and add 9 inches. The total is the approximate number of inches of binding you will need.

Quilt Diagram

DOTS AND DASHES

Color Plan

Photocopy this page and use it to experiment with color schemes for your quilt.

Quiltmaking Basics

This section provides a refresher course in basic quiltmaking techniques. Refer to it as needed; it will help not only with the projects in this book but also with all your quiltmaking.

Quiltmaker's Basic Supply List

Here's a list of items you should have on hand before beginning a project.

• **Iron and ironing board:** Make sure these are set up near your sewing machine. Careful pressing leads to accurate piecing.

• **Needles:** The two types of needles commonly used by quilters are *betweens,* short needles used for hand quilting, and *sharps,* long, very thin needles used for appliqué and hand piecing. The thickness of hand-sewing needles decreases as their size designation increases. For instance, a size 12 needle is smaller than a size 10.

• **Rotary cutter, plastic ruler, and cutting mat:** Fabric can be cut quickly and accurately with rotary-cutting equipment. There are a variety of cutters available, all with slightly different handle styles and safety latches. Rigid, see-through acrylic rulers are used with rotary cutters. A 6 × 24-inch ruler is a good size; for the most versatility, be sure it has 45- and 60-degree angle markings. A 14-inch square ruler will also be helpful for making sure blocks are square. Always use a special mat with a rotary cutter. The mat protects the work surface and helps to grip the fabric. Purchase the largest mat practical for your sewing area. A good all-purpose size is 18 × 24 inches.

• **Safety pins:** These are generally used to baste quilts for machine quilting. Use rustproof nickel-plated brass safety pins, preferably in size #0.

• **Scissors:** You'll need several pairs of scissors—shears for cutting fabric, general scissors for cutting paper and template plastic, and small, sharp embroidery scissors for trimming threads.

• **Seam ripper:** A seam ripper with a small, extra-fine blade slips easily under any stitch length.

• **Sewing machine:** Any machine with a straight stitch is suitable for piecing quilt blocks. Follow the manufacturer's recommendations for cleaning and servicing your sewing machine.

• **Straight pins:** Choose long, thin pins with glass or plastic heads that are easy to see against fabric so that you don't forget to remove one.

• **Template material:** Sheets of clear and opaque template plastic can be purchased at most quilt or craft shops. Gridded plastic is also available and may help you to draw shapes more easily. Various weights of cardboard can also be used for templates, including common household items like cereal boxes, posterboard, and manila file folders.

• **Thimbles:** For hand quilting, a thimble is almost essential. Look for one that fits the finger you use to push the needle. The thimble should be snug enough to stay put when you shake your hand. There should be a bit of space between the end of your finger and the inside of the thimble.

• **Thread:** For hand or machine piecing, 100 percent cotton thread is a traditional favorite. Cotton-covered polyester is also acceptable. For hand quilting, use 100 percent cotton quilting thread. For machine quilting, you may want to try clear nylon thread as the top thread, with cotton thread in the bobbin.

• **Tweezers:** Keep a pair of tweezers handy for removing bits of thread from ripped-out seams and for pulling away scraps of removable foundations. Regular cosmetic tweezers will work fine.

Selecting and Preparing Fabrics

The traditional fabric choice for quilts is 100 percent cotton. It handles well, is easy to care for, presses easily, and frays less than synthetic blends.

The yardages in this book are generous estimates based on 44/45-inch-wide fabrics. It's a good idea to always purchase a bit more fabric than necessary to compensate for shrinkage and occasional cutting errors.

Prewash your fabrics using warm water and a mild soap or detergent. Test for colorfastness by first soaking a scrap in warm water. If colors bleed, set the dye by soaking the whole piece of fabric in a solution of 3 parts cold water to 1 part vinegar. Rinse the fabric several times in warm water. If it still bleeds, don't use it in a quilt that will need laundering—save it for a wallhanging that won't get a lot of use.

After washing, preshrink your fabric by drying it in a dryer on the medium setting. To keep wrinkles under control, remove the fabric from the dryer while it's still slightly damp and press it immediately with a hot iron.

CUTTING FABRIC

The cutting instructions for each project follow the list of materials. Whenever possible, the instructions are written to take advantage of quick rotary-cutting techniques. In addition, some projects include patterns for those who prefer to make templates and scissor cut individual pieces.

Although rotary cutting can be faster and more accurate than cutting with scissors, it has one disadvantage: It does not always result in the most efficient use of fabric. In some cases, the method results in long strips of leftover fabric. Don't think of these as waste; just add them to your scrap bag for future projects.

Rotary-Cutting Basics

Follow these two safety rules every time you use a rotary cutter: Always cut *away* from yourself, and always slide the blade guard into place as soon as you stop cutting.

Step 1: You can cut several layers of fabric at a time with a rotary cutter. Fold the fabric with the selvage edges together. You can fold it again if you want, doubling the number of layers to be cut.

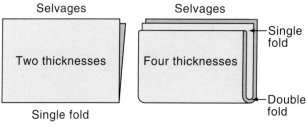

Diagram 1

Step 2: To square up the end of the fabric, place a ruled square on the fold and slide a 6 × 24-inch ruler against the side of the square. Hold the ruler in place, remove the square, and cut along the edge of the ruler. If you are left-handed, work from the other end of the fabric.

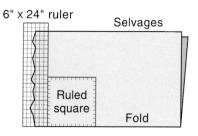

Diagram 2

Step 3: For patchwork, cut strips or rectangles on the crosswise grain, then subcut them into smaller pieces as needed. The diagram shows a strip cut into squares.

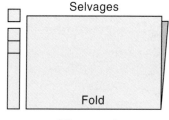

Diagram 3

Step 4: A square can be subcut into two triangles by making one diagonal cut (A). Two diagonal cuts yield four triangles (B).

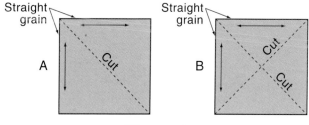

Diagram 4

Step 5: Check strips periodically to make sure they're straight and not angled. If they are angled, refold the fabric and square up the edges again.

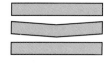

Diagram 5

ENLARGING PATTERNS

Every effort has been made to provide full-size pattern pieces. But in some cases, where the pattern piece is too large to fit on the page, only one-half or one-quarter of the pattern is given. Instructions on the pattern piece will tell you where to position the pattern to continue tracing to make a full-size template.

MAKING AND USING TEMPLATES

To make a plastic template, place template plastic over the book page, trace the pattern onto the plastic, and cut out the template. To make a cardboard template, copy the pattern onto tracing paper, glue the paper to the cardboard, and cut out the template. With a permanent marker, record on every template any identification letters and grain lines, as well as the size and name of the block and the number of pieces needed. Always check your templates against the printed pattern for accuracy.

The patchwork patterns in this book are printed with double lines. The inner dashed line is the finished size of the piece, while the outer solid line includes the seam allowance.

For hand piecing: Trace the inner line to make finished-size templates. Cut out the templates on the traced line. Draw around the templates on the wrong side of the fabric, leaving ½ inch between pieces. Then mark ¼-inch seam allowances before you cut out the pieces.

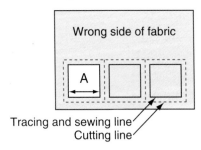

Diagram 6

For machine piecing: Trace the outer solid line on the printed pattern to make templates with seam allowance included. Draw around the templates on the wrong side of the fabric and cut out the pieces on this line.

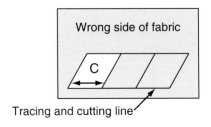

Diagram 7

For appliqué: Appliqué patterns in this book have only a single line and are finished size. Draw around the templates on the right side of the fabric, leaving ½ inch between pieces. Add ⅛- to ¼-inch seam allowances by eye as you cut the pieces.

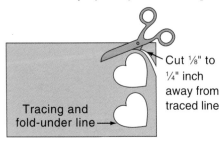

Diagram 8

PIECING BASICS

Standard seam allowance for machine piecing is ¼ inch. For hand piecing, the sewing line is marked on the fabric.

Hand Piecing

Cut fabric pieces using finished-size templates. Place the pieces right sides together, match marked seam lines, and pin. Use a running stitch along the marked line, backstitching every four or five stitches and at the beginning and end of the seam.

When you cross seam allowances of previously joined units, leave the seam allowances free. Backstitch just before and after you cross, then resume stitching the seam.

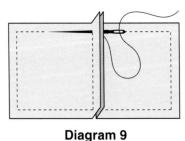

Diagram 9

Quiltmaking Basics   225

Machine Piecing

Cut the fabric pieces using templates with seam allowances included or using a rotary cutter and ruler without templates. Set the stitch length at 10 to 12 stitches per inch.

Place the fabric pieces right sides together, then sew from raw edge to raw edge. Press seams before crossing them with other seams, pressing toward the darker fabric whenever possible.

Chain piecing: Some of the quilts in this book were assembled using a technique called chain piecing, or assembly line piecing, in which like segments are fed through the sewing machine one after another, without lifting the presser foot or clipping threads on individual segments. The end result is a chain of sewn segments connected to one another by a short length of thread, as shown in **Diagram 10.**

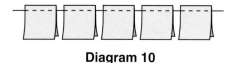

Diagram 10

Chain piecing is a good choice if logs have a finished width of 1 inch or more. Wider strips are easier to handle than very narrow ones, and if slight variations do occur, they won't be as noticeable in a wider strip. Another benefit of chain piecing is its speed. Since it is assembly line sewing, chain piecing usually makes block construction faster. You can perform the same step on all the blocks before moving on to the next step.

QUICK-PIECED TRIANGLE SQUARES

Many Amish quilts, including a handful featured in this book, feature triangle squares. A triangle square is made of two right triangles sewn together along their longest sides to make a square, as shown in **Diagram 11.**

Diagram 11

Both of the techniques described here will help you assemble accurate triangle squares more quickly than you could using the traditional method of sewing individual triangles together. Examples for both methods produce finished triangle squares that are 2¾ inches. However, if you need triangle squares in a different size, follow the directions below.

Method 1: Grids

The grid method is a good choice if you plan to make many identical triangle squares. Two pieces of fabric are cut oversize, placed together with right sides facing, then marked, sewn, and cut apart into individual triangle squares. This technique requires careful marking and sewing, but it produces multiples of identical triangle squares quickly and allows you to avoid working with bias edges. It is an especially useful method when working with very small triangle squares because your results may be more accurate than with other piecing methods.

To make a scrap quilt that's full of visual texture, variety is important and can be achieved by using grids with fewer squares. Adjust the number of squares in the grid to suit the design you are trying to achieve.

Step 1. To determine the correct size to cut the fabric, you must first determine the number of triangle squares you wish to make and the dimensions of the squares in the grid. Each square drawn in the grid will result in two triangle squares and is equal to the finished size of the triangle square, plus ⅞ inch.

In this example, the finished size of the triangle square is 2¾ inches. The number of identical triangle squares required is 60, so:

60 triangle squares required ÷ 2 completed triangle squares in each grid square = a grid of 30 squares

Grid size = finished size of 2¾ inches + ⅞ inch = 3⅝-inch grid required

A grid of 5 squares by 6 squares produces 60 triangle squares and measures 18⅛ × 21¾ inches.

To allow a bit of extra fabric on all sides, choose two pieces of fabric that are at least 19½ × 22¾ inches.

Note: If your fabric cuts are narrow, adjust the grid layout. For instance, a grid of 3 squares by 10 squares will yield the same number of triangle squares but can be drawn on a piece of fabric that measures approximately 11½ × 37 inches.

Step 2. On the wrong side of the lighter fabric, use a pencil or permanent marker to draw a grid of squares, as shown in **Diagram 12A**. Begin approximately ½ inch from the edge of the fabric. Referring to **12B**, carefully draw a diagonal line through each square in the grid; these lines will be cutting lines.

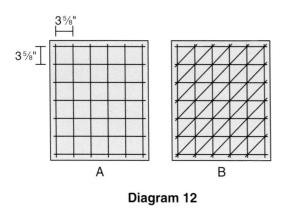

A   B

Diagram 12

Sew Quick

To eliminate the need to draw lines directly on fabric, use a hot-iron transfer pen to draw the grid on a sheet of paper, then iron the image onto the wrong side of your lightest fabric.

Step 3. Position the marked fabric and the second piece of fabric with their right sides together. Press to help the two pieces adhere to each other and use a few straight pins to secure the layers. Using a ¼-inch seam allowance, stitch

along both sides of the diagonal lines, as shown in **Diagram 13**. Use the edge of your presser foot as a ¼-inch guide, or draw a line ¼ inch from each side of the diagonal line to indicate sewing lines.

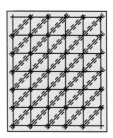

Diagram 13

Sew Easy

To help you distinguish sewing lines from cutting lines, use a different color ink to mark each line.

Step 4. Use a rotary cutter and ruler to cut the grid apart. Cut on all the grid and diagonal lines, as shown in **Diagram 14A**. Carefully press the triangle squares open, pressing each seam toward the darker fabric. Trim off the triangle points at the seam ends, as shown in **14B**. Continue marking and cutting triangle squares until you have made the number required for the quilt you are making.

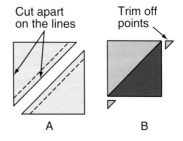

A   B

Diagram 14

Method 2: Single Squares from Squares

If you prefer a scrappier look or if you would like to make use of small pieces of fabric, the individual square method may be useful. Squares of different fabrics are sandwiched and sewn togeth-

Quiltmaking Basics   **227**

er, then cut apart diagonally to yield two identical triangle squares.

Step 1. Determine the required size of fabric squares by adding ⅞ inch to the desired finished size of your triangle squares. For a 2¾-inch triangle square, you must cut 3⅝-inch squares of fabric.

—— Sew Easy ——

To make the finished size of your squares as accurate as possible, cut fabric squares slightly larger than necessary, then trim back the completed triangle squares after assembly.

Step 2. Select two fabrics for a triangle square and cut a 3⅝-inch square from each. Draw a diagonal line from one corner to the other on the wrong side of the lightest square. Position the squares with their right sides together, taking care to align all edges. Sew a seam ¼ inch from each side of the drawn line. After sewing the seams, cut the squares in half on the drawn line. Press the seam in each triangle square toward the darkest fabric (see **Diagram 15**).

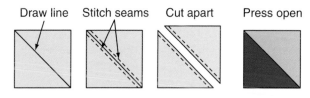

Diagram 15

Step 3. Continue making triangle squares until you have completed the total number required for your quilt. If you are sewing many triangle squares, chain piecing will help speed up the process. Draw diagonal lines and pair each square with its counterpart. Feed the units through the sewing machine one after another in a continuous chain, without breaking the threads.

SET-IN SEAMS

For Schoolhouse and other blocks: While many of the Schoolhouse blocks in this book call for simple, straight seam sewing, occasionally the

design of a block will require that you sew a set-in seam. A set-in seam is one that requires you to fit a piece (or pieces) into the quilt block by pivoting at a key point. Although this is not especially difficult, it does call for some advance planning.

The need for a set-in seam can be seen in the roof and skyline of House 2 in **Diagram 16**. While House 1 can be completed by adding Rows 2 and 3 with simple, straight seam sewing, the A and A reverse pieces cannot be added to House 2 quite so simply. Because of the angled seams, you will need to turn a corner to get the pieces to fit.

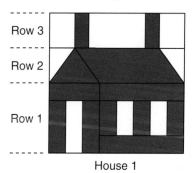

House 1

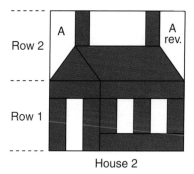

House 2

Diagram 16

Step 1. Sew the roof unit to the top of the house, as shown in **Diagram 17**.

Diagram 17

Step 2. Place a fabric A piece along the chimney edge, with right sides together and top edges aligned. Use a pencil to mark a dot ¼ inch from the bottom edge of A, as shown in **Diagram 18A.** Pin, then begin sewing at the dot, taking a ¼-inch seam allowance. Start with a backstitch and stitch outward in the direction indicated by the arrow. Wait to press.

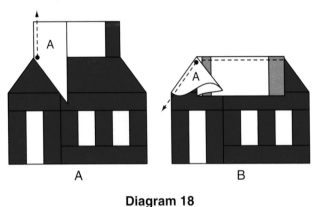

Diagram 18

Step 3. Maneuver the A piece so that its angled bottom edge is aligned with the angled edge of the large pieced unit, as shown in **18B.** Pin, taking care that the marked dot is secured at the pivot point. Once again, begin sewing at the dot, taking a ¼-inch seam allowance. Backstitch, then stitch outward in the direction indicated by the arrow. Finish by pressing both seams away from A.

Step 4. Repeat Steps 1 through 3 to attach the A reverse piece to the opposite side of the block.

While it is generally easier to stitch outward from a pivot point, this is not always possible. In quilts with complex designs, you may need to complete a series of long seams, turning corners as you go.

To do this, begin by marking all of the ¼-inch pivot points before you start to sew. Work from pivot point to pivot point, pinning and taking the standard ¼-inch seam allowance. Adjust your stitching so that you finish with the sewing machine needle in the down position as you reach each pivot point. Pin to the next pivot point, turn the quilt top under the machine needle, and continue sewing. Work your way from point to point until the rows are completely joined.

Sew Easy

While it is advisable to press seam allowances toward the darker of the two sewn fabrics, this is not always possible, especially when set-in seams are involved. You can eliminate the problem of darker seam allowances shadowing through lighter fabrics by carefully grading the seam allowances. Trim the darker allowance to a *scant* ¼ inch (or ³⁄₁₆ inch) so that it hides behind the lighter—and wider—seam allowance.

For 8-Pointed Star blocks: Pattern pieces must sometimes be set into angles created by other pieces, as shown in the diagram. In **Diagram 19,** pieces A, B, and C are set into the angles created by the four joined diamond pieces.

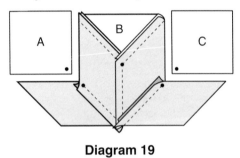

Diagram 19

Step 1. Keep the seam allowances open where the piece is to be set in. Begin by sewing the first seam in the usual manner, beginning and ending the seam ¼ inch from the edge of the fabric and backstitching at each end, as shown in **Diagram 20.**

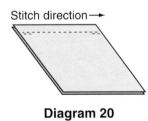

Stitch direction →

Diagram 20

Step 2. Open up the pattern pieces and place the piece to be set in right sides together with one of the first two pieces. Begin the seam ¼ inch from the edge of the fabric and sew to the exact point where the first seam ended, backstitching at the beginning and end of the seam, as shown in **Diagram 21**.

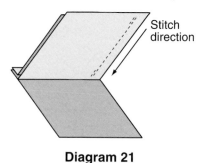

Diagram 21

Step 3. Rotate the pattern pieces so that you are ready to sew the final seam. Keeping the seam allowances free, sew from the point where the last seam ended to ¼ inch from the edge of the piece, as shown in **Diagram 22**.

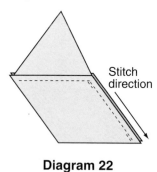

Diagram 22

Step 4. Press the seams so that as many of them as possible lie flat. The finished unit should look like the one shown in **Diagram 23**.

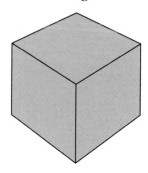

Diagram 23

SEWING CURVED SEAMS

Most of the assembly procedures you'll encounter in Wedding Ring quilts involve matching curved seams. Center points are marked on the pattern pieces, so be sure to copy the points to your tem-plates for easier matching. Also, to help you align pieces accurately, templates have been drawn to eliminate excess seam allowances at the points. The step-by-step directions below give information about successfully sewing the different types of curved seams you'll encounter. With a little practice, you'll be able to sew curves with confidence and ease.

Sewing Arcs to Melons

Step 1. Mark the center of each side of the melon and background pieces. If your quilt is made with solid rather than pieced arcs, mark the centers of the arcs, too. You may make a small mark with a pencil or fine-tip permanent pen. Or simply make a small snip at the center point with the tip of your scissors. Be careful not to cut deeper than ⅛ inch into the seam allowance. See **Diagram 24**.

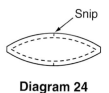

Diagram 24

Step 2. With right sides together, match the center of a melon to the center seam of a pieced arc, then pin at this point. See **Diagram 25A**. Match and pin the ends of the arc and melon. Place more pins along the seam if you like. See **25B**.

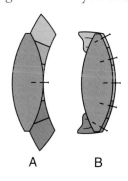

A   B

Diagram 25

Step 3. With the melon on top, sew the two pieces together using a ¼-inch seam allowance. If you haven't pinned along the seam, manipulate the fabric with your fingers to fit the curve. Remove the pins as the needle approaches them. Press the seams toward the arc unless directed otherwise in the project instructions. Open out the melon piece, pressing the seam toward the arc unless directed otherwise. See **Diagram 26.**

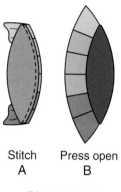

Stitch
A

Press open
B

Diagram 26

Step 4. Sew the pieced arcs with connecting wedges to the opposite or unsewn side of the melon. Match the center of the melon with the center seam of the longer arc and pin at that point. Then pin at each end. It is also helpful to place pins at the seam intersections at each end of the melon, matching the seams where the ends of the arc are sewn to the melon with the seams of the connecting wedges on the arc. See **Diagram 27A.**

Use a few more pins along the side, or simply manipulate the fabric with your fingers as you sew. Again, sew with the melon on top, using a ¼-inch seam allowance. It may be necessary to stop occasionally and reposition the fabric. If you do, be sure to stop with the needle down. Stitch all the way to the end of the arc. Open out the melon piece, pressing the seams toward the arcs unless directed otherwise. See **27B.**

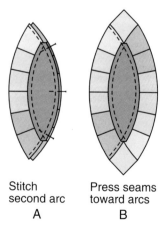

Stitch
second arc
A

Press seams
toward arcs
B

Diagram 27

Sewing Arcs to the Background

With right sides together, pin the center of one side of a background piece to the center of an arc/melon unit, with the background piece on top. Stick a pin in the background piece, ¼ inch from one end. Match that point with the seam on the arc between the connecting wedge and the next inner wedge of the arc. Repeat on the opposite end of the background piece. Add more pins along the length of the curve if you like. Sew the pieces together with a ¼-inch seam allowance. See **Diagram 28.**

Important: Start and stop your seams ¼ inch from each end, and backstitch. If you don't leave the ¼-inch seam allowance open, you won't be able to attach the arc/melon unit on the adjacent side.

Press the seams away from the arcs unless directed otherwise in the project instructions.

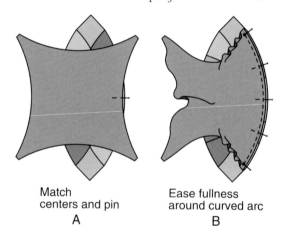

Match
centers and pin
A

Ease fullness
around curved arc
B

Diagram 28

Sew Easy

To help ease your fabric along the curves, try clipping into the seam allowances on the concave curves. By making several small snips (no deeper than ⅛ inch) into the seam allowance, you'll give your fabric the flexibility to bend and manipulate around the convex curve of the melon to which you are attaching it.

Sewing Rings into Rows

Step 1. Sew additional arc/melon units to the quilt top following the project instructions. **Important:** When adding remaining arc/melon units, remember to match the seams where connecting wedges meet the rest of the arc, with the point ¼ inch from the tip of the background piece. Be sure to keep the ¼-inch seam allowance unsewn at the beginning and end of each curved seam.

Step 2. Once you have four arc/melon units coming together where four circles interconnect (see **Diagram 29**), you will need to stitch the connecting wedges together. To do so, match the raw edges of two adjacent connecting wedges and stitch from the edge to ¼ inch from the inner point where the wedges are connected to the arcs. Backstitch. Repeat for the other pair of wedges. Finger press the two seams you've just sewn in opposite directions, pin the remaining raw edges of the wedges together, and stitch, backstitching ¼ inch from each end.

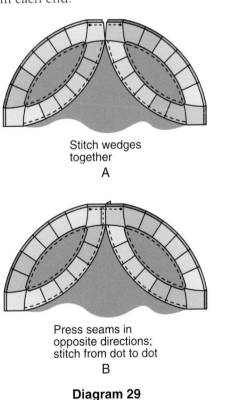

Stitch wedges
together
A

Press seams in
opposite directions;
stitch from dot to dot
B

Diagram 29

Step 3. Sew the quilt top together as illustrated for your project, using the same techniques described here for aligning curves and finishing the connecting wedge seams.

Appliquéing Rings to a Border

In a few projects in this book, the Wedding Ring quilt tops are appliquéd to a border unit or background. Any appliqué method will work for this step, but a freezer paper technique may help seam allowances stay in place easily.

Step 1. To make a stabilizing template for appliqué, connect the individual template pieces for the pieced arc, including the connecting wedges on opposite ends. Be sure you don't include seam allowances when constructing the shape of the complete arc. See **Diagram 30.**

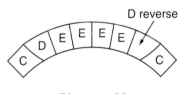

D reverse

Diagram 30

Step 2. Trace the shape onto the nonwaxy side of freezer paper and cut it out. Make a freezer paper template for each outer arc to be appliquéd.

Step 3. Align a freezer paper arc, waxy side up, to the wrong side of an outer pieced arc. The freezer paper should fit snugly against the inner seam allowance where the arc connects to the background piece. Use the tip of a medium-hot iron to press the outer seam allowance of the ring onto the freezer paper. See **Diagram 31.** This eliminates the need for basting or turning under edges as you work and holds the seam allowance securely as you appliqué the rings to the border.

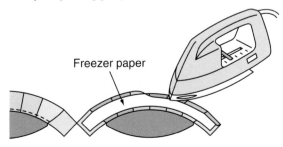

Freezer paper

Diagram 31

── Sew Easy ──

The tip of a clean, hot-glue gun makes a convenient "iron" for adhering freezer paper to the fabric seam allowance. The small tip can help you manipulate fabric more easily and will help avoid burned fingertips that some-times come from using an iron.

Repeat, ironing a new freezer paper template onto each outer arc in your quilt. Construct the border and center the top on it, as described in the project directions. Appliqué the ring edges to the borders. Remove all freezer paper templates when the appliqué is complete.

FOUNDATION PIECING

Many Log Cabin designs are perfect candidates for the foundation method of piecing. Nineteenth-century quilters used this technique to construct their quilts, sewing fabric pieces to either the front or back side of a foundation onto which a copy of the block had been drafted. Foundation piecing is enjoying a strong revival today, with more and more quilters designing blocks specifically for use with this method.

Foundations help ensure that your quilt will be square. Log Cabin and Pineapple blocks won't pucker up in the middle when they are pieced on a foundation. In addition, foundation piecing is often the best choice for blocks with narrow logs. It's much easier to construct a perfect block full of ½-inch logs when those logs are sewn to a rigid foundation with premarked lines. Sewing individual narrow strips together with an exact ¼-inch seam allowance is possible, of course, but accurate results are more difficult to achieve.

One disadvantage of the foundation method is the fact that a separate foundation must be prepared for each individual block. This requires additional preparation time as well as added materials. But there are benefits that help offset this extra preparation: You save cutting time by not having to cut individual logs to exact sizes. Working with long strips that are trimmed as you go means the actual sewing moves along quickly.

Foundation Basics

With the foundation method, an entire block is first drawn to scale on the chosen foundation material. The only seam allowance included is the one around the outer perimeter of the design. **Diagram 32** illustrates a typical template for the foundation method.

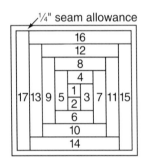

Diagram 32

The foundation technique used in this book involves positioning the fabric on one side of the foundation (the reverse side) and sewing on the opposite side (the front, marked side). Seams are stitched directly onto one of the marked lines of the template. If you are unfamiliar with this technique, it may at first seem awkward. But if you position the fabric correctly and are careful to sew on the lines, every log will be perfect, no matter how narrow its finished width.

Some quilters choose to piece on the front of a foundation, but that method requires that you use exact seam allowances. One advantage to choosing foundation piecing in the first place is its simplicity and speed, so it seems awkward to slow the process down by including a step that requires more precision.

There is one thing you must keep in mind as you work: Since the fabric will be sewn to the back of the foundation, the finished block will always be a *mirror image* of the template. For some blocks, this does not create a problem—the light and dark areas are clearly defined. For others, getting the fabrics in the right place can sometimes be confusing. Where color or value may change from block to block, or where blocks are not symmetrical, misplaced fabric can alter your entire design.

It may be helpful to premark all or part of the logs of your foundation, on either the front or back side, as shown in **Diagram 33**. Jotting down simple designations such as light, dark, or the actual color of a log will save time and keep frustrating seam-ripping sessions to a minimum.

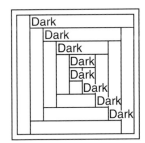

Diagram 33

Foundation Materials

There are two types of foundations—permanent and removable—and both are exactly what their names imply. Several types of materials fall into each category, all with advantages and disadvantages. Though the following list is by no means exhaustive, the descriptions may help you decide which type will be best for your project.

Permanent Foundations

Muslin is the most common example of a permanent foundation material. Some advantages include the following:

• The foundation will remain in the finished quilt permanently. The extra layer of fabric makes hand quilting more difficult, but since it adds more depth to the finished top, extensive quilting may not be necessary or desired. Many Log Cabin

quilts with permanent foundations are tied rather than quilted.

• The extra fabric often eliminates the need for batting.

• The foundation will permanently stabilize the fabric, making careful placement of fabric grain less of a consideration.

• The foundation will help reinforce stitching, so seam allowances can be trimmed back a little more. This may help make outline quilting somewhat easier.

Some disadvantages of this type of foundation include:

• The material can stretch as it's handled. Be careful not to tug on the foundation too much as you work, or the block may become distorted. Tightly woven muslin will minimize the problem.

• The block sometimes seems to shrink as you add pieces. This is caused by the slight loft created by each new seam. The amount of shrinkage is usually very small but should be considered if you plan to use a pieced border that must fit the quilt top exactly.

Two other options in the permanent foundation category include flannel and sheer interfacing. Flannel may be a bit harder to hold on to as you work, but it adds more depth and body than muslin. Spray-on starch or sizing will stiffen the flannel slightly, making it easier to handle. As for the interfacing, the additional layer it adds is easier to hand quilt through than muslin. Sheer interfacing is a good choice for those who intend to hand piece on a foundation.

Removable Foundations

Paper is the most commonly used removable foundation. Among its advantages are the following:

• The foundation will be removed after the top is assembled, and thus will not add an extra layer of fabric to your quilt.

• The paper will remain rigid as you work. There is no need to worry about distorting or shrinking the block.

• The cost of materials is very low.

Some of the disadvantages of paper as a foundation include:

• It can sometimes be time-consuming to remove, especially if pieces are very small.

• It will not remain in place to permanently stabilize the fabric, so cutting and positioning pieces on grain is more of a consideration.

Many types of paper can be used as foundation material. For example, blank newsprint is a good choice. It is sturdy enough to remain intact while handling but pulls away easily when your top is complete. Newsprint is available in pads from 9 × 12 inches up to poster size, so it works well for blocks that are too large to draft onto a piece of 8½ × 11-inch paper.

Inexpensive copier paper, onion skin, and tracing papers are options for small blocks. Other foundation choices in the removable category include vanishing muslin, a loosely woven fabric that deteriorates and falls away when ironed, and tear-away paper, which is designed to be used as a stabilizer during machine embroidery.

Transferring the Image

There are several ways to transfer the template onto your foundation material.

Transfer Pens

Use a hot-iron transfer pen to draw the full-size block onto tracing paper. The image can usually be ironed onto a foundation material five or six times. Retrace over the original transfer for additional ironings, being careful to mark over the existing lines exactly. A transfer pen can be used on both fabric and paper foundations, but do a test first to be sure it will work on your chosen material.

Photocopies

Photocopies are an option for smaller blocks. The major disadvantage of photocopying is the slight distortion that's almost certain to occur. To minimize that distortion, make sure the page being copied is completely flat against the glass screen of the copier. Always check your copies to make sure blocks are square. Copiers can alter size slightly, too, so measure your copies carefully if a slight variation in block size will affect the finished quilt top. Always use the same generation of copies in your project, since copies of copies will usually be a slightly different size.

Computer Printouts

Those of you who use a computer to design quilt blocks can print the images directly onto paper. Most drawing programs have a "tile" feature that allows you to print large designs in segments, then tape the segments together to make a whole. For small blocks, some quilters feed freezer paper–backed muslin through their printers—but check with your printer's manufacturer before attempting that! In general, if a printer will accept card stock, it will probably process fabric. Printer ink should be tested for permanency on a piece of scrap fabric.

Light Box

A simple light box, or a lamp placed underneath a glass table, can be used to help you see the template clearly enough to trace it directly onto a foundation. However, with this method only one block can be drawn at a time. Blocks may be different due to slight tracing variations.

Other Considerations

Pens and other markers can be used to mark foundations. If you are using permanent foundations, be sure the markings on them are permanent, too, or that they will wash out completely without staining. You don't want your finished quilt to be ruined by bleeding ink during its first bath. Always check a new marker on scrap fabric before using it in a project, even if it's a brand you have used before. If the ink bleeds, try to heat set it by ironing a marked scrap for a few minutes with a medium-hot iron. Check again for color-fastness. If the ink still bleeds, do not use it on permanent foundations.

Permanent inks are not necessary for removable foundations. Just be sure to choose a marking system that won't wear off onto fabric as you work.

FABRIC GRAIN

For maximum strength and stability and minimum distortion, fabric should be cut along its lengthwise or crosswise grain. Ideally, the straight of grain should be parallel with the outer perimeter of your block. For most pieces in Log Cabin quilts, this means positioning the grain line parallel to the seam. The rectangles, squares, and occasional triangles used to assemble quilt blocks in this book are simple shapes that will be easy to cut on grain. Grain placement is most important if you are using removable foundations that won't remain in the quilt as permanent stabilizers.

STITCH LENGTH

Most foundation piecing is done with a slightly shorter than normal stitch length. Twelve to 14 stitches per inch will produce good results. Be sure not to make your stitches too small, or they could cause unnecessary wear to the fabric. Also, very small stitches will be more difficult to remove if an error occurs.

Smaller stitches will "punch" your paper foundations, making them easier to remove. And smaller stitches are less likely to be distorted when foundations are pulled away.

PIECING A BLOCK

This section takes you step by step through the construction of one sample Log Cabin block. You may want to make a sample block here to learn the technique, or you may decide to select a particular project and jump right in. Even if you don't make a sample block, it's a good idea to read through all of the steps in this section so that you

understand the process thoroughly before beginning any of the projects.

All of the foundation piecing instructions in this book contain recommended sizes for strip widths. It's easiest to cut long strips of fabric, then trim the logs to length as the block is assembled.

The strip width is based on the finished size of the log. The finished width of each log in this sample block is ¼ inch. If we add ¼ inch to each side to allow for seam allowances, the cut size becomes ¾ inch. When you first learn to piece on a foundation, it's usually best to add an additional ⅛ to ¼ inch to the calculated size. The extra bit of fabric will give you more flexibility as you position your strips onto the back of the foundation, and the excess will be trimmed away after sewing.

The Cutting Chart in each project takes this into consideration, calling for wider than necessary strips. However, since it will only take a practice block or two for you to become a foundation piecing pro, you may not want to cut extra-wide strips for the entire quilt. Cut just enough to construct one or two blocks to start with, then reevaluate the strip width, reducing it when you feel comfortable doing so. Never cut the strips narrower than the finished width plus ¼-inch seam allowance on each side.

For the sample block, make a foundation from the pattern on page 210. Start by cutting 1¼- to 1½-inch-wide strips across the width of your fabrics. Since the extra width will be trimmed away after sewing, the method may at first seem wasteful, but remember that you'll probably decrease the width after one or two blocks. Even if you prefer to continue using wider than necessary strips, the time you'll save and the perfect results you'll achieve by piecing on a foundation will likely make the use of additional fabric an unimportant consideration.

Step 1. Pieces are sewn to the foundation in numerical order. Cut a 1¼-inch square from the fabric you set aside for the center piece, log 1. Place it right side up on the back side of your foundation, centering it over the lines surrounding the area for log 1, as shown in **Diagram 34.** Use tape, a dab of glue stick, or a pin to hold the fabric in place.

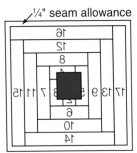

Diagram 34

Step 2. Hold the foundation up to the light with the back side away from you. You should be able to see the shadow of log 1. Does the shadow overlap all drawn lines for log 1? Is the overlap sufficient to create a stable seam allowance when those lines are sewn? If not, reposition the piece and check again before continuing.

Step 3. Find the strip of fabric set aside for log 2 and position it on the back side of your foundation, right side down. Align the strip along the left and lower edges of log 1, as shown in Diagram **35A.** The strip will entirely cover log 1.

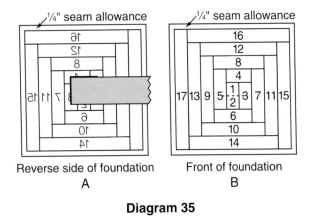

Diagram 35

Step 4. Holding the strip in place, flip the foundation over. Sew on the line separating log 1 from log 2, beginning and ending approximately ⅛ inch

on either side of the line, as shown in **35B** in the previous step. Remove the foundation from the machine.

Step 5. Flip again to the back side of your foundation. Trim away the excess tail of fabric from log 2 just past the end of the seam line, as shown in **Diagram 36A.** If necessary, trim away excess fabric from the seam allowance you've created. If you used tape to secure the first piece, remove it now.

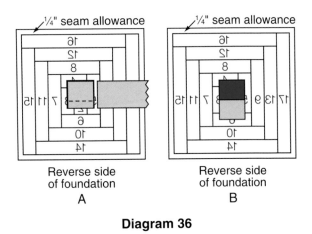

Diagram 36

Step 6. Flip log 2 into a right-side-up position, finger pressing it firmly into place. If you prefer, keep an iron near your work area to press pieces as you go. The back side of your foundation should now resemble **36B.**

Step 7. Hold the foundation up to the light with the back side away from you. You will now be able to see the shadow created by the fabric for log 2. Its raw edges should overlap all unsewn seam lines for log 2. This assures you there will be sufficient seam allowance on all sides when you add the adjacent logs.

One way to judge whether your strip has been placed correctly is to take a look at your seam allowance before trimming away the excess. Is it overly wide? If so, the piece you've just sewn may have been positioned incorrectly on the foundation. **Diagram 37** shows two examples of log 2 placement; here log 2 appears transparent to make the differences easier to see. In **37A,** the strip is aligned against the left and lower edges of log 1, as directed in Step 3. In **37B,** the strip is aligned lower on log 1.

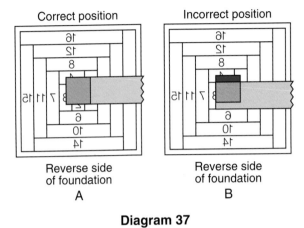

Diagram 37

When the seam in **37B** is stitched, it will have a larger than necessary seam allowance, stealing width from the log 2 fabric. The remaining width may not be adequate to cover the area for log 2 and create a stable seam allowance on its remaining sides when the fabric is flipped into place. **Diagram 38** shows the result: This strip is now too narrow to have an adequate seam along its lower edge.

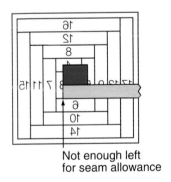

Diagram 38

Step 8. Log 3 is added in exactly the same way as log 2. Position a strip of fabric right side down on the foundation, aligning its top with log 1 and its left edge with the left edges of logs 1 and 2, as shown in **Diagram 39A.** The strip will completely cover the sewn pieces.

Flip the foundation over, and sew on the vertical line separating log 3 from logs 1 and 2, begin-

ning and ending approximately ⅛ inch on either side of the line. Remove the foundation from the machine.

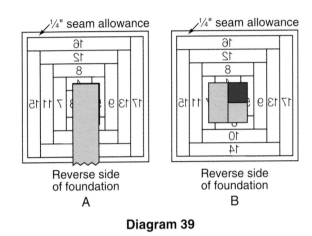

Diagram 39

Step 9. Trim the excess tail from log 3. Trim excess seam allowance if necessary. Flip log 3 into a right-side-up position, finger pressing it firmly into place. The reverse side of your foundation should now resemble **39B.**

Step 10. Position log 4 right side down on the foundation, as shown in **Diagram 40A.** Holding the fabric in place, flip the foundation over and sew on the horizontal line separating log 4 from logs 1 and 3. Remember to begin and end the seam approximately ⅛ inch on either side of the line. Remove the foundation from the machine.

Step 11. Turn the foundation over to the back side, and trim the excess tail of fabric from log 4,

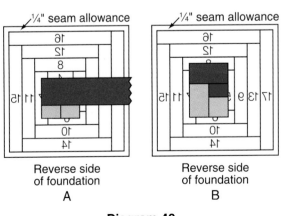

Diagram 40

just as you did with the previous logs. Trim excess seam allowance if necessary, then finger press log 4 into a right-side-up position. The back side of your foundation should now resemble **40B** on page 237.

Step 12. Sew all remaining logs to the foundation in exactly the same way. After adding log 7, the back of your foundation should resemble **Diagram 41A** and the front side should resemble **41B**. Notice that each new seam acts as a stabilizer for those it intersects.

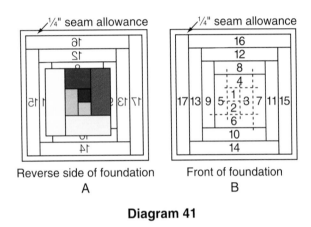

Reverse side of foundation
A

Front of foundation
B

Diagram 41

Step 13. Log 17 is the final piece for this block. After it has been added, press the entire block lightly. Align your plastic ruler with an *outer* line of the seam allowance, and cut directly on the line with your rotary cutter. Be careful not to cut off the seam allowance. Repeat for the remaining outer lines. Leave removable foundations in place until your quilt top is assembled.

Sew Easy

Although you can use scissors to trim your blocks, rotary-cutting equipment is more accurate. The ruler holds the unstitched outside edges of the logs firmly in place as you cut with the rotary cutter.

APPLIQUÉ BASICS

Review "Making and Using Templates" on page 224 to learn how to prepare templates for appliqué. Lightly draw around each template on the right side of the fabric using a pencil or other nonpermanent marker. These are the fold-under lines. Cut out the pieces ⅛ to ¼ inch to the outside of the marked lines.

In this section, we include a number of additional techniques to assist you with the specific projects in this book. You may find that a combination of methods will work best within the same quilt, depending on the individual shapes involved. We suggest that you experiment with each of these techniques to see which best suits your sewing style.

The Needle-Turn Method

Pin the pieces in position on the background fabric, always working in order from the background to the foreground. For best results, don't turn under or appliqué edges that will be covered by other appliqué pieces. Use a thread color that matches the fabric of the appliqué piece.

Step 1. Bring the needle up from under the appliqué patch exactly on the drawn line, as shown in **Diagram 42**. Fold under the seam allowance on the line to neatly encase the knot.

Cutting line   Drawn line

Diagram 42

Step 2. Insert the tip of the needle into the background fabric right next to where the thread comes out of the appliqué piece. Bring the needle out of the background fabric approximately ¹⁄₁₆ inch away from and up through the very edge of the fold, completing the first stitch, as shown in **Diagram 43**.

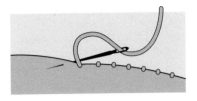

Diagram 43

Step 3. Repeat this process for each stitch, using the tip and shank of your appliqué needle to turn under ½-inch-long sections of seam allowance at a time. As you turn under a section, press it flat with your thumb and then stitch it in place, as shown.

Diagram 44

Sew Easy

Here are a few extra pointers for needle-turn appliqué.

• For a neater finished edge, clip inner points and curves before sewing. Make a perpendicular cut into an inner point, almost to the turn line. Make small V-shaped cuts on inner curves, again almost to the turn line. Make as many cuts as necessary to help you achieve a smooth fold. Take a few extra appliqué stitches at cuts to reinforce fabric. Use a drop of Fray Check as necessary to prevent raveling.

• Turn under points by cutting off the tip slightly. Fold the remaining seam allowance under to the turn line. Next, turn the seam allowance on one side of the point, then the other. To achieve a sharp point, it may be necessary to trim excess fabric at the folds as you work.

FREEZER PAPER APPLIQUÉ

Freezer paper can help make many appliqué projects easier. The paper acts as a stabilizer, allowing crisper points and smoother curves.

You can purchase plain white freezer paper at most grocery stores. Gridded freezer paper is available at many quilt shops.

Two different methods of freezer paper appliqué are explained here. Read through the directions for both, then choose the method that suits you best.

Method 1: Freezer Paper Appliqué

Step 1. Use a template to draw your patterns onto the dull (nonwaxy) side of the freezer paper.

Step 2. Cut out the shapes on the lines. Do not add a seam allowance.

Step 3. Use a medium to hot, *dry* iron to press the shiny (waxy) side of the shapes onto the right side of your fabric, as shown in **Diagram 45**. The iron will adhere the paper to the fabric.

Diagram 45

Step 4. Cut out the shape from the fabric, adding a ³⁄₁₆- to ¼-inch seam allowance around all edges of the paper template, as shown in **Diagram 46.**

Diagram 46

Step 5. Peel away the freezer paper and center it, waxy side up, on the reverse side of your fabric. Press the seam allowance over the template, as shown in **Diagram 47**. The waxy coating will soften and hold your seam in place. This method eliminates basting, but you will still need to clip the curves and points.

Diagram 47

Step 6. Appliqué the pieces to the block, then make a small slit in the background fabric and use a pair of tweezers to remove the freezer paper.

Method 2: Freezer Paper Appliqué

Follow Steps 1 through 4 under "Method 1: Freezer Paper Appliqué." Leaving the freezer paper adhered to the right side of your fabric, pin the piece to the background fabric. As you stitch the appliqué to the background, turn under the seam allowance on the edge of the freezer paper. Use the edge of the paper as a guide for the fold of your fabric. After your appliqué is stitched in place, gently peel off the freezer paper.

MAKING BIAS VINES

Some of the projects in this book include sashing or borders with appliqué bias strips for vines. The directions specify the size fabric square required for the individual project, as well as the number of strips needed. The strip width given is the width you will need to cut the strips if you are using bias bars. If you are not using bias bars, the instructions here indicate the formula for determining the width to cut the bias strips.

Step 1. Mark and cut a 45-degree angle on the vine fabric, as shown in **Diagram 48A.**

Step 2. Cut bias strips parallel to the first 45-degree cut, as shown in **Diagram 48B**. If you are using the fold method described in Step 3, multiply the desired finished width of the vine by 3, add ¼ inch to that figure, and cut. For example, if you want a vine to finish at ¾ inch wide, the bias strips should measure 2½ inches.

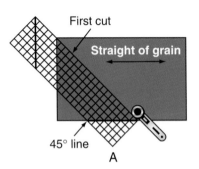

A

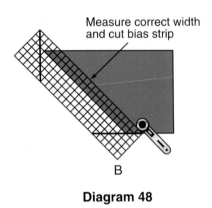

B

Diagram 48

Step 3. Fold each strip into thirds, as shown in Diagram 49. Make sure that the raw edges will be concealed by the folded edges. Press carefully. Position, pin or baste, then appliqué the vines in place, as instructed in the project directions.

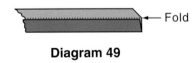

Diagram 49

USING BIAS BARS

Using bias bars is particularly helpful when you need long, narrow stems or vines. Bias bars, which are sold in sets of several widths, are made to withstand the heat of an iron.

Step 1. Cut a bias strip, as shown in **Diagram 48.** The chart below lists cut widths for three sizes of bias strips. **Note:** These widths apply only to strips cut for bias bars.

Finished Width	Cut Width
$\frac{1}{8}$ inch	$\frac{7}{8}$ inch
$\frac{1}{4}$ inch	$1\frac{1}{8}$ inches
$\frac{3}{8}$ inch	$1\frac{3}{8}$ inches

Step 2. Fold the strip in half lengthwise, with wrong sides together. Press lightly to hold the edges of the fabric together as you stitch. To avoid stretching, set the iron down to press one section, lift the iron, set it down and press a different section, and repeat until the entire strip has been pressed. Sew the raw edges together, using a $\frac{1}{4}$-inch seam allowance. Trim the seam allowance to approximately $\frac{1}{8}$ inch, as shown in **Diagram 50A.**

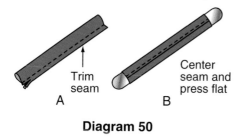

Diagram 50

Step 3. Insert the appropriate-size bias bar into the tube. Turn the tube slightly to center the seam along the flat edge of the bar, as shown in **Diagram 50B.** Dampen the fabric with water or spray starch, and press the seam allowance to one side.

Step 4. Flip the tube over, and check to make sure the seam will be hidden when the strip is appliquéd to the quilt. When you are satisfied with the appearance, press the top side of the tube and remove the bias bar. If the vines are particularly long, you will need to slide the bias bar along the inside of the fabric tube to press the entire length before removing the bar.

PRESSING BASICS

Proper pressing can make a big difference in the appearance of a finished block or quilt top. It allows patchwork to open up to its full size, permits more precise matching of seams, and results in smooth, flat work. Quilters are divided on the issue of whether a steam or dry iron is best; experiment to see which works best for you. Keep these tips in mind:

• Press seam allowances to one side, not open. Whenever possible, press toward the darker fabric. If you find you must press toward a lighter fabric, trim the dark seam allowance slightly to prevent show-through.

• Press seams of adjacent rows of blocks, or rows within blocks, in opposite directions. The pressed seams will fit together snugly, producing precise intersections.

• Press, don't iron. Bring the iron down gently and firmly. This is especially important if you are using steam.

• To press appliqués, lay a towel on the ironing board, turn the piece right side down on the towel, and press very gently on the back side.

ASSEMBLING QUILT TOPS

Lay out all the blocks for your quilt top using the quilt diagram or photo as a guide to placement. Pin and sew the blocks together in vertical or horizontal rows for straight-set quilts and in diagonal rows for diagonal-set quilts. Press the seam allowances in opposite directions from row to row so that the seams will fit together snugly when rows are joined.

To keep a large quilt top manageable, join rows into pairs first and then join the pairs. When pressing a completed quilt top, press on the back side first, carefully clipping and removing hanging threads; then press the front.

MITERING BORDERS

Step 1. Start by measuring the length of your finished quilt top through the center. Add to that figure two times the width of the border, plus 5 inches extra. This is the length you need to cut the two side borders. For example, if the quilt top is 48 inches long and the border is 4 inches wide, you need two borders that are each 61 inches long (48 + 4 + 4 + 5 = 61). In the same manner, calculate the length of the top and bottom borders, then cut the borders.

Step 2. Sew each of the borders to the quilt top, beginning and ending the seams ¼ inch from the edge of the quilt. Press the border seams flat from the right side of the quilt.

Step 3. Working at one corner of the quilt, place one border on top of the adjacent border. Fold the top border under so that it meets the edge of the other border and forms a 45-degree angle, as shown in **Diagram 51**. If you are working with a plaid or striped border, check to make sure the stripes match along this folded edge. Press the fold in place.

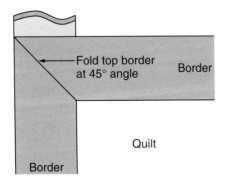

Diagram 51

Step 4. Fold the quilt top with right sides together and align the edges of the borders. With the pressed fold as the corner seam line and the body of the quilt out of the way, sew from the inner corner to the outer corner, as shown in **Diagram 52.**

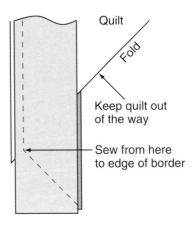

Diagram 52

Step 5. Unfold the quilt and check to make sure that all points match and the miter is flat. Trim the border seam allowance to ¼ inch and press the seam open.

Step 6. Repeat Steps 3 through 5 for the three remaining corners.

MARKING QUILTING DESIGNS

To mark a quilting design, use a commercially made stencil, make your own stencil using a sheet of plastic, or trace the design from a book page. Use a nonpermanent marker, such as a silver or white pencil, chalk pencil, or chalk marker, that will be visible on the fabric. You can even mark with a 0.5 mm lead pencil, but be sure to mark lightly.

If you are using a quilt design from a book, either trace the design onto tracing paper or photocopy it. If the pattern will be used many times, glue it to cardboard to make it sturdy.

For light-color fabrics that you can see through, place the pattern under the quilt top and trace the quilting design directly onto the fabric. Mark in a thin, continuous line that will be covered by the quilting thread.

With dark fabrics, mark from the top by drawing around a hard-edged design template. To make a simple template, trace the design onto template plastic and cut it out around the outer edge. Trace around the template onto the fabric, then add inner lines by eye.

PIECING THE QUILT BACKING

Depending upon the size of your quilt, you may not have to piece the quilt back, such as for the Chinese Coins Variation wallhanging on page 124, which is only 46¾ × 35 inches in size. However, if you are making a larger wallhanging or a bed-size quilt, piecing the backing is necessary. **Diagram 53** shows how quilt backings are generally pieced together for each quilt size. Refer to the project directions, however, for information on yardage, how to cut the backing fabric, and how to seam it.

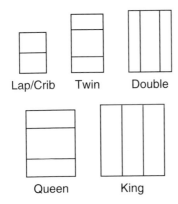

Lap/Crib   Twin   Double

Queen   King

Diagram 53

LAYERING AND BASTING

Carefully preparing the quilt top, batting, and backing will ensure that the finished quilt will lie flat and smooth. Place the backing wrong side up on a large table or clean floor. Center the batting on the backing and smooth out any wrinkles. Center the quilt top right side up on the batting; smooth it out and remove any loose threads.

If you plan to hand quilt, baste the quilt with thread. Use a long darning needle and white thread. Baste outward from the center of the quilt in a grid of horizontal and vertical rows approximately 4 inches apart.

If you plan to machine quilt, baste with safety pins. Thread basting does not hold the layers securely enough during machine quilting, plus the thread is more difficult to remove when quilting is completed. Use rustproof nickel-plated brass safety pins in size #0, starting in the center of the quilt and pinning approximately every 3 inches.

HAND QUILTING

For best results, use a hoop or a frame to hold the quilt layers taut and smooth during quilting. Work with one hand on top of the quilt and the other hand underneath, guiding the needle. Don't worry about the size of your stitches in the beginning; concentrate on making them even, and they will get smaller over time.

Getting started: Thread a needle with quilting thread and knot the end. Insert the needle through the quilt top and batting about 1 inch away from where you will begin stitching, as shown in **Diagram 54**. Bring the needle to the surface in position to make the first stitch. Gently tug on the thread to pop the knot through the quilt top and bury it in the batting.

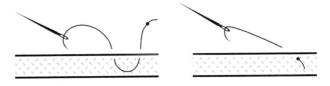

Diagram 54

Taking the stitches: Insert the needle through the three layers of the quilt. When you feel the tip of the needle with your underneath finger, gently guide it back up through the quilt. When the needle comes through the top of the quilt, press your thimble on the end with the eye to guide it down again through the quilt layers, as shown in **Diagram 55**. Continue to quilt in this manner, taking two or three small running stitches at a time.

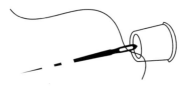

Diagram 55

Ending a line of stitching: Bring the needle to the top of the quilt just past the last stitch. Make a knot at the surface by bringing the needle under the thread where it comes out of the fabric and up through the loop of thread it creates. Repeat this knot and insert the needle into the hole where the thread comes out of the fabric. Run the needle inside the batting for an inch and bring it back to the surface, as shown in **Diagram 56**. Tug gently on the thread to pop the knot into the batting layer. Clip the thread.

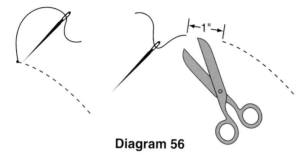

Diagram 56

Machine Quilting

For best results when doing machine-guided quilting, use a walking foot (also called an even feed foot) on your sewing machine. For free-motion quilting, use a darning or machine-embroidery foot.

Use thread to match the fabric colors, or use clear nylon thread in the top of the machine and a white or colored thread in the bobbin. To secure the thread at the beginning of a line of stitches, adjust the stitch length on your machine to make several very short stitches, then gradually increase to the regular stitch length. As you near the end of the line, gradually reduce the stitch length so that the last few stitches are very short.

For machine-guided quilting, keep the feed dogs up and move all three layers as smoothly as you can under the needle. To turn a corner in a quilting design, stop with the needle inserted in the fabric, raise the foot, pivot the quilt, lower the foot, and continue stitching.

For free-motion quilting, disengage the feed dogs so you can manipulate the quilt freely as you stitch. Guide the quilt under the needle with both hands, coordinating the speed of the needle with the movement of the quilt to create stitches of consistent length.

Making and Attaching Binding

Double-fold binding, which is also called French-fold binding, can be made from either straight-grain or bias strips. To make double-fold binding, cut strips of fabric four times the finished width of the binding, plus seam allowance. In general, cut strips 2 inches wide for quilts with thin batting or scalloped edges and 2¼ to 2½ inches wide for quilts with thicker batting.

Straight-Grain Binding

To make straight-grain binding, cut crosswise strips from the binding fabric in the desired width. Sew them together end to end with diagonal seams.

Place the strips with right sides together so that each strip is set in ¼ inch from the end of the other strip. Sew a diagonal seam, as shown in **Diagram 57**, then trim the excess fabric, leaving a ¼-inch seam allowance.

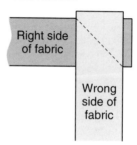

Right side of fabric

Wrong side of fabric

Diagram 57

Continuous Bias Binding

Bias binding can be cut in one long strip from a square of fabric that has been cut apart and resewn into a tube. To estimate the number of inches of binding a particular square will produce, use this formula: Multiply the length of one side by the length of another side, and divide the result by the width of binding you want. Using a 30-inch square and 2¼-inch binding as an example: $30 \times 30 = 900$; $900 \div 2\frac{1}{4} = 400$ inches of binding.

Step 1. To make bias binding, cut a square in half diagonally to get two triangles. Place the two triangles right sides together, as shown, and sew with a ¼-inch seam, as shown in **Diagram 58**. Open out the two pieces and press the seam open.

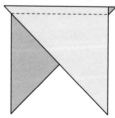

Diagram 58

Step 2. Using a pencil and a see-through ruler, mark cutting lines on the wrong side of the fabric in the desired binding width. Draw the lines parallel to the bias edges, as shown in **Diagram 59**.

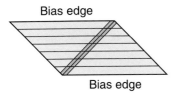

Bias edge

Bias edge

Diagram 59

Step 3. Fold the fabric with right sides together, bringing the two nonbias edges together and offsetting them by one strip width (as shown in **Diagram 60**). Pin the edges together, creating a tube, and sew with a ¼-inch seam. Press the seam open.

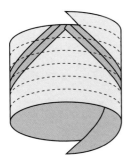

Diagram 60

Step 4. Cut on the marked lines, turning the tube to cut one long bias strip, as shown in **Diagram 61**.

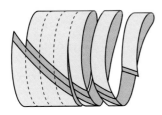

Diagram 61

Attaching the Binding

Trim excess batting and backing even with the quilt top. For double-fold binding, fold the long binding strip in half lengthwise, with wrong sides together, and press. Beginning in the middle of a side, not in a corner, place the strip right sides together with the quilt top, align raw edges, and pin.

Step 1. Fold over approximately 1 inch at the beginning of the strip and begin stitching ½ inch from the fold, as shown in **Diagram 62**. Sew the binding to the quilt, using a ¼-inch seam and stitching through all layers.

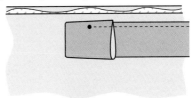

Diagram 62

Step 2. As you approach a corner, stop stitching ¼ inch from the raw edge of the corner. Backstitch and remove the quilt from the machine. Fold the binding strip up at a 45-degree angle, as shown in **Diagram 63A**. Fold the strip back down so there is a fold at the upper edge, as shown in **Diagram 63B**. Begin sewing ¼ inch from the top edge of the quilt, continuing to the next corner. Miter all four corners in this manner.

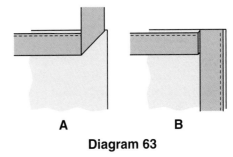

A   **B**

Diagram 63

Step 3. To finish the binding seam, overlap the folded-back beginning section with the ending section, as shown in **Diagram 64**. Stitch across the fold, allowing the end to extend approximately ½ inch beyond the beginning.

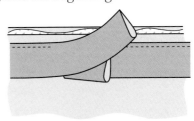

Diagram 64

Step 4. Turn the binding to the back of the quilt and blindstitch the folded edge in place, covering the machine stitches with the folded edge. Fold in the adjacent sides on the back and take several stitches in the miter. In the same way, add several stitches to the miters on the front, as shown in **Diagram 65.**

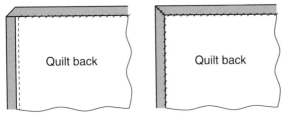

Diagram 65

Binding Curves

It is important that you use bias binding, which has more stretch, for quilts with curved outer edges. Refer to "Making and Attaching Binding" on page 244 for detailed information about making French-fold bias binding. You will need to make your bias binding 2 inches wide.

Step 1. To estimate the length of bias binding needed, measure around the perimeter of one outside arc. Multiply this measurement by the number of arcs around the outside of the quilt, then add 15 inches to the measurement. The calculation is the approximate number of inches of bias binding you will need.

Step 2. Begin sewing on the binding at the midpoint of a ring. With raw edges even, sew the binding around the curve, easing in the fullness. Do not stretch the binding to make it smooth.

Step 3. When you get to the inner point of two arcs, clip the seam allowance of the quilt for a flat fit, as shown in **Diagram 66.** Keep the needle down through all thicknesses of fabric, pivot at the inner point, and then continue stitching around the next curve, easing in the fullness of the binding.

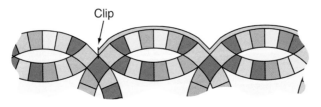

Diagram 66

Step 4. Continue sewing around each curve, clipping as necessary to help the binding turn at the corners. As you sew, make sure the portion of the quilt where binding has been attached is lying flat and is not buckled or puckered by binding that is pulled too tight.

When you have completed sewing the binding to the front of the quilt, fold the binding to the back of the quilt and stitch it in place by hand. As you near an inner point, fold the binding on one side of the point and stitch it to the inner corner. Then fold in the binding on the other side of the corner. The binding will automatically form a miter. Continue hand stitching in place.

Treat outer, pointed areas of connecting wedges, such as those on the Is This Wedded Bliss? quilt, as you would a quilt corner, mitering each outer point as described in Step 2 of "Attaching the Binding" on page 245.

Sew Easy

After you have stitched the binding to the back of the quilt, you may want to take a stitch or two by hand to hold the two binding edges together where they meet going into and out of the inner point where the curves meet, as shown. This extra stitch will help your binding appear smooth and less bulky at each inner point.

Stitch here

SIGNING YOUR QUILT

Be sure to sign and date your finished quilt. Your finishing touch can be a simple signature in permanent ink or an elaborate inked or embroidered label. Add any other pertinent details that can help family members or quilt collectors 100 years from now understand what went into your labor of love.

ACKNOWLEDGMENTS

Reflections, made by Patricia Mahoney of Santa Maria, California. A quilter for more than 30 years, Patricia pieced this quilt by both hand and machine, working on much of it during her husband's illness. This quilt won honors at three quilt shows in 1991, including the California State Fair, and was also published in *Award-Winning Quilts and Their Makers* in 1991. Patricia is a member of the Santa Maria Valley Quilt Guild.

Memories of SS #3, made by Doreen Hugill, Mount Elgin, Ontario, Canada. SS #3 was a one-room stone schoolhouse with one teacher for all eight grades. Doreen made this quilt as a commissioned project for a family who also attended the school and who were her friends and classmates at the school. Doreen thought the Schoolhouse block would be a perfect choice to relive their shared memories of SS #3.

Logs Hexagonal, made by June Ryker, Littleton, Colorado. June is a well-known quiltmaker, teacher, and author who has spent a great deal of time exploring and expanding the traditional Log Cabin. She has squeezed, stretched, and rounded the basic block into new and unique shapes. June has been quilting since 1973. Her patterns are published under the name The Quilted Lady.

Sparkle Plenty, made by Joan Dyer of Redondo Beach, California, and hand quilted by Mrs. Simon Ray Miller of Ohio. Joan presented this quilt to her daughter and son-in-law, Cheryl and Jesse Berg, of Berkeley, at their February 1994 wedding. Joan has been quilting since 1989. This quilt was included in the American Quilter's Society 10th Annual Quilt Show in Paducah, Kentucky.

House Medallion, made by Susan Loveless Bengtson, Rising Sun, Indiana. Susan has been quilting since 1972. Her love of quilting has prompted her to take classes, teach classes, work in quilt shops, and enter quilt shows, where she has won a number of ribbons. She also enjoys collecting antique quilts.

Feathered World without End, made by Valerie Schadt of Fayetteville, New York. A quilter for more than 15 years, Valerie designed and hand quilted the patterns on this quilt, which won an honorable mention in 1995 at the Pennsylvania National Quilting Extravaganza in Fort Washington, Pennsylvania. It was also displayed at Quilting by the Lake in Morrisville, New York.

Is This Wedded Bliss?, made by Maureen Carlson, Moline, Illinois. This quilt was shown at the 1994 Quilters' Heritage Celebration in Lancaster, Pennsylvania, and the 1994 International Quilt Festival in Houston, Texas. Maureen loves hand-dyed fabrics, and she dyed the purple fabric for this beauty herself.

Oklahoma Nine Patch, made by Carolyn Miller, Santa Cruz, California. Carolyn was inspired to create this quilt when she saw a similar one in a small photo in a book on Oklahoma heritage quilts. Except for adding the border, she pieced and quilted it entirely by hand. Carolyn was a quiltmaker for years before deciding in 1987 to, as she puts it, "make quilts seriously." She has since won several ribbons at local shows. Her favorite projects are heavily hand-quilted scrap quilts.

Summer Night, made by Karen K. Stone, Dallas, Texas. Karen's quilt is actually two-sided; the front and back are constructed simultaneously in a reversible Log Cabin technique taught by Emiko Toda Loeb. Karen began quilting in 1987 when she was expecting her first child. She quickly became hooked and now shares her enthusiasm through teaching.

Antique Indigo Schoolhouses, made by Sally Tanner, Tampa, Florida. Sally drafted her Schoolhouse quilt as a way to use a box of old blue scrap fabrics. It has been exhibited in the Third Continental Quilting Congress in Tampa; the World of Quilts in Rochester, Michigan; and in the Florida Keys Quilters show. This quilt was also featured in the September 1983 issue of *Quilter's Newsletter Magazine.* Sally is a charter member of Quilters Workshop of Tampa Bay, as well as the founder of the Florida Keys Quilters Guild.

Crazy Wedding Ring, made by Joanne Winn, Massillon, Ohio. This quilt is an example of the types of circular patterns that Joanne offers through her pattern company, Canada Goose Designs. This pattern design is known by several other names, such as Tea Leaf, Orange Peel, and Pincushion.

Summer's End, made by Judy Miller, Columbia, Maryland. This quilt is the happy result of an idea that, according to Judy, had been "simmering in me for quite awhile." Combining scraps she had on hand with fabrics she purchased at summer sales, Judy created a contemporary-looking quilt using a traditional pattern and setting. The quilt was exhibited at the Quilters' Heritage Celebration in Lancaster, Pennsylvania, in 1993, where it was awarded an Honorable Mention. Judy has been quilting since 1977, when she made a quilt from embroidered blocks she had started 20 years earlier.

My Stars! . . . They're Plaid!, made by Betty L. Alvarez of Marietta, Georgia. A quilter since 1978, Betty is the past president and quilt show chairperson of the East Cobb Quilter's Guild. Making this quilt helped her explore designing quilts with "movement." In 1991 and 1992, it won awards at several shows and was featured in *Quilt World* magazine.

Chinese Coins Variation, made by Karan Flanscha of Cedar Falls, Iowa. Karan is a quiltmaker and teacher and has served as president of both the Iowa Quilters Guild and the Keepsake Quilters Guild. The quilt was shown in the Invitation Exhibit at the Kentucky Fall Festival of Quilts in 1989 and was featured in the June 1991 issue of *Quilter's Newsletter Magazine*.

Straight Furrows, formerly owned by Woodin Wheel Antiques, Kalona, Iowa. The only thing known about this cheerful 1930s-era quilt is that it was made in Ottumwa, Iowa. The quilt appears here courtesy of Marilyn Woodin, the owner of Woodin Wheel Antiques and the Kalona Quilt and Textile Museum. Marilyn has been a quilt collector for more than 20 years, and she lectures on antique and Amish quilts.

Sister's Choice, owned by Angela Dominy of Livingston, Texas. The blocks for this quilt were made by members of the Kingwood Area Quilt Guild. It was designed and assembled by Bev Rogers and machine quilted by Dori Hawks. The block was chosen to celebrate the sisterhood among quilters everywhere. The quilt won second place for group quilts in Houston in 1994, and it appeared in the April 1995 issue of *Quilter's Newsletter Magazine*. Angela won the quilt in a raffle.

Feed Sack Wedding Ring, made by Lizzie Stover and owned by her granddaughter, Bertha Rush, Hatfield, Pennsylvania. Bertha is a prolific quilter and a member of the Variable Star Quilters. Feed Sack Wedding Ring was shown at the 1992 Variable Star Quilt Show and in a quilt exhibit sponsored by the Eastern Mennonite Historical Society from 1994 to 1995. Bertha also hand quilts for other people.

81 Patch, owned by Shelly Zegart of Louisville, Kentucky. Shelly was a founding director of the Kentucky Quilt Project, the first state quilt documentation project. She collects, writes, advises quilt survey groups, and sells fine quilts. She also lectures on all aspects of quilt history and aesthetics and has curated exhibitions here and abroad. Shelly is a founder and editor of *The Quilt Journal*.

My Cabin Made of Logs, made by Jane Graff, Delafield, Wisconsin. Jane has been quilting for more than 15 years and competes on local, state, and national levels. She also teaches and lectures on quiltmaking. Her Schoolhouse quilt was juried in the 1994 American Quilter's Society show, and won First Prize in the pieced category as well as the Judges Recognition Award at the 1994 Wisconsin State Fair. Jane is a fabric collector and confesses that for this queen-size quilt, she only had to purchase the backing fabric—the rest was already part of her collection!

Scrap Baskets with Nine-Patch Sashing, by Wilma Sestric, Ballwin, Missouri. Wilma started out as a painter, teaching tole and decorative painting to students at her art shop. She started quilting almost 20 years ago and loves the creative outlet it provides.

Scrap Half Log Cabin, made by Sharyn Craig, El Cajon, California. Sharyn is a nationally known quiltmaker, teacher, and author who enjoys challenging quiltmakers to exercise their creativity. Her designs are based on traditional patterns, but she adds a subtle twist to create an original statement. Sharyn views her quiltmaking as a link to past and future generations and encourages all quilters to keep that current flowing.

Job's Tears, designed and made by Suzzy Chalfant Payne, Fairport, New York, and Susan Aylsworth Bushnell, Meadowbrook, Pennsylvania, for their book *Creative American Quilting Inspired by the Bible*. In 1976, they developed timesaving methods for making traditional patchwork and authored *Quick and Easy Patchwork on the Sewing Machine* and *The Quick and Easy Giant Dahlia Quilt on the Sewing Machine*. They've presented hundreds of quilting classes and programs. Their quilts have been featured in several magazines, including *Good Housekeeping*.

Sunshine and Shadow, made by Bettina Havig; owned by Joyce Gross, Petaluma, California. This quilt was a gift to Joyce from Bettina. Joyce is a well-known quilt collector, quilt historian, and has been publisher and editor of *Quilter's Journal* for over 15 years. In 1993, she was honored by the American Museum of Quilts and Textiles in San Jose, California, with the exhibit "Portrait of a Quilter, Scholar, Author: Joyce Gross." Joyce was also inducted into the Quilters Hall of Fame in Marion, Indiana.

Dots and Dashes, made by Sharyn Craig, El Cajon, California. Sharyn was inspired to create this quilt after she saw a photo of an antique pillow in a magazine and decided that its design would look great as a quilt. She is proud of the fact that the whole quilt top is made of leftovers recycled from two earlier quilt projects.

INDEX

Underscored page references indicate boxed text or tables.